The Power of

IMPACT
CIRCLES

ALISSA M. QUINN

PRAISE FOR *THE POWER OF IMPACT CIRCLES*

Alissa M. Quinn's *The Power of Impact Circles* is an inspiring exploration of creating supportive spaces during pivotal moments in her life, including battles with cancer and personal transitions. Ms. Quinn weaves her stories within a framework of empowerment, growth, and healing, giving readers real-life examples of informal and formal circles she created and participated in. The common thread in each chapter lies in the transformative power of having the courage to reach out to build meaningful relationships and communities.

I had the honor of being a founding member of one of Ms. Quinn's formal impact circles formed in the late eighties—a time when women in leadership roles were a small minority. This experience was transformative for me, as it provided a supportive network of like-minded professional women who were determined to overcome the resistance from traditional networks.

Ms. Quinn's vision was to create a network so successful that professionals would approach us seeking to do business with us. This goal was not only ambitious but also empowering, as it challenged the status quo and paved the way for women to thrive in their careers. For me, being part of this circle was a truly empowering experience that helped me build my business, celebrate milestones, and support each other in our professional journeys.

The Power of Impact Circles is a must-read for those who may be navigating their own life's challenges—whether personal or professional.

In addition to sharing the key benefits of joining an impact circle, Ms. Quinn includes an appendix filled with practical tips and guidelines for creating circles. I am grateful to Ms. Quinn for having the courage to share her personal stories of mourning, loss, triumph, and success.

Martha A. Roblee, retired, corporate tax executive

Alissa takes us through her life's journey and shows us how to cherish life and live it to the fullest despite loss and disappointment. Through her wonderful storytelling, we witness how a strong and vibrant woman embraces the goodness life has to offer and the impact of surrounding yourself with people who really see you. Alissa showcases the power of building community, informal and formal, in every sphere of her life. And the women she brings together in her impact circles don't just cheer her on; they challenge her, uplift her, and remind her of her worth. They are mentors, mirrors, and morale-boosters.

What makes this memoir stand out is how clearly it illustrates that empowerment doesn't always come from grand gestures—it's often built in the quiet moments of connection, the chance encounters, the sharing of dreams and goals, and the value of honest conversations.

This book is a celebration of community, of intentional sisterhood, and of the life-changing magic that happens when women support women. Whether you're seeking your own circle or simply looking for hope in human connection, *The Power of Impact Circles* is a story that will leave you inspired and uplifted.

Ellen Sax, Consultant

The Power of Impact Circles is not only a story, it is an open calling to take the leap of faith and lead differently. A circle has a point of beginning but by design has no ending. This is the story of how we can call upon our tribe to share our deepest heartaches and greatest triumphs with love and support to move forward knowing we are not alone. The guide is the ultimate gift as we create our circles; a must read for anyone who wants to bring people together with purpose and intention.

Kathy Lanni, Chief Community Officer, Broadview Federal Credit Union

An accomplished business professional, ballroom dancer extraordinaire and a devoted, loving mother, Ms. Quinn lives life with passion and purpose. Her inspiring story details the power of connections and the deep friendships and enduring support that flow from them. As she faced her own personal challenges and life transitions, she confronted them head on by reaching out to other women—friends and new acquaintances—to gather together and share ideas, frustrations and goals, and gain insights and valuable advice and support from one another.

These "impact circles" were a sanctuary of friendship, caring and support through both the challenges and joys of life, creating deeply meaningful experiences for all. This power of connection enabled Ms.

Quinn to find greater joy, fulfillment and meaning in her life and she generously shares her tips for others to enrich their lives by creating their own impact circles.

Pat Bucklin, Former Executive Director, New York State Bar Association

This charming book is both a deeply personal memoir and a "how to." It is how to create a life of passion and purpose with actual guides at the end.

Written from the heart, Alissa's book shows her many amazing accomplishments, her incredible work ethic and the power of her loving family to shape her, her values, and her intellect.

Alissa weaves tales of success, synchronicity and growing spirituality among some of life's most difficult experiences. Her writing about her cancer journey is most moving and convincing when she talks about the power of impact circles in dealing with the medical community.

She learns about networking for lifesaving purposes and shares that urgency with the reader. Her descriptions of the process of forming her health team make one wonder how anyone deals with the medical system without one's own impact circle of connected medicos and others.

As one who has known Alissa since she was that blossoming 14 year old, it truly is an honor to see and experience her growth and impact as a powerful woman in a predominantly male world. She rightfully has earned that long list of accomplishments, as the reader will come to know.

Elizabeth Dunn, retired LCSW

For nearly two decades, I've watched and experienced Alissa Quinn bring women together with her warmth, support, and relentless positivity. Her gift for connecting people is truly remarkable. So when she asked if I'd be interested in speaking to her third Impact Circle—a group of professional women who have been touched by cancer—I immediately said, "Yes!"

I realized then that I had never shared my own cancer experience.

My treatment involved surgery, which seemed minor compared to the chemotherapy and radiation I had seen family members and patients endure. But once Alissa learned that I was also a cancer survivor, she warmly invited me to join her Passion & Purpose Impact Circle. I eagerly became part of this community of resilient, powerful women.

The wealth of support, knowledge, friendship, and strength within these circles is a much-needed antidote to the fractured and often lonely world we live in. *The Power of Impact Circles* is both a guide and a call to action—for women and men alike—to build supportive networks and forge deep connections in their own communities.

Sandy Camper, M.Ac., Dipl. Ac., Oncology Acupuncture Specialist

Having been a member of one of Alissa's Impact Circles, I expected her book to focus on the extraordinary value of these circles—the trust, shared wisdom, and deep support that form when women come together with intention. But what I found was something even more personal: an inspiring journey of a woman who truly defines resilience, determination, and the ability to forgive. Alissa's story unfolds with honesty and vulnerability, weaving in powerful lessons about leadership, community, and healing. It's a tribute not just to the strength of women, but to the magic that happens when we show up for each other. Her journey is as heartfelt as it is empowering.

Kara Conway Love, Social Tails, LLC

"Impact. Whether through positive support circles, having a vision and setting goals, giving back to the community, or making a difference in a stranger's life with a warm smile, having a positive impact is one of life's greatest joys.

Alissa did a masterful job detailing how the power of deep connection and shared trust can change lives; be it your own or others'. She has given us a proven recipe for how to support one another during and after some of life's greatest challenges.

Throughout the book, we discover how Alissa has learned, grown and inspired—equally through triumph and turmoil. Regardless of where you start your own journey, the takeaways from *The Power of Impact*

Circles will motivate you to reach your goals and overcome your most significant obstacles through meaningful connections and mutual support."

Amy Aldrich, Owner State Farm Agency

The Power of Impact Circles beautifully captures how intentional communities can transform lives. Having personally experienced one of Alissa Quinn's professional women's circles, I know firsthand the lasting friendships and strength that come from connecting with women through shared experiences. Alissa's story is inspiring, authentic, and offers a roadmap for anyone seeking deeper support and meaningful relationships. Her story reinforces the concept that vulnerability and authenticity lead to lifelong friendships through shared experiences. A heartfelt and empowering read."

Anne Saile Lifelong women's empowerment advocate, former Hospital CEO, philanthropist, entrepreneur, author.

This book is a moving and powerful reflection on the circles of women executives the author has cultivated over the years—spaces created with care, intention and purpose for every phase of life and leadership. Through these circles, she highlights the transformative power of authentic connection, shared experience and collective wisdom.

More than a narrative about community, this work is a testament to the author herself—her unshakable commitment to her family, her resiliency, tenacity and vision. She reminds us that women don't rise alone. They rise with and for each other. With honesty, vulnerability, and strength, she invites us to consider what it means to lead with purpose and to show up fully for others while evolving ourselves.

This book is both a call to action and a celebration of what becomes possible when women gather in truth, hold space for growth, and lift one another toward their highest potential. Life lessons are abundant.

Angela S. Dixon, President/Founder, Dixon Consulting II, LLC

What I was expecting was a book about "Impact Circles" was actually only a fraction of what this book offers. Instead, it offers a window into a life that had incredible challenges but was lived with hope, optimism, kindness, gratitude, and the ability to remain focused on what is actually meaningful; family and impactful and sometimes magical relationships. It gave me chills and brought some tears. This moving story was delivered in an inspiring memoir which ended in the way Alissa lived her life. Thinking of others before herself.

Dawn Abbuhl, President, Repeat Business Systems, Inc.

I initially met Alissa Quinn in 2007 when my husband and I relocated to a house adjacent to her and her family. For the following 13 years, we had occasional interactions marked by waves or smiles as we went about our daily activities. In 2020, while discussing the impacts of the Covid pandemic, I confided that I was experiencing one of the most challenging times of my life. It was during this period that I truly "met" Alissa. She promptly extended her support by providing resources she believed would be beneficial, a gesture she continues to offer. When she mentioned that she was authoring a book, I recognized her genuine intent to assist others.

The term "Impact circle" may not be familiar, but its value becomes clear throughout the book. I realized that, had I read this earlier in my career, I might have created my own support network during times of isolation instead of relying solely on myself, a burden that proved to be exhausting. The book moved me to tears and made me reflect on how different my life could have been if I had truly "met" Alissa in 2007 rather than in 2020. She would have empowered me to seek support from others or I might have been invited to join a circle she created. In return, how I wish I would have been there for her when she was navigating cancer. I was after all, right next door.

Today, I can attest firsthand to the value of impact circles. Knowing I was struggling with several major life transitions, Alissa invited me to be part of her newly created Next Chapter Circle. New to the concept, I started out a little tentative as to how this would work, but with Alissa's encouragement, I was determined to give this a try—what was there to lose? After the first meeting, I felt so fortunate to be part of this circle. Immediately, I found myself receiving such support from women I had just met, and it has become so fulfilling to be able to offer support back. I now look forward to our monthly circle and make every effort to prioritize being there for myself and for the members.

PRAISE FOR *THE POWER OF IMPACT CIRCLES*

The gift of this book is that it offers both inspiration and guidance for enriching your life by simply connecting with others. You will see how Alissa illustrates it is never too late to start your own impact circle, formal or informal. I've recently been inspired to start to gather friends, who live locally but get together rarely, on an informal (for now) impromptu basis, not only to socialize but, to serve as a safe space to share life's challenges with old friends knowing there will be others there to offer support. I have Alissa to thank for that inspiration!

Julie Shaw, retired CEO

A great book for those who are looking to navigate life in a different and more fulfilling way. As Alissa transparently shares her life experiences, she illustrates how a trusted, caring, goal-aligned and committed community of friends can buoy you in life through the highs and lows. Besides her interesting personal reflections, she also shares many tips and guidelines for establishing powerful impact circles and ensuring that each group enriches all who engage. Her life lessons are invaluable, no matter what phase of life you are in. The concepts support personal growth but translate beautifully to business success, as Alissa's story clearly demonstrates.

Having been blessed to be a member of several of Alissa's impact circles, I will heartily confirm that my life has been richer because of them!

Kathy Rowe, retired Technology and Healthcare Sales Executive

Alissa Quinn's, *The Power of Impact Circles,* is a MUST read. Insightful, inspirational, informative, and moving, it is a modern-day, self-improvement go-to-guide for realizing your best self.

Ann Marie Lizzi, Owner, Majestic Media Group LLC

The Power of Impact Circles is honest, brave, thoughtful, and deeply human. Alissa doesn't just tell you about the power of connection; she shows you, through her own life, how intentionally creating community can change everything.

PRAISE FOR *THE POWER OF IMPACT CIRCLES*

What I love most is that this book isn't just a memoir — it's a playbook. Alissa offers real-life lessons on resilience, authenticity, and leadership, along with practical tools for creating your own Impact Circles.

At its heart, the message is simple but powerful: we are stronger together.When we come together intentionally, we unlock wisdom, support, and growth we could never reach on our own.

Alissa has a rare gift for bringing people together — whether they're facing career challenges, illness, or life's big "what's next" moments. This book is a generous, heartfelt invitation to build the kind of connections that lift you up, challenge you, and remind you who you really are.

Robbin Jorgensen, Founder and CEO, Women Igniting Change

The Power of Impact Circles
Published by Alissa M. Quinn
Slingerlands, New York, USA

QUINN, ALISSA M., Author
THE POWER OF IMPACT CIRCLES
ALISSA M. QUINN

Library of Congress Control Number: 2025905069

ISBN: 979-8-9928856-0-6 (paperback)
ISBN: 979-8-9928856-1-3 (hardcover)
ISBN: 979-8-9928856-2-0 (ebook)

SEL031000 SELF-HELP / Personal Growth / General
BUS012030 BUSINESS & ECONOMICS / Careers / Career Advancement & Professional Development
BUS107000 BUSINESS & ECONOMICS / Personal Success

Editing: Ayshea Wild
Art Direction: Pique Publishing, Inc.
Cover Images: Joan Heffler (Author Photo); Pexels / AnnaMitsu (Background Image)

The Power of
IMPACT
CIRCLES

ALISSA M. QUINN

In honor of my parents, Frank and Angela Calabria, for my children, John and Rachel Quinn, and anyone open to harnessing the power of human vulnerability, authenticity, and collective wisdom

TABLE OF CONTENTS

FOREWORD

I remember the day Alissa walked up to me and introduced herself. It was at an Albany hotel, and a large crowd of women was networking before a Community Foundation annual lunch. Of course, I knew who she was—a community leader, a successful businesswoman. I remember her directness: "Has your life been affected by cancer?"

Wow. Big topic, lots of intimacy, and something I did not talk to many people about. But this woman, Alissa, was looking right into me, directly and kindly.

I said, "Yes, yes twice," surprising myself because I rarely talked about my cancers then. I've rarely talked about them since. I never wanted to be known as "that woman with cancer." I knew, or intuited, there was stigma—especially for women—around people in the workplace with cancer. I wanted my performance and career to come first, and I led with that. Here was Alissa in front of me, offering me a different way to be with my cancer and cancer history: *with* other women in an impact circle for professional women touched by cancer.

Later I would learn that this was not the first time this dynamic and über-successful businesswoman had created an impact circle. The noteworthy thing is that she created impact circles for what she most needed, and it turned out that in creating them for herself, she gave incredibly and generously to many other women. First, she created support for women leaders—a sounding board of directors. Then, as her life progressed, she formed an impact circle for women who were trying to balance raising families and developing careers.

Cancer appeared in Alissa's life next. She created an impact circle for how to navigate cancer treatment and recovery while working and raising a family. Alissa's way of taking whatever appeared in her life and using it to help other women was formidable. It's as if she said, "If this is a challenge for me, it must be a challenge for some other women, and we can help each other."

You'll read in this book how Alissa started her impact circles and how she continues to foster them. You'll read about her life and how the circles grew from her career, parenting, cancer journey, and life transitions. She connects with her impact circles by reaching across and sharing pain, grieving losses, embracing resources and strategies, and celebrating joys with other women who really get it.

Alissa's generosity in writing this book gives us a way to face difficult parts of our lives and seek support for whatever is in front of us. She shows us how to find a few people who share a common goal, make a circle, and help each other. The impact will be enormous. Thank you, Alissa, for this beautiful, powerful gift.

~Diane Cameron Pascone

INTRODUCTION

ver the course of my thirty-eight years in the financial services industry, I've created four formal professional networking groups: the Professional Women's Network (PWN) in 1989, a group of professional women in exclusive industries helping each other grow our businesses and positions; the Executive Network (EN) in 1996, for high-level professional women focused on balancing and integrating work and family life; Passion, Purpose, and Legacy (PPL) in 2014, a healing circle for executive women touched by cancer; and Next Chapter (NC), a group of executive women in transition who are navigating divorce, losing parents or spouses or jobs, experiencing shifts in identity and purpose, or preparing for retirement.

I now refer to these groups as "impact circles." I define an impact circle as an intentional gathering of like-minded individuals focused on a common mission of supporting each member's needs with synergy and wisdom that comes from collaborative engagement. I find power in connecting the right people who are willing to improve the quality of their lives, share their vulnerabilities, be fierce supporters of their fellow members, and give and receive insights for the greatest good of each member and the group's mission.

In these pages, I share my personal journey: why and how I created these four formal impact circles, the influence they had on my life and the lives of members, and the informal circles I actively engaged with along my path. I hope to show you the power of impact circles and inspire you to create your own. The synergy of my impact circles comes from my approach to life and from connecting like-minded people with the common goal of helping one another. Together, let's imagine a world where impact circles can unleash synergy, wisdom, love, and hope. Embracing the strength of enduring relationships can benefit us all.

CHAPTER ONE:
Childhood

O
n a perfectly delightful summer's day, I gathered my three best girlfriends, locked arm in arm, and walked to the Farmer in the Dell, a mini-mart convenience store that sold candy a mile or so from where my family lived. I was in search of BB Bats, a rectangular, taffy-like lollipop that could break your teeth if you were not careful. Our family's three-bedroom starter home was in Albany, New York, on a tiny little street in the Capital Region. Having a sweet tooth at a very early age, I led my little pack of girlfriends down Frantone Lane, took a left on Tipton Drive, a right on Albany Shaker Road, passed the farmhouse where our family purchased unbleached brown eggs and milk in glass bottles with foil tops, and arrived at the store. My posse picked out our favorite BB Bats lollipops in chocolate, vanilla, strawberry, and banana flavors. Then, mission accomplished, we headed for home, licking our treasured candy. I was the ringleader of "my girls" at four years old.

Looking back, I am truly shocked that I managed such a feat, as I have zero sense of direction, and I can get lost going anywhere. I do recall being scared but hoped I would find my way. My parents had driven me there many times, so I just trusted my memory and was pleasantly surprised we made it there and back unscathed. The tasty lollipops were absolutely worth the trip. Nowadays, I can't imagine four very small girls walking such a path unaccompanied by an adult. Thankfully, the story has a happy ending. My mother didn't find out about my little adventure for a month or so. I distinctly remember my mom in her study, putting down our black rotary-dial telephone with its long, curly cord and sharing that she'd just heard from one of the other girl's mothers that we had crossed several major streets and had a significant excursion. My mother did not know what to make of the adventure, and too much time had passed for any real punishment, but I knew I was in big trouble. That is my earliest memory of creating an impact circle, a small group of like-minded individuals, focused on a common goal—in this case, getting my beloved candy. I still have an insatiable sweet tooth today.

MAMA AND PAPA

My father, Frank Calabria, was born in 1924, one of four children to two Italian immigrants, Rosina Scarcelli (Nanny) and Ernesto Calabria (Poppy), who had both immigrated to the United States from Reggio di Calabria, known as the southern boot of Italy. Ernesto was from the small town of Fuscaldo, and Rosina from the tiny village of Santa Sofia d'Epiro, both provinces of Cosenza, separated by one huge mountain. When my family went to explore our Italian roots, we discovered that if my grandparents wanted to see each other, it involved a very long car ride up and down a massive mountain peak that is literally in the clouds and one of the scariest roadways any of us had ever traveled.

My grandfather Ernesto immigrated to the United States via Ellis Island, like so many immigrants, and settled in Brooklyn, NY, until he could save enough money to bring his bride Rosina to the US. Ernesto was a sculptor, commissioned to work on a variety of federal buildings and churches in New York City, including the Basilica of Regina Pacis, still standing at 1230 65th Street, Brooklyn. I visited it decades later, awed to find a young priest there from Reggio di Calabria, just like my grandparents. My father had two older sisters, Aquilina and Antoinette, and a younger brother, Ernesto Jr. They lived in a two-story duplex in Bay Ridge, near the Verrazzano Bridge. Their love endured for over fifty years, despite their different personalities, Rosina's strong-willed and Ernesto's more even-keeled.

I remember celebrating my grandparents' golden anniversary with a seven-course Italian feast: antipasto salad, chicken soup with pastina, penne pasta with marinara sauce, fried baccalà (salted cod), chicken cacciatore, anniversary cake with strawberries and cream, and espresso with anisette to mark the end of the meal. Afterward, Nanny and Poppy showed their grandchildren how to play the card game Canasta, which they played almost every night. I distinctly recall many Thanksgivings and Christmases with them. On Christmas Eve, they would make noises to pretend Santa Claus and his reindeer were on the roof, which still makes me giggle with delight. We rose at midnight to open one present, as is traditional in Italian families. There was Victorian-era décor, clear plastic on the sofas, and a small black-and-white television in the living room with Italian nougat and colorful sweet-and-sour candies in glass dishes. However, we spent most of our time in the kitchen, with the incredible aroma of my Nanny's Italian spices wafting through the air.

My father served in World War II as an athletic instructor and was decorated with a Victory Medal, a Good Conduct Medal, and an American Theater Service Medal. After his service in the army, my father focused on obtaining his formal college education. To pay for this, my father worked as a ballroom dance instructor at the Byrnes & Swanson Dance Studio in Brooklyn, NY, earning his undergraduate degree from the City College of New York and his PhD in clinical psychology from New York University. He was also focused on fitness and health, using bodybuilding to recover from a leg injury that had confined him to a wheelchair as a young adult.

My mother, Angela Calabria, was born in 1928 and grew up in Guayaquil, Ecuador, spending summers in the capital, Quito, and escaping from the sweltering heat of her hometown. My mother was one of three children; she had an older sister,

Maruja, and a younger brother, James, born to Delia Benavides (Abuelita) and Jose Canelos (Abuelito). To make a living, my mother's parents built up a fleet of buses and managed a few rental properties.

When my mother was twelve years old, she and numerous friends contracted typhoid fever from eating the cream at the top of bottles of unpasteurized milk. Learning that the death rates from typhoid fever were extremely high at their local hospital, my grandmother, Delia, chose to care for my mother herself in one of the apartment buildings they had been renting out. Once the tenants learned there was typhoid fever in the family, there was no problem with them vacating. After two months of isolation, intravenous feedings, cold baths, and ice packs, my mother's 104-degree fever finally subsided. Then, after one week of solid food, her fever returned vigorously for another month. Treatment continued until my mother finally recovered, but sadly, none of her friends who were treated at the local hospital survived. That experience caused my grandmother's and my mother's profound distrust of medical systems, which significantly impacted our entire family.

In 1946, my abuelita, uncomfortable with the economic and political climate in Ecuador, decided to move her family to the United States. She left with three young-adult children in tow: my Uncle Jimmy, approximately fifteen years old; my mother, eighteen years old; and my Aunt Maruja, twenty years old. They settled in Queens, without my abuelito, who was reluctant to leave his home country. They came via large ship through the Panama Canal to Ellis Island. My abuelita found work as a dressmaker in New York City to pay for a small apartment that she rented from an Ecuadorian friend. She was paid by the piece to make wedding dresses. I owe much gratitude to my abuelita, who was a force of nature to have done such a thing at that time—strong-willed, independent, and willing to do anything for her family, including whatever work was available outside of the home.

My mother and her sister saw a job advertisement in the local newspaper that read NEEDED: GIRLS WHO KNOW HOW TO DRAW, and they secured jobs in a silk-screen printing company in Lower Manhattan. They painted on Mylar® sheets, copying patterns separated by color. In Ecuador, my mother and her sister had attended Catholic schools, where they learned to draw, sew, and knit. In the US, their first jobs helped pay for living expenses and their younger brother's medical school bills. My abuelito came to the US a short while later to reunite with his family, and he and my abuelita rented and maintained a six-unit apartment building for many years. My grandmother provided bookkeeping services for the apartment building, while my grandfather oversaw its maintenance. They divorced several years later, but my abuelita's fierce determination provided the foundation for a better life for her family and all the generations to follow.

It was my mother's sister who encouraged her to go to the ballroom dance, where she met my father. He worked part-time as a ballroom dance host while he completed his PhD. As the host, it would have been customary for my father to dance with all the single ladies, but once he met my mother, she had more dances with him than most for the rest of the evening. They married a year later, traveled to Europe for their honeymoon, and danced together for an additional fifty-four years.

My parents moved into my paternal grandparents' duplex in Brooklyn after their honeymoon. One funny story from that time is that my father made the mistake of inadvertently criticizing my mother's cooking. My mother was helping her mother-in-law make traditional southern Italian meatballs at a Sunday-night family dinner. In disgust, my father gasped. "Mom, what did you do to the meatballs?" Apparently, my mother had accidentally added cilantro to the meatballs instead of the parsley the recipe called for. (The herbs look similar, and I made the same mistake decades later.) My Nanny, to her credit, attempted to cover for her daughter-in-law, but once my father figured out what had happened, he apologized. This was one secret to their long marriage.

My paternal aunt Aquilina, known as Jackie, had one daughter, Gina Sanchez. My paternal aunt Antoinette, known as Biege, had three children: Heather, Vincent, and Dawn, who lived in my Nanny and Poppy's first-floor duplex. While I was young, Dawn, the youngest, tragically died of a childhood illness, and my Aunt Biege died of cancer. We all navigated the grief as a family, and I felt their passings very significantly, especially when facing my own mortality later.

Shortly thereafter, my father received his first full-time job offer, an associate teaching position in the Psychology Department at the State University of New York at Albany, bringing my parents to the Capital Region. His next position was at Russell Sage College. He taught in the evening division, where he had adult students and formed many dear, lifelong friendships. To this day, I hear from adult students who adored my dad and his humanistic teaching methods, which warms my heart.

FOUR SIBLINGS

My parents had four children, approximately two years apart, while our family lived in our small two-bedroom apartment in Loudon Arms, Albany. My oldest brother, Carl, was born in 1958, my brother Mark in 1960, I in 1962, and my younger sister, Mayela, in 1965. Albany Memorial Hospital, where the first three of us were born, did not allow siblings to visit. When I was born, Mark was waiting outside with my dad and yelled for my mother to just toss me out the window into his arms so he could meet his baby sister: "Can you just throw her down here for a minute?" My mother was on an upper level, so my parents had a good laugh. A few years later, they moved to a ranch-style home on Frantone Lane in Loudonville, New York, and shortly thereafter, Mayela was born. My earliest memory is of my third birthday and receiving a pink, plastic jewelry kit and a toy harmonica with colorful buttons. I still have two childhood Christmas toys as treasured keepsakes: a golden-tan stuffed Henry dog called Snoopy and a sweet doll with an angelic face and blinking black eyelashes in a pink, frilly dress with matching bloomers.

When I was four years old, my father secured a prominent position as a professor of psychology at the prestigious Union College, and my parents purchased an eight-bedroom home with three floors and a full basement in the historic district of Schenectady, NY, known as the General Electric Realty Plot. Our family went from a modest single-family ranch-style home to a large home in a beautiful historic neighborhood, which was their pride and joy their whole lives. Our home was located just one block up from Union College, two blocks over from Ellis Hospital, and next door to the Steinmetz Memorial Park, named after renowned General Electric scientist Charles P. Steinmetz, who was a mathematician, electrical engineer, and professor at Union College.

Our home was one plot down from the Unitarian Universalist Society of Schenectady, and my parents embraced Unitarian Universalist values as they raised a family. They were both raised and married in the Catholic church but remained members of the Unitarian Universalist congregation for the rest of their lives. Our Percival Lewin home had been built in 1908 and was previously owned by Dr. Fuchs, who ran his medical practice from the basement. My father also ran his part-time psychologist practice there.

I was blessed to grow up in a household with loving parents and siblings. I have been extremely close to my family my whole life, and as I was growing up, my parents honored the unique, independent, and strong personalities of their children. I hold treasured memories of my father taking us to Schenectady's Central Park. We all went sledding and had hilarious snowball fights—my sister and me in the back of our tiny Volkswagen Bug and our brothers on the outside throwing snowballs at us. We also learned to ice skate, looking like little penguins. Most nights, we sat around our kitchen table for dinner, sharing stories from the day. We had an idyllic childhood, catching fireflies in tin cans and playing with other children in our neighborhood: kick the can, hide-and-seek, and monster-in-the-lair. We were also fortunate to have open space to run and play at Steinmetz Memorial Park next door. We explored nature at Hans Groot's Kill, which we referred to as the ravine, located nearby. We took exhilarating trips to Jones Beach in Long Island with its rocky ocean bottom and strong riptides, and to Maine's coastal waters to collect boulders for my mother's exquisite Japanese garden that she nurtured for many years at our Wendell Avenue home. We also visited our wonderful extended family of grandparents, aunts, uncles, and cousins for many holidays in Brooklyn and Long Island.

Early on, my parents had household help from South America, with families living in our basement from time to time, but later we each had chores of cooking, cleaning, vacuuming, taking out the garbage, and yard work. My parents ran a tight ship but made sure we were all loved beyond measure. Once, when my brothers Mark and Carl were bickering and chasing each other around the living room, Mark was fortunate to jump over my parents' beloved rectangular marble cocktail table, but Carl regrettably landed right in its center, cracking the table in half. There were a few times when my parents had a stern word or a slap on the behind for us. That was one of those times for my brothers. My sister and I hid.

Despite a few misdeeds, each sibling blossomed into a well-rounded individual. Carl set a high academic standard, mentoring and role modeling for the rest of us. We also had our own interests outside of academics, enjoying extracurricular activities and excelling in different ways. Our parents had clear expectations that, for the best possible outcomes, academics would be the foundation of our lives.

On Sunday mornings, we walked to our Unitarian church, which provided a spiritual foundation for us to choose how we wanted to incorporate religion or spirituality into our lives. We attended weekly Sunday school. Unitarian Universalist teachings encourage individuals of all ages to choose for themselves whether to believe in a higher power or not, how to treat others, and how to support their communities. Each winter holiday season, we attended a candlelight solstice service and brought child-size gloves, scarves, and mittens to place on a large live evergreen tree to share with others in need.

ARTIST IN RESIDENCE

was incredibly fortunate to witness our mother, a self-taught sculptor, creating pieces in a variety of media, including plaster, metal, wood, clay, and lead, all on our kitchen table or in her basement studio. She took a few classes at Skidmore College and Union College and trained under two highly regarded local artists, Schenectady resident Robert Blood and Lefu Gu from Saratoga. My mother created, right in front of my eyes, a myriad of busts, dancing figures, guitar players, abstract pieces, still-life paintings, and Japanese brush paintings of landscapes. Inspired by a trip she and my father made to Kyoto, Japan, she decorated the inside of our family home in an Asian design style and created a serene Japanese garden, which she embellished for over fifty years. My mother was very proud to participate in several house and garden tours for the Schenectady County Historical Society.

To this day, all my siblings cherish having several of our mother's sculptures and paintings, along with my grandfather Ernesto's exquisite Italian sculptures, in our homes. I greatly admired the artistic skills of my mother and Poppy. My mother created a childhood home of beauty and love, inside and out—a cherished environment and a true blessing to me.

ROLL UP THE CARPETS

As far back as I can remember, my father would put on some of his favorite vinyl record albums and encourage all four kids to move to the music in whatever way felt right. Around age six, attempting to mirror my ten-year-old brother Carl—the "smooth operator" of the family, as my dad used to call him—I did my own version of rock and roll freestyle. My dancing, however, was more like an awkward gyration with my arms gawkily moving back and forth. Some of us are born with natural dance movement, but as evidenced by a video I later discovered, I was not. It is hilarious to see my early dancing, and let us just say, it was not a graceful beginning. Although I felt redeemed when I recently saw a video of others dancing during that era, as I truly danced like them. I laughed so hard because I knew I had looked exceptionally clumsy, but apparently, it was the style back then. Who knew! Mark, eight years old at the time, did a breakdancing routine, spinning around on the floor with silly antics, while Mayela, aged four with a cherubic face, began reciting lines from one of her favorite books, *Way Up in the Sky*. While she was reciting from memory, she was quite animated, using her arms in graceful movements to illustrate "the wing on the left" and "the wing on the right" and how "the big sun comes up." She was using her arms to dance, just like I do in ballroom waltz today. We all had an early introduction to dance, encouraged by our parents. I am profoundly grateful that we were all supported to embrace our individuality and find our own style; our parents respected our distinctive personalities in dance and in life.

A few special times a year, my parents would throw parties in our Schenectady home to celebrate a variety of milestones: birthdays, anniversaries, and other holidays. My mother was an excellent cook who had learned from her Italian mother-in-law, Rosina Calabria. As soon as I was old enough, I helped my mother in the kitchen, learning to cook all our treasured family recipes: chicken cacciatore, rice pilaf, shrimp toast, roasted red peppers, empanadas, poppy-seed cake, pearl-tapioca pudding, crescent cookies, and rice pudding. After dinner, our bellies were full. We celebrated each occasion with extended family from Long Island—aunts, uncles, cousins—as well as local friends, who were all on hand to mark any worthy milestone. We enjoyed a buffet of delicacies and the aroma of rich spices from around the world that permeated the kitchen, family room, living room, hallway, staircase, and dining room.

We listened to soothing jazz music in the background, carefully selected by my father from his extensive music collection. He would play tunes by Herb Alpert, Louis Armstrong, Count Basie, and Nana Mouskouri. Musical talent ran in my father's family, and he and his brother Ernie both played classical guitar. Uncle Ernie released an LP in 1971, *Prelude to Love,* with his wife Barbara Massey on vocals and piano. On incredibly special occasions, Uncle Ernie, my father, and his dear classical guitar instructor, Maria Zemantauski, would play guitar in our living room, a cherished treat to be remembered. My father was extremely diligent about his guitar playing, which did not come easily to him, repeating scales and pieces of music over and over. Normally, my dad only played guitar for himself, practicing mostly at night while my sister and I fell asleep. This is a precious memory of mine, and to this day, I listen to classical guitar music to soothe my soul, thinking of my father and those nights of falling peacefully asleep to his playing.

After the guitar performances, my father would start the process of rolling up the living room carpet, exposing the beautiful oak hardwood floors for the final highlight of the evening: the dancing. My dad would shift the tempo, putting on his favorite Latin music—rumbas, cha-chas, salsas, merengues, and mambos—and encouraging everyone to get on the floor and dance. Any kind of dance was encouraged in our household, a reflection of our parents' inclusivity in all forms of human expression. Almost everyone was on the dance floor. The most spectacular part of the evening was when my parents would do an impromptu dance performance, a medley of their favorite sultry Latin dances. My dad would typically start leading my mom in a slow, sensual rumba, then shift to a racy cha-cha, throw in an energetic merengue, and always culminate with a spicy mambo. My parents beamed with delight, dancing in their beloved, grand home, surrounded by their dearest family members and friends, and receiving robust applause from everyone.

FOLK DANCING

On Friday nights, after a long workweek, my dad would rally my mom to attend the local folk dances at the YWCA of Schenectady. During the week, my mom was engaged in raising four children, in addition to working part-time for a local silk-screen company in our home. She was doing the same copy-and-transfer design work used to reproduce fabrics and wallpaper that she did at her first job in New York City. My mom also helped oversee two rental properties in Riverdale, New

York, when her mother, who had dementia, came to live with us. My dad would start playing upbeat dance music, which would entice my mom to collect her dance shoes, and off they would go. Very few children attended folk dances with their parents, but given the chance to stay home on my own on a Friday night or go to a folk dance with my parents, my choice was to dance. This reminds me of a song by Lee Ann Womack, released in 2000, called "I Hope You Dance." At first, I just sat and watched the dancers, but with some encouragement, I started to learn some of the basic figures and soon became a regular participant. I vividly remember learning these favorite dances: the Israeli Hora (to the song "Hava Nagila"), the Armenian Miserlou, the Greek Zorba, and the Russian Troika. Some of the dances were done shoulder to shoulder, or in my case, hand to hand, as I was nowhere near tall enough to reach adult shoulders.

At Union College, my father's creative teaching style often included movement and experiential-learning exercises, which illustrated or incorporated psychological and educational principles. Some of my cherished childhood memories are of the parties my parents hosted for my dad's Union College students. The students would come for dinner with no idea what was in store for them. They were treated to a buffet of ethnically diverse foods made by my mom with assistance from my sister and me. After dinner, my dad would put on his favorite folk-dance music from countries around the globe. We would roll up the carpets again, and my parents would demonstrate a traditional folk dance and then give a mini dance lesson. Once the students started to relax, they enjoyed their nontraditional class in our living room.

SEAMSTRESS SHOP

As a teenager, in addition to babysitting for a variety of local families during the academic school year, my very first summer job was ironing clothes in a local seamstress shop on Van Vranken Avenue, a mile or so from my home. I was paid a modest amount for each piece I ironed, so I was not getting rich that summer. It did, however, give me an appreciation for hard work.

I smile when I think about my parallel work connection to Abuelita, who also had a first job in a seamstress shop when she came to the US and settled in Manhattan. In her case, she was sewing and altering dresses; I was ironing them. To this day, when I am ironing an outfit for work or a special occasion, I think back to my very first job ironing clothes and the connection to both Abuelita and my mother, who was an excellent seamstress, making many of our clothes growing up, including double-stitched jean overalls when they were in style. My mother also knitted Easter dresses for my sister and me, and sweaters for my father and brothers.

COURTSHIP

I met my boyfriend, John, when I was in high school, as he and my brothers and other friends used to work on cars in our Wendell Avenue driveway. Initially, my parents were not too keen on my having a steady boyfriend at age fourteen, especially one almost three years older than I was, but John and I formed a close relationship and became high school sweethearts. I had several friendships with male classmates in the Mont Pleasant Technical Program I attended across town and a few close girlfriends while John and I dated, attending his senior ball, my junior prom, and my senior ball together. John came to basketball games where I was a cheerleader, picked me up from piano lessons, and after he got off work at a local pizzeria, brought me ice cream sundaes while I babysat across the street from my home. We had a traditional courtship while I focused on my academic work. We went to the movies often, something we both enjoyed, which is the foundation of my enduring love of popcorn and red licorice.

One unique thing John and I had in common was that neither of us ever felt a need to drink alcohol, a pastime most other students our age had. My father genuinely enjoyed his homemade Italian wine with dinner, and we always had the opportunity to try some, but I preferred my sweets. I don't recall trying to make a statement about not drinking alcohol; I simply did not like the way it made me feel, which was mostly lightheaded, the same reaction my mother felt. I also didn't like the idea of not being in control around others when drinking alcohol.

My parents hosted a sweet sixteen birthday party for me in our home, as my mother felt strongly about honoring her Latin roots, and it was like having a quinceañera at age fifteen to mark the transition from girlhood to womanhood. I invited John, my high school friends, and dear cousins, and we rolled up the carpets and danced. I remember wearing a light-purple dress, a long necklace, and high-heeled, T-strapped shoes to look my best. Once the music played and the lights were dimmed, I enjoyed dancing with my friends and family. It was a bit awkward having John and my high school friends at the same venue, as they were from two different parts of my life, and somehow they never seemed to gel. John and I dated on and off during my Union College years, although my predominant focus was continuing with academics, studying around the clock, and laying the foundation for my future career.

EARLY LIFE LESSONS

*M*y dad was affectionately known as Crazy Frank. He was most certainly not crazy, but more like a creative genius, willing to use unique teaching methods with his students. Later in my life, many of my father's students who I met mentioned how much they loved my dad and his nontraditional teaching style, recalling the joy of dance lessons they had in our family living room. I witnessed firsthand, at an early age, how dance and a willingness to think outside the box can bring together people of all ages, backgrounds, and abilities. I recall hearing stories of how my father hosted classes outside in Union College's Jackson's Garden, where he asked students to blindfold each other and use senses other than sight to explore their surroundings. I heard another student share how they were encouraged to use creative writing and puppet-making skills to explore different types of communication in my father's humanistic psychology classes. I feel a heartwarming connection to his unique teaching methods, paralleling my personal and professional approaches to life; we were both willing to think outside of traditional ideas.

I was filled with pride recently to be reminded by a friend that while I was in middle school, I stood up for a fellow classmate who was being picked on by mean girls in our physical education class for her lack of athleticism. I went directly to the school gym teacher, reported the unacceptable conduct, and insisted it stop. My friend reminded me of how it had affected her to see me standing up for another student at a formative age. I am proud of my younger self.

My mom prided herself on raising four children with my father, stretching his full-time professor's salary and her part-time income from silk-screen work and rental properties as far as she could with her frugal budgeting strategies. Throughout her life, my mom kept a handwritten ledger of every single household expense and filled it in monthly. We grew up in a big house, but it was chillier than most with the thermostat set low, especially at night, to save on electricity. My parents both took tremendous pride in having a large home and preferred to minimize household expenses, including fancy clothes, haircuts, and heat. I learned a great deal about household budgeting from my mother, an important financial lesson that was instrumental in my life and future career.

Later, when I was in high school, focused on very high academic achievement, playing the piano at a competitive level, and doing competitive team gymnastics at the YWCA, my mother noticed the pressure I was experiencing in my teenage life. She suggested it was time to forgo my piano lessons because the intense stress of preparing for recitals at Albany's performing arts center, known as The Egg, was taking too great a toll on me. I was struggling to keep a balanced life as a dating teenager with academic pursuits and extracurricular activities as my top priorities, believing they would be an essential foundation for my life. The stress was affecting me, a worrier from a young age, in significant ways. I am grateful my mother suggested it was time to reassess my priorities, helping me find balance at that stage in my life.

Not everything in my childhood was idyllic. I had one repressed memory from my very early life that I shockingly remembered while I was in college well over a decade later. I was watching a movie called *Born Innocent*, which addresses the topic of repressed memories, and it triggered my own. I recalled that when I was five years old, on two occasions, I was kissed and fondled by a teenage son of the household help living in our basement. I have attempted to keep that memory in my past and not allow it to have any power over me, but it is disturbing, especially when I hear stories of so many other women with experiences of sexual abuse.

CHAPTER TWO:
Education

M y father, a Renaissance man, always believed in me 100 percent, telling me that I could be anything professionally, including president of the United States, if I wanted. I chuckled and grinned from ear to ear. I had such an incredible foundation of love and support from my parents, who were always focused on my formal and informal education. Our culturally enriching exposure to music, dance, and food from around the world, in addition to travel, made for an incredibly inspirational foundation for the rest of my life. With a father who was a college professor, education was always a priority, but never with a heavy hand. All siblings were expected to do our best in all aspects of our academic lives, but not at a cost to our health or wellness.

My siblings and I attended Zoller Elementary School and Oneida Middle School, walking to and from school with neighbor friends our age. I loved stopping by the Normanskill convenience store on our way home to get sweet treats. I did get myself into trouble when I took two cents from my mother's wallet to buy a freeze pop that cost four cents when I was in kindergarten. I only had two cents. When my mother caught me, I had to pay my two cents to her, a formidable life lesson at a very young age. I am grateful to have had a very positive Schenectady public school experience—academically, socially, and emotionally.

MECHANICAL ENGINEERING / ECONOMICS

I graduated from Mont Pleasant High School in 1980, salutatorian of our class and number one in my college preparatory technical program. This was one of only two programs in New York State. I was one of approximately thirty students who finished the program, following in the footsteps of my two older brothers. My sister, not having an interest in the technology curriculum, attended Linton High School, later known as Schenectady High School, which was a better fit for her.

During the program, I designed and built a model residential deck and made an architectural drawing for a private residence, complete with a grand ballroom, circular atrium for plants, and Roman columns. I learned about the Tinius Olsen machine and how to test a variety of metal alloys. This included finding the breaking point of steel, aluminum, and brass, and studying chemical etchings to learn more about their breaking principles. I was also a basketball cheerleader, a member of the yearbook committee, a tennis player on the men's team, as they did not have a women's team, a participant in Spanish Club and the Spanish National Honor Society who placed fourth in the National Spanish Contest, and a fundraiser who enjoyed selling doughnuts and pizza to connect with fellow classmates. I dressed up every Halloween in homemade costumes to enjoy the less serious side of myself, including a football player, Raggedy Ann, and a pink bunny with a huge cotton tail and bendable ears.

I had one memorable mean-girls experience when I discovered beer and cigarettes had been dumped into my pocketbook at a local dance, which is a sad recollection. Because I did not drink or smoke, I was perceived as somewhat of a goody two shoes. I never did seem to fit in 100 percent with the boys or the girls, as I was predominantly focused on academic pursuits.

I was proud to get into Union College, as my father's employment benefits included full tuition coverage if we attended Union, or half tuition coverage at any other college or university in the US. My parents were only required to pay for room and board expenses and encouraged me to live on campus all four years, despite our home only being one block from campus, as they believed it would be an important personal growth opportunity for me.

Although I had expected college to be difficult academically, I hadn't expected it to be so exceptionally rigorous. My first semester was one of the most intellectually challenging times in my life. I was taking chemistry, calculus, and economics on a trimester system, which required absorbing a significant amount of information in a short period of time. I was adjusting to living on campus in an all-women dormitory, attempting to be proactively engaged in campus networking activities, but I was struggling academically for the first time in my life. I went from being at the top of my high school program to studying around the clock, only to get my first C+ in chemistry. Up to that point, I had always done extremely well in math and science classes and was majoring in mechanical engineering. Carl had just graduated from Union College with an electrical engineering degree, and Mark was in his second year of mechanical engineering at Northeastern University in Boston, Massachusetts, so I was following in their footsteps. After classes, I went to my chemistry professor for help on a regular basis, hoping to improve my grade through extra credit, but I simply could not grasp or memorize the complex concepts in the required material. I worked extremely hard to attempt to learn the principles in the allotted time. Thankfully, I got A's in both calculus and economics, so my grade point average was within the accepted range, but it was shocking for me because I had always excelled educationally and taken my academics very seriously.

Studying around the clock left little time for a vibrant college social life, except for befriending the women in my Richmond

House dormitory and dating John. The women in my dormitory bonded over common academic challenges and formed good friendships. I made positive connections with women friends during my college years, creating a small, informal impact circle. We genuinely cared about each other. I recall one student who didn't know how to polish her shoes. She came from a wealthy family and had no idea what I was doing when I started polishing my shoes to attempt to keep them looking new.

I was fortunate to have great first roommates, but in subsequent years, I found it was helpful to have my own space because I studied at all hours of the day and night. Once my academic rigors began to moderate, I participated in additional extracurricular activities such as the Society of Women Engineers and acted as an Orientation Advisor and Campus Tour Guide. I stayed on campus longer than many students, as I was driven to succeed academically and certainly did not want to disappoint my parents or myself.

COLLEGIATE SPORTS

was surprised to be recruited as a walk-on to the Union College women's tennis team during my sophomore year. Although I was on the Mont Pleasant High School men's tennis team, I never expected to play collegiate sports. I was most definitely not one of the strongest tennis players on the team, and I played in one of the last singles slots, but I attended every practice, went to every match, kept mentally strong, and was consistent in getting the ball over the net, despite not having a great serve or a strong backhand. I simply fought to win every single point for my team. At the end of the fall season, I was asked to make sure to attend the sports banquet and was astonished to have been selected as Most Valuable Player. Apparently, I won more points for my team than anyone else.

This was a valuable life lesson because I was far from the best player on the team, just the most consistent. I was extremely fortunate to have a coach who valued more than just team placement on a roster.

While I was focused on my mechanical engineering course-work, I found my classmates tended to be male students. One day, a fellow student invited me to join his friends in a Tae Kwon Do class. I had no idea what Tae Kwon Do was at the time but learned it was a "hand-foot" art form. I met the instructor, an impressive woman student who had her black belt. I was in a class of approximately twenty-five boys and five girls, which was much like the gender ratio I was experiencing in my engi-neering curriculum. I was used to being one of very few women in my classes. The end goal was to learn a series of structured, flowing moves that formed a routine. Each student would be expected to perform personal routines in front of a group of judges at the end of a ten-week session.

We were encouraged to invite guests to the final testing event, so I invited John and my parents. I was mentally and physically ready to do my routine. I watched a series of students, admiring them as they executed their routines. When it was my turn, I was laser focused on the task at hand. I had to perform several dozen moves in a flowing manner with grace and intensity in front of the panel of judges, who would decide whether students passed on to the next level. The routine was a blur for me, except for the components where we were required to do what is called a "kiai," basically a yell that sounds like "kia!" to stress the level of intensity of a particular move. I was pleasantly surprised by the power that came out of my 5'1" body as I made a noise that silenced the room each time. Upon completion, my parents were beaming with pride; they had witnessed their eldest daughter perform a unique physical art form, delivering an excellent demonstration in front of a small crowd, in stark contrast to my prior, graceful gymnastics routines and lyrical piano recitals.

When it came time for the judges to present the belt-testing results, I was elated to receive the highest rank in the class, a yellow belt with two green stripes. The judges said they were almost ready to award me a green belt, which rarely occurred. I found the entire experience to be incredibly empowering; I was most definitely out of my comfort zone, doing something physically demanding, and distinguishing myself with honors. It was an intense and powerful way to use my physical and mental strength, which I learned could come in several forms and still be feminine. This experience, as a young woman in college, gave me a renewed sense that I could use my voice and my physical strength, increasing my level of self-confidence. I also took a self-defense class for women that was offered in my dormitory, hoping to increase my personal safety. Both classes were important foundations for my individual power.

SUMMER INTERNSHIPS

My summer internship as a mechanical engineering student was pivotal in my career trajectory. I worked in a small machine shop, Mohawk Development Services, in Duanesburg, New York, doing electrical wiring and soldering for General Electric turbine-vibration-panel testers and working on architectural drawings for gas turbines. During my technical high school classes, one of my favorite projects had been designing my dream home and building a miniature deck to scale out of balsa wood. During the last week of my internship, the president of the company asked me to fix a six-inch square, metal mechanical clock. I distinctly remember looking at the clock and thinking to myself, I have absolutely no interest in doing this. I was unlike my older brothers, who would have relished the opportunity. I preferred to think about where it might go on a fireplace mantel or how I could embellish it. In that moment, I decided I was not well suited to becoming an engineer. My brain simply didn't process information the way an engineer's did. I made it through the rigorous coursework, but I could not see myself in a professional engineering role. Knowing how important it was to keep my career options open, I saw the value in continuing with mechanical engineering, but I learned there was a separate major in Industrial Economics that combined engineering and economics.

During my next two summers, I worked as a bank teller at Mohawk National Bank, around the corner from where I lived. This suited my academic background, extroverted personality, and fashion sense much better—I preferred suits, dresses, and high heels to wearing jeans and T-shirts in the machine shop. As a bank teller, I only made one financial error, when I gave an elderly customer an extra one hundred dollars, but thankfully, she came in to return it the next day. Otherwise, I balanced my cash drawer every day and gained an interesting foundation for my future career in wealth management.

TERM ABROAD IN SPAIN

Before I headed to Spain on my college term abroad, my parents gently encouraged me to consider taking a break from my relationship with John, who I had been dating since I was fourteen and he was seventeen, as this was my first significant relationship. Following their suggestion, John and I took a break. I studied in Seville, traveling with a girlfriend in my junior year. We traveled to London, Cambridge, Bath, Oxford, Paris, and Barcelona before the term started, and after it ended, we ventured to Rome, Florence, and Venice. It was a fabulous itinerary, embraced by my parents.

On one of our adventures in England, we went in search of my girlfriend's ancestral town in Wales. We made it as far as the small town of Wells, where we had a good laugh because we hadn't understood the bus driver's accent and had ended up in the wrong place! We explored each city with gusto, soaking in every adventure. When we were in Paris, we stayed in a tiny flat in the heart of the city, thrilled to be there. However, it was the first time it had snowed there in twenty years. Not having proper attire and finding ourselves in an unheated apartment for our first Christmas away from our families, we wore every piece of clothing we had. We bought ourselves a roast chicken and a tiny Christmas tree, then strung popcorn garlands for a very simple holiday. While trying to sleep on the floor and freezing under every blanket and towel I could find in the small apartment, I got a call from John to wish me a Merry Christmas. I quietly began sobbing, because I couldn't reckon how he could have found a phone number for the flat, as I didn't even have it. Admittedly, it was a welcome call, as I was feeling a little homesick.

My term abroad was a transformative experience. In Seville, I lived with a widow who was hosting students predominantly for money, so it was not an ideal situation. She provided a warm breakfast and a bed to sleep in, but beyond that, I was on my own. I lived several miles from where all the other Union College students lived with families who had children. I was, however, lucky enough to be connected to one Spanish boy through Centro Norteamericano, where we were taking classes in town. Each semester, they introduced an American girl and a Spanish boy to each other. Antonio became a wonderful friend, making my Seville experience immensely more enjoyable and introducing me to his special friend group. They wanted to know everything I could share about what it was like to be an American girl, and I wanted to learn everything I could about life in Seville. After school and homework, my Seville friends took me everywhere, including to the famous Giralda, to town squares, and to the best traditional restaurants and bars, where we had tapas of *patatas bravas,* Spanish tortilla, fried calamari, and *churros y chocolate,* a quintessential Spanish treat. This circle of friends transformed my term-abroad experience. I felt welcomed, despite living with a widow who did not embrace my being there and having to walk several miles to school in the dark every morning by myself. With my poor sense of direction, this made for a scary experience, as it was well before cell phones, MapQuest, or GPS.

On our last adventure together, my Spanish friends rented a rowboat to show me all the unique parts of their city. They taught me how to dance their traditional Sevillana folk dances, reminding me of the folk dances I had learned with my parents at the YWCA. At the end of our boat ride, one of the boys gave me his father's wedding ring as a symbol of dear friendship, which totally blew me away. It was not a romantic relationship in any way, just a friendship between an American girl and Spanish boy. The ring reminds me it's possible to have a meaningful platonic friendship with someone within a short amount of time. Decades later, after we were all married and had families, I reconnected with several of those friends. The impact we had on each other was palpable. I had changed their opinion of Americans from negative, based on what they had seen on their televisions, to positive. I can now see this was another early, informal impact circle.

With the Union College term-abroad students, I traveled to Toledo, Malaga, Granada, and other small towns in Spain. It was riveting to see famous works of art in person, such as Leonardo da Vinci's *Mona Lisa* at the Louvre in Paris and Pablo Picasso's *Guernica* in Spain, surrounded by heavily armed security guards, bringing to life the slides from my art history class, which was my favorite elective course.

I recently found a letter I wrote to my parents in cursive after I graduated from Union College, expressing my deep gratitude to them for my education and study abroad. I am proud that I could directly share my appreciation with them in a beautiful, sentimental letter at that age. I was grateful for such a remarkable experience. Upon return from my European travels, John and I unexpectedly bumped into each other when I was at a local discotheque called Sneaky Pete's with both of my brothers. It was a few weeks after I had dropped off a tiny Venetian gondola, a souvenir I had purchased after our Christmas Day call in Paris, at the pizza shop where John worked. We started dating again.

SENIOR THESIS

My senior thesis, "The Impact Computers Have on Factory and Office Employment," was an important part of my academic experience at Union College and the first time I applied real-world business concepts to my coursework. I remember reading the book *Megatrends* by John Naisbitt and exploring the burgeoning personal computer industry and how it might affect future jobs. Using Union College's library, I uncovered research pieces written by Al Gore. It was exciting to research how global business worked and how the trends of the future might impact my life, personally and professionally. I was conducting serious statistical research with a practical purpose, helping to broaden my future professional endeavors, and exploring potential careers. From that business research, I felt my budding entrepreneurial spirit building on the pizza-and-doughnut-sales success I had in high school, with my sweet tooth and love of Italian food in action.

Before I graduated from Union College in 1984 with a degree in Industrial Economics, I had absolutely no idea what I wanted to do as a career. I used the college's career center and investigated a variety of paths but honestly didn't know which direction I would head in. I remember being intrigued by the fashion industry, but after learning about the compensation structure and what it took to get to a high-level position, I decided I needed to explore a path that could get me to a more prominent position sooner. I sent cover letters and my résumé to over fifty local companies, including engineering firms, and met with Union College alumni, but had discouraging results. I was disappointed about being turned down for training programs in bank management and financial management that male accounting classmates were offered instead. This was my first taste of what felt like gender discrimination, considering my high academic standing and extensive summer internships.

CHAPTER THREE:
Career

After graduating from college, I got my first apartment with a girlfriend on Union Street in Schenectady, sharing a third-floor space in a large house. I was less than a mile from my childhood home and beginning my journey to financial independence. I continued looking for my first official job, typing my résumé and sending it to be printed in bulk. After researching many industries, I sent out dozens of customized cover letters to companies with entry-level positions. I was surprised how handy my high school typing class proved to be; I had not anticipated needing those skills in my future career or the ensuing personal computer revolution.

After three months of serious job searching in the summer of 1984, and anxious to put my formal education to use, I turned to employment openings advertised in local newspapers. I applied for a position at Lela Computers, a small retail shop that sold personal computers, and I finally got my first job offer on the spot.

COMPUTER SALES

Before accepting that position, I thought it prudent to research the entire local computer retail industry. I interviewed with the local IBM office, but they did not have open positions in Albany. Instead, they set me up with an interview in Parsippany, New Jersey, two and a half hours away. John drove back and forth with me to that job interview. Apparently, my luggage was never loaded into the car, so John drove all the way back to retrieve it in a snowstorm. On another occasion, John had walked to and from his home in Altamont to mine in Schenectady, which was over ten miles away, during another snowstorm because his parents wouldn't let him drive on such a snowy day. At that point, John showed a serious commitment to our relationship, performing loving deeds, for sure, and giving me many endearing Hallmark cards.

I never got an employment offer from IBM, but I secured a competitive offer from The Computer Room, the Capital Region's largest personal computer dealer, to sell IBM, Apple, Hewlett-Packard, and Epson brands. My first full-time professional role was as a Computer Sales Representative in a stand-alone building located at 1492 Central Avenue in Albany, New York. There was no real sales training; I just watched seasoned managers on the retail floor.

A few months into my job, one of the salesmen I worked with in our tiny office came to get me, saying somebody was there to see me. I walked over, greeted the customer, and asked a few questions about what he was looking for. The man pulled out a long list of items he wanted to purchase: an Apple computer with the most processing power, a printer, printer cartridges, an extra hard drive, software packages (then on floppy disks), and connecting cords. This was a comprehensive computer system and my largest sale to date: $7,000. At the end of the conversation, I inquired why he had asked for me. He said, "I didn't ask for you. I said I wanted a Lisa." Mystery solved. I grinned, trying to maintain my professional composure, as I shared that my name was Alissa, pronounced "a-lee-sa." The name of the computer he requested was called "Lisa" after Steve Jobs's daughter. We both had a good laugh.

(Thank you, Mom, for my name! My whole life, I have struggled with people mispronouncing and misspelling my name as Alicia, Alyssa, Aleesa, Alice, Elissa, Eliza, Elise, and more. I always share with people that my name is pronounced like "Mona Lisa," and that tends to help a little bit. To this day, I still have many long-standing friends, colleagues, and clients who mispronounce and incorrectly spell my name. I am, however, grateful for its uniqueness.)

Within a year, I was promoted to Corporate Marketing Representative, when our company merged with Future Information Systems, and I shifted from retail to corporate sales, selling computer solutions to businesses. I clearly needed to figure out a way to fulfill this role my way, as the managers I worked under used a sales style known in the day as "smoke-stack chasing," visiting businesses unannounced. This was not likely to be my best approach. Instead, I researched and reached out to local businesses, discovered how to listen to the needs of potential business clients, and presented customized computer system solutions.

I also learned how to configure motherboard chipsets, the collection of electronic components that manage data flow between the computer processing unit, the graphics process-ing unit, and random-access memory. It did put some of my engineering technology skills to work. Soon, I had a routine and figured out what sales process and cycle worked for me. For each sale, I connected all system components, downloaded computer software, loaded all the bulky computer boxes into the back seat of my first new car, a gray Honda Prelude, and hand-delivered and set up computer systems in corporate office settings.

It was a good first full-time job. I developed sales and market-ing skills and earned a higher income than I would have in the management training programs I was denied. Sweet victory! More importantly, I developed lifelong friendships with two of my initial managers. After three years, I noticed a trend: Once corporations knew what types of computer systems and software they needed, they could use the burgeoning mail-order industry, which provided cheaper pricing. Seeing the writing on the wall, I believed it was time to explore a different career path. I could appreciate my abuelita's ability to think in advance about the challenges she and her children might encounter in their home country. I was feeling the same in my professional role and felt I should explore a new path.

BUSINESS AND PROFESSIONAL WOMEN'S CLUB

I received a lovely handwritten note from the president of the local Business and Professional Women's Club (BPW) of Schenectady after she saw my Union College graduation announcement. She invited me to come to a club dinner, where I met an amazing group of professional women with long careers behind them. I truly enjoyed getting to know these women and hearing about their career paths just as I was beginning mine. I joined the network and began making connections of all kinds.

As part of BPW, I was asked to participate in the Individual Development Program's public-speaking training class. I had no idea what my professional career might bring in the coming years, but I figured it certainly would not hurt for me to have practice in public speaking. The program's instructor was Judi Clements, who led a small class through a series of exercises, practicing writing and giving speeches. At the end of the program, there was a public-speaking contest at the local level. Students were asked to write a speech and then deliver it in front of their peers. I was the youngest member of the class. I was pleasantly surprised to be voted as the winner, and I was asked to deliver the same speech at the regional BPW meeting, where I won the contest again. This time, I was asked to represent our club at the New York State BPW Convention in Lake Placid and deliver my speech in front of over a hundred professional women from across the state.

My topic, from the beginning, had been smoking in the workplace. At that time, smoking was permitted in New York State (NYS) offices, and I shared a small workspace with several smokers. I came home each night with clothes that reeked of cigarette smoke. It was unpleasant and unhealthy to work in those conditions. I recall having nicotine withdrawal going home some nights. The most impactful part of my speech was the story of a coworker, whose father was a smoker. She said that when she was four years old, she went to the windowsill of her second-story bedroom, opened it, and screamed to her father, "If you don't quit smoking, I am going to jump. I mean it!" Her father quit on the spot.

To my delight, I won the NYS public-speaking competition and was asked to go to Milwaukee, Wisconsin, to present my speech in front of four hundred delegates from BPW clubs across the US. I delivered my speech after dinner in a room that was so filled with smoke I could barely see past the first row. I was clearly more nervous delivering my topic under these smoky conditions but was determined to give it my best effort. Although I did not win the national contest, I vividly recall one woman coming up to me after my presentation with a cigarette in her hand, saying that she didn't particularly appreciate the topic of my speech but that I had delivered it brilliantly. I grinned and was proud of my courageous twenty-three-year-old self.

That experience would prove to be a great foundation for my business journey in the years ahead. Judi Clements and I have remained in touch ever since, and I'm grateful for her professional guidance and support. We recently reconnected at a Schenectady BPW dinner and reminisced about the impact her class had on me and my professional journey.

Another Schenectady BPW member, Joanne Valentine, a financial consultant at Prudential-Bache, invited me to lunch to discuss her professional role and a potential career path for me. She said, "You would be really good at what I do." I remarked that I had no idea what she did. My parents had never disclosed anything about their investments to me, nor was I aware that they had a financial consultant. All I knew was that my mother kept exceptionally detailed expense ledgers of our family budget, was frugal, and was focused on raising four children on my father's salary with additional income from her part-time silk-screen work. Joanne outlined what her career path had been and said there were many firms that had comprehensive financial-management training programs. She shared that investment sales experience was not required, but that my computer sales experience could be an excellent foundation.

I decided to explore what a career in financial management might look like. I interviewed at the main local brokerage firms: E. F. Hutton, Merrill Lynch, First Albany, and Shearson Lehman Brothers. My BPW informal impact circle completely changed the trajectory of my burgeoning career, and connecting with its members provided one of the most powerful results I experienced.

FINANCIAL ADVISOR

nly one financial services company in the Capital District was willing to take a chance on me, a twenty-four-year-old woman with three years of sales experience. After seven interviews; personality, competency, and aptitude tests; and conversations with other financial consultants in the firm's office, the hiring manager said, "I have good news and bad news. The good news is we would like to offer you a position as a trainee financial consultant, but I am moving on to a different role and will not be your manager."

I had to digest that the one person willing to take a chance on me would not be there. Instead, I met with the new manager for a cup of tea at Peaches Café, immediately across the street from their downtown Albany office. I was extremely impressed with the new manager and thought he was genuine, articulate, and supportive. He shared that I would have to pass five major exams on the first attempt: the Series 7 General Securities Representative Exam, Series 66 State Law Exam, Series 3 National Commodities Futures Exam, and NYS Life and Health Insurance Exams. Otherwise, I would be terminated. I would be sent to New York City's Twin Towers for eight weeks. With no safety net, I chose to take the position with little actual understanding of what I was getting myself into. I was taking a large step back from a salaried job where I also earned a commission to accept an opportunity for uncertain future gain.

I started studying the curriculum known as Broker in a Box, which had dozens of individual booklets for each financial management concentration. I had little basis for the content I was about to learn, as I had only studied the basics of capital markets, company balance sheets, and accounting at Union College, writing one research report on a publicly traded company. I was extremely diligent and took my studying seriously. I certainly did not want to be terminated before I even got a chance to explore this new career path. My NYC job preparation included rooming with five women in an apartment suite across from the World Trade Center for eight weeks and learning financial product knowledge, sales skills, and cold calling in a class of fifty-one trainees from across the East Coast. Eleven of us were women. Thankfully, after months of studying around the clock, I passed all five exams on the first try, allowing me to keep my job and attempt a career as a financial consultant. Soon thereafter, our titles changed to financial advisor.

I worked exceptionally long hours, having no idea if I would be able to make a living on this career path. At the beginning of the training program, in the auditorium, we looked around and were told that only two out of three trainees were likely to finish. I was the only woman financial advisor in my office of twenty-five men in Albany, and by the end of the eighteen-month training program, I was also the only woman left out of eleven trainees from the whole East Coast. At the end, only one-third of the initial trainees were left, a sobering statistic. I was, surprisingly, voted the most likely financial advisor to succeed by all five of my trainers.

I was proud to prove them right by being named the #1 financial advisor at the end of the program, based on the number of client relationships we developed. They apparently had more faith in me than I did at the time; by my third year as a financial advisor, I had begun exploring other potential career options, because I truly had no idea if I could survive in an entrepreneurial career with no base salary. Thankfully, my first manager was exceptional and mentored me, encouraging me to keep doing what I was doing. I did so with tremendous perseverance and hard work.

PROFESSIONAL WOMEN'S NETWORK

As the sole woman financial advisor in my Albany office, I knew I had to figure out how to attract clients in my own way instead of cold calling, as we had been taught in our training program. I needed to think of a different strategy for what success would look and feel like to me. All five trainers had voted for me as most likely to succeed. What was it they saw in me that was different from the other trainees? The answer is they recognized that my approach to sales was relationship-based. I knew my strengths were in developing relationships and connections with professionals, despite my youth and inexperience. I had been actively involved in the BPW and felt I needed to build on those types of connections. I loved the concept of networking with women in my community but felt I needed a more fine-tuned approach to business development. I would leverage my relationship capabilities and highlight my firm's resources to address the needs of potential clients, listening carefully to their needs and presenting solutions.

In 1989, I came up with an idea of forming a new group of businesswomen, whose primary focus was business development and who were willing to help each other succeed in a professional network of like-minded business owners and high-level women executives. I hand-selected professional women from a variety of fields, meeting with one woman at a time and sharing the concept I had in mind. Members had to be willing to focus on their own business or professional development, but also willing to be part of something bigger than themselves. My first official impact circle, the Professional Women's Network (PWN), was born.

PWN was a group of approximately twenty executive women and women-owned businesses, including an attorney, a physician, a certified public accountant, a psychologist, a public relations business owner, an integrative nurse practitioner, a general business manager, a human resources professional, a mortgage broker, a commercial insurance agent, a real estate broker, a news anchor, a chamber of commerce professional, a women's leadership coach, an IBM executive, a print-shop specialist, and a corporate-gift business owner. We met for breakfast over the course of more than twenty years to focus on helping each other build our businesses and on our professional advancement.

As founder and first president, I went around the boardroom table with three simple questions: What do you need? What do you have to give or share? How can we help? We engaged in deep, meaningful conversations, helping each other within our fierce network of supporters. We invited speakers on a wide variety of topics, held full-day retreats, and even developed a philanthropic foundation, volunteering for causes we cared about and donating our time, talent, and treasure to make a collective impact.

Five years into our impact circle, one of our members had an unanticipated flash of vulnerability, shedding tears and sharing raw emotion with us all. It was at that moment that our group of professional women went from "suits to souls," genuinely caring first about our members and second about our business development. Over the years, our network focused on work-life integration and balance, using our strong "sounding board of directors."

Over the next two decades, we met for meals, had discussions, and hosted speakers on a variety of topics: breaking the glass ceiling, board work, stress management, personal fulfillment, business development, and entrepreneurial endeavors. We also enjoyed social outings. One favorite group memory was going to New York City, a first for one member, where we celebrated milestone birthdays, had tea at The Plaza, saw a Broadway show, *Mamma Mia!*, and went late-night disco dancing, allowing for deep bonding. We leaned on each other's professional skill sets, engaged in Myers-Briggs personality testing, and embraced strategies of how best to work with our teams and each other. We embraced the uniqueness of our extroverted and introverted personalities to grow as individuals as well as growing our businesses. We explored complementary healing modalities, including sound healing and integrative medicine through the medical resources in our group. We leaned on our legal, medical, accounting, banking, and financial expertise to help members in their business endeavors.

Our most memorable retreats were those at the Rensselaerville Institute and the excursions to country labyrinths with unique leadership training, where we focused on each member's personal and professional growth through vision-boarding, sharing hopes, dreams, and goals for deep, authentic healing. Our business relationships deepened and our friendships flourished.

One of my favorite PWN activities was when we volunteered at a local women's shelter and completely transformed one room, cleaning, painting, reorganizing, and decorating a safe space for a mother and her children. We made an impressive and meaningful difference. My involvement was shopping and decorating to help create a beautiful, inviting room. This is a skill set I have embraced my whole adult life, and this time I used it for an important outcome.

Our PWN was a trailblazing concept with long-lasting effects on our members, including friendships and professional relationships that endured over three decades. Here is a synopsis of what PWN meant, written by Jaruloch Whitehead, our third network president.

Alissa,

PWN and its members are very special to me; in my short life, I have yet to be able to trust so many women at the same time. Collectively, PWN is a group of the most genuine and trustworthy women I have known. Individually, PWN is a bunch of good friends, girlfriends.
I am really honored to be a part of this group of women, and I am flattered to be recognized [for making] some contributions to its success. More importantly, to me, you have all contributed to my growth, and I want to thank each of you...
For being my teacher
For your courage to stand up and smile
For your courage to take risks, to give challenges, to be fair, and to love

> *For the lesson [that] there is more than one right answer (at least nineteen, at the last count)*
> *For listening, with your hearts first and then with your brains*
> *For teaching me, by example, that it is OK and courageous to be your natural self; that you don't have to put on airs or act the part*
> *For the lesson that I am worth it, all of it*
> *For teaching that my weakness is also my strength*
> *For teaching me that it is OK not to know the answer*
> *For your faith, your wisdom, your belief*
> *For the lesson that there is more to life than achievements; there is the light side of life, there is fun!*
> *For the appreciation of beauty for its own sake*
> *For bringing out the dark side of me and forcing me to deal with my strengths and my weaknesses*
> *For teaching me to accept, to forgive, and to move forward*
> *For showing me different perspectives to life, to wealth, to love*
> *For showing us that underneath the successful veneer of a suit, we are so different, yet so similar*
> *This is a real list. I went down the membership list and asked myself what each member has taught me, and this is what I came up with, among others.*
> *Most of all, I admire your courage, your wisdom, your strength, your beauty, and I treasure your friendship, your generosity, of your time and your "selves."*
> *Thank you for all of that and for "the present."*
>
> *From my heart,*
> *Jaruloch*

Her passage beautifully summarized what I hoped our formal impact circle could provide. In 2024, we celebrated the thirty-fifth reunion of our PWN, with personal friendships and professional relationships that have endured over three decades.

SALES MANAGER

n 1997, ten years into my professional career in the financial services industry, and still with very few women in
leadership positions, I was surprised to be tapped for a sales
manager role in our Albany office. This position had not existed
before. Another financial advisor in the office was asked to be
an assistant manager, with the idea that we would both work
with the branch manager in a leadership team structure. I
was quite taken aback by the ask. My initial reaction was one
of skepticism. I was unclear about the motivation behind the
request. Was it to groom me for a path to leadership at a branch
office? Was it to increase sales in our office? Were they looking
to increase leadership diversity? I was not sure.

I did not initially see the benefits of such a role, as my primary
focus was building an income stream to support my family.
There was an unspoken rule of "Never give up your client base,"
as that is what generates income and provides job security.
Without it, you become expendable. The sales manager salary
would be nominal compared to the income I was commanding at that point in my career, finally hitting my professional
stride. That type of role was typically considered a stepping-
stone to branch management, and with very few women in
management roles in the financial services industry, there was
very little precedent. I had virtually no female role models. If I
chose that path, I would have to forge my own way, hoping my
style of collaborative leadership would be embraced.

As I contemplated all the possible outcomes, I decided to lean
on my PWN impact circle. We were a strong group of independent thinkers. Who better to bounce this idea off? I called a
barn-raising meeting, which we held whenever it was helpful to
focus on one member of the group for an important need that
arose. I hosted it at the Fort Orange Club and invited members

who were available to strategize about this important career decision. This included several members who were clients at the time.

The outcome of our roundtable discussion was surprisingly different from what I had anticipated. I shared the background information: If I chose to take the role of sales manager, I would remain a financial advisor and dedicate potentially 25 percent of my time to the role of office sales manager. I shared my concerns about the risks of my leadership style in a male-dominated industry, the nominal salary, and the long-term challenges of choosing a path in branch management. These included the potential need to move my family on a regular basis from smaller branches to larger branches around the country. This intelligent and caring network listened and then began asking thought-provoking questions.

One member shared "You have been extraordinarily successful in your career so far. What if you look back on not taking this position with regret? What is the downside to taking the position, committing to it for a year, and if you don't find it valuable, stepping aside at that time?"

That approach had not occurred to me, as I was focused on the long-term picture. I listened to the collective wisdom of the group and thought carefully about what my next step should be.

The following week, I accepted the role of sales manager, as I believed this opportunity might not present itself again, and I did not want to look back on this decision with regret. Shortly thereafter, I did an assessment training session in our NYC corporate offices, meeting with senior leaders from our firm and evaluating my potential for leadership. This was an extremely valuable experience, and I was viewed very favorably by senior leaders.

I began consulting with the financial advisors in my office one-on-one, focusing on business development and account-ability in their sales practices and sharing ideas at our weekly sales meetings. I met with our leadership team on a systematic basis, and we gauged the impact our new roles were having. The role was daunting, and I could see myself spending more than 25 percent of my time working to impact office sales.

JUNIOR PARTNER

round this time, an older financial advisor in our office was having health issues and asked me if I would be willing to take over the client base he had built up over the last thirty-five years. I was thrilled that he had selected me. I knew that as a sales manager focused on business development, a mother of a four-year-old son, and a volunteer for not-for-profit organizations I cared about, taking over another financial advisor's client base could topple my work-life balance. Because of this, I considered hiring a junior partner. This choice would be a pivotal moment in my career. I gave the matter careful consideration, and I began a search for a right-fit junior partner. My thought was that I would take over the larger client relationships and have a junior partner work with clients with less complex needs. I began inquiring about potential candidates and, surprisingly, two connections—a PWN member and a client—recommended the same person.

The woman who would become my best friend was just finishing her accounting degree at Siena College and cleaning houses part-time to help pay for her education. She had been widowed in her early thirties and gone back to school to complete her bachelor's degree. To support her house-cleaning business, I decided to hire her to clean my house; then I would ascertain whether to take the business conversation any further. When she shared a little of her background, I was intrigued and interested in talking with her professionally.

I asked the candidate to meet me at the Fort Orange Club, in the first room off the parking lot, later that week at noon. As this was my first official interview for a junior partner, I arrived thirty minutes early to review a series of questions I had printed in preparation for our discussion. I hoped she would be on time because, with my personal work ethic, I defined "on time" as at least ten minutes early in those days. At noon, as the grandfather clock started chiming, her head appeared around the corner; she had been sitting in the first room off the parking garage, called the Coat Room. I was in the next room, the Newspaper Room. She had been sitting there for thirty minutes thinking the same thing: My new partner had better be early, or this relationship is not going to work.

When she peered around the corner, we both faced a full-length mirror and saw ourselves reflected there. We were approximately the same height, around five feet tall, and we were wearing similar blue business suits, cream V-necked blouses, and blue pumps, similar hairstyles, and were even both of Italian heritage. We chuckled, as the reflection said a thousand words. During our business lunch, we found we shared many more things in common: We were both married to husbands named John, we owned the same Lenox ecru china pattern, we shared a similar work ethic and financial-planning philosophy, and we each drove out of the parking lot in a black BMW 3 Series car. I interviewed a few other candidates but ultimately hired her as my junior partner.

Without warning, the financial advisor who had planned to transition his clients to me decided to hire his son-in-law to take over his client base. This was devastating. Knowing family ties were stronger than business partnerships, my business partner and I simply chose to focus on building our own businesses in a strategic-alliance fashion, despite our disappointment. This setback gave me even more incentive to just focus on the families I served and on my business motto, which has always been "People don't care how much you know until they know how much you care."

Because I wanted to do an excellent job, I found myself spending more than 25 percent of my time in the sales manager role, and I was training my new business partner at the same time. As I had initially anticipated, I could see that the career path of sales management would likely require moving from branch to branch, potentially across the country, if I wanted to excel.

With the limited compensation structure in mind, I chose to step down after the year was over, focusing instead on my client base and my financial advisory role with my new junior partner. I was proud of myself for taking the sales management role because otherwise I might have looked back with regret, as one of the members of my PWN impact circle suggested. I was grateful to have had the opportunity to try a role in leadership, but from a career stability and compensation standpoint, I needed to provide for my family. I have never given it a second thought since, knowing I made the best choice.

I trained my business partner, mentored her, and appointed her as lead financial advisor on select accounts. I was proud to support her development in the industry. I continued to strongly believe in her potential and had her officially join my team in 2009, when we shifted to a different wealth management firm. We followed a colleague I had worked with since 1989, who was the assistant manager while I was the sales manager. Most of his career was in branch management, and we had an excellent working relationship based on trust and respect.

CHAPTER FOUR:
Adulthood

ohn and I were engaged on Valentine's Day 1985, after dating for over ten years and focusing on establishing our professional careers first. I was excited about starting the next journey of our lives—marriage—and the potential for a family, my life's dream. In preparation for our wedding, we took a few ballroom dance classes at Guilderland High School, where John had attended school. We learned to do a basic waltz, hoping to do more than a simple, slow first wedding dance. This was my first official connection with ballroom dancing. I wouldn't take the sport more seriously for another sixteen years, when I was forty years old, but I witnessed my parents' love affair with dance that lasted their whole lives.

MARRIAGE

hortly after I passed all my financial advisor entrance exams, John and I were married on June 27, 1987, at the Unitarian Universalist Society of Schenectady near my childhood home. I was twenty-four, and he was twenty-seven. There were approximately 120 guests. I was the first of my siblings to get married. We had a limited wedding budget, as my parents' focus had always been on providing a college education, culturally enriching experiences, and terms abroad for all four of their children.

We kept things very simple. I bought a white dress off the rack at Macy's, had an embroidered wedding train made to attach, and added a simple veil. It was a mishmash of things, but with my fashion sense, I made it look like it all went together. Mayela was my maid of honor; Kristen Sanchez and Christine Gesky, my second cousins, were my junior bridesmaids; and Amanda

Mitchell, a girl I used to babysit, was my flower girl. They were all special to me. My mother and a few of her Latin women friends catered the event in the banquet room at the church to keep expenses down. My father, the former ballroom dance instructor, beamed with pride to cut in and dance a waltz with his daughter, leading me gracefully around the floor on my wedding day. This was a dear moment to have shared with my father.

Our wedding budget may have been limited to $4,000, but I remember the day as a beautiful experience. The official ceremony was the most important part to me. The minister read a passage from *Gift from the Sea* by Anne Morrow Lindbergh, which I selected. I also read the same passage at my siblings' weddings, as it describes how relationships are like a dance that if navigated well, can be a lovely partnership, which resonated with me.

At the time of the wedding, I was living independently at Woodlake apartments in Guilderland, New York, around the corner from John's similar apartment. From my parents' perspective, it was unthinkable for us to live together before marriage, as they adhered to the traditional family values of the time. Once we were married, we moved into a small condominium in Clifton Park, and shortly thereafter to a starter home we could afford together. We had nice neighbors and got our first dog, Oliver, who was a cocker spaniel that I fell in love with at a pet shop. This puppy-mill puppy had originally been sold, but we ended up rescuing him after learning he might be euthanized due to cataracts and a heart murmur. I remember going across the street to Friendly's restaurant and crying at the thought of him not having a forever home.

During the first few years of marriage, John and I were both focused on our professional careers. We had weekly date nights, usually dinner and a movie, took weekend trips within a few hours' radius of our home to New York, Vermont, Connecticut, or Massachusetts, once going to Disney World with friends who won a trip and invited us to be their guests. I believed we had a good life and that we were nicely connected with family and friends.

CHILDREN

I had been steadily building my financial advisory practice since 1987, with many mergers and acquisitions, all at the same company in downtown Albany. I was extremely proud to become a mom and a vice president in the same year, 1993, with the birth of our son, John William Quinn, in January, which was a most treasured blessing for our family. I negotiated a maternity leave, as there were no other women financial advisors of childbearing age in my office at the time. I was able to get eight weeks off, collecting any sales commissions I was entitled to.

I had focused much of my energy on building my income so that John and I could afford to raise a family together. I started a college savings fund before I knew we could even have children. I had a birth plan that didn't exactly go as anticipated—I was in labor for a very long day and night. The umbilical cord was wrapped around our son's neck, which resulted in a forceps-assisted delivery and a challenging physical recovery. After eight weeks, I nearly returned to the hospital due to complications from breastfeeding and lack of sleep. We had good full-time daycare and were extremely fortunate to have both sets of loving grandparents in town—my in-laws, Marguerite (Colleen) and John E. (Jack) Quinn, and my parents—so we could continue to have date nights on the weekends.

EXECUTIVE NETWORK

During the early part of my career, I was very focused on work and family life. I noticed that my PWN impact circle had many businesswomen who were focused on their professional career tracks, but not all were choosing to have families at the same time. Once my focus was a full-scale blend of my professional career and family, I decided it was time to prioritize work-life integration. As a result, the Executive Network, my second formal impact circle, was born on November 20, 1996. This networking group provided the opportunity to connect with women who were balancing parenting and executive careers. We discussed various family matters, including childcare, aging parents, sleep issues, and balancing time between children's activities and professional events.

The Executive Network had a huge impact on us all as we focused on being the best mothers we could be as well as breadwinners in our families. We leaned on one another for parenting advice while striving to excel in our careers, allowing each other grace as we navigated our individual journeys and figured out what worked best for us personally and professionally. I take great pride in the authentic, enduring friendships that were formed and lasted for decades. This group of women proved to be an incredible source of support as I navigated significant life challenges. The vulnerability, authenticity, and magic I felt in this impact circle were real. I am proud to have provided a platform that allowed meaningful friendships and professional relationships to flourish; they are still fundamental to our lives today.

At that point, my biggest life decision was whether to have a second child or not. John and I took several years to decide due to the physical challenges of delivering our firstborn, my demanding professional role, and John's career path, which had a variety of twists and turns. It was an emotional struggle. As someone who grew up as one of four siblings, I felt strongly that there was someone missing.

A friend in my first PWN impact circle had invited me to join her for a three-day long weekend at Canyon Ranch, an upscale holistic spa in the Berkshires of Massachusetts. I was not exactly sure what to expect, but I met with an intake professional, who suggested a sample itinerary for the weekend. It was a very structured process that proved to be life-changing.

I selected various classes and personalized sessions including morning exercises such as yoga, tai chi, and stretching, and attended what I believed was a stress-management appointment. I quickly realized that I was in my first therapy session with a psychologist. I didn't figure that out until after he'd asked me four questions, and I was in a puddle of tears. He got right to the heart of why I was there and identified my emotional turmoil about whether to have a second child. I tried to imagine what our lives would be like if we welcomed a second child into our family and what adjustments we would need to make.

I saw that if I let go of some of my professional volunteer roles that I was involved in for business-development reasons, it would allow me more time to focus on family. I chose to step down from the board of Junior Achievement and my position as Chair of the Corporate Committee at the Albany Institute of History and Art. I had to have faith in my entrepreneurial skills to provide for my children's financial futures. I will never forget the anguish of finding myself sobbing on our back porch because I was imagining my life without a second child. I realized I desperately wanted our son to have a sibling, hoping for one as incredible as my siblings were to me. I was finally at peace knowing that I wanted to have a second child.

When we learned we were having a baby girl, I was beyond

elated, as I had assumed our second child would be another boy. I didn't even let myself consider the possibility, and potential joy, of having a girl. When I had my ultrasound, which confirmed that I was having a girl, I sobbed big, sloppy tears of joy. I was over-the-moon excited, beside myself with more delight than I could possibly have imagined. I felt incredibly blessed and grateful to have both a boy and a girl.

After weeks of looking at girls' names in a baby-name book, I finally settled on Lauren Elizabeth. When our four-year-old son Johnnie heard the name, he immediately requested that her name be Rachel. Rachel was the name of his best friend at preschool, and he wanted to have a Rachel of his own. I didn't hesitate to change our daughter's name to Rachel Lauren at birth, knowing the importance of sibling bonds from very early on. Our son John and his little sister have had a phenomenal brother-sister relationship ever since.

My family was always my top priority, though I always did my very best professionally. I had a strong determination to save enough money for our children to attend private colleges. My parents had provided private higher education for me and my siblings, and it was extremely important for me to provide the same.

I never missed any important events in my children's lives. I was certain that I would never put work before my children. The Executive Network impact circle proved to be an incredible sounding board, where we could encourage each other to embrace unique challenges and opportunities, including balancing work and family.

Here is what one of our Executive Network members shared about the impact our group had on her life.

This group was a lifesaver. When I first joined, my girls were ages five and eight, and when we ended, they were nineteen and twenty-two. During this time, I held high positions in travel, sales, and then leadership. For the fourteen-plus years that I was blessed to participate in this group, it was a valuable monthly safe haven, where I could freely share my personal and professional goals, successes, fears, challenges, and joys. These women were a treasured group. Some were ahead of me in their phase of life and career, others were around the same age, and some a little younger. Everyone brought insights that encouraged and sometimes stretched me.

These friends were sensitive and discerning but truthful and real. We were all pretty vulnerable with each other and sometimes raw, which was refreshing. We live in a small region, where there are probably just two degrees of separation between people, so it was scary at first to trust there would be confidentiality. But trust was our foundation. We didn't feel we needed to pretend everything was all right when it wasn't. We cried and celebrated together. We discussed business and career issues with the same intensity as concerns about our marriages, kids' health, school challenges, college journeys, and struggles with aging parents.

With my constant business travel during those years, and the remote nature of my job, it was challenging to form friendships and keep local women friends. But our Executive Network was a group I could depend on, thanks to Alissa's strong commitment to our continuity. Having this special group of women as a reality check and a sounding board in my life kept me sane and helped me weather very difficult business and personal issues. I think it's interesting to note that some women were only involved for a few years and new women joined even in the final years, but somehow that was OK because Alissa carefully vetted our members and was firm about the rules for our group. I will always be grateful to Alissa for inviting me into this precious circle of friends and her dedication to keeping us together for that period.

This passage lovingly and meaningfully summarizes the magic I felt in the parenting / work-life balance impact circle we created.

FORESHADOWING

arly in our marriage, I discovered that my spouse and I had different values around money, as he was accumulating debt. He was a car enthusiast and owned dozens of vehicles over the first several years of our marriage. The breaking point for me was when there were more cars than could fit in our driveway at one time. There was discussion of him building another garage for his vehicles in addition to a pool-house garage, our attached two-car garage, and our expanded driveway. I attempted to embrace my husband's hobbies, but I could not condone him spending money outside of our family budget. It began to sink in that my husband and I had opposing values around money. We did not share the same goal I had around saving for college tuition for our children. From my perspective, it was the essential foundation of my children's futures, and I was determined to provide it.

I felt I had a choice: let this difference in our financial values damage our marriage or attempt to move on. I chose to focus on my children's financial futures and believed I needed to pay off my spouse's debts to wipe the slate clean. It was admittedly gut-wrenching to have to liquidate a significant portion of the money I had painstakingly saved for our children's college educations, but I did so out of love and hope.

HAPPY LIFE

chose to focus on the positives John and I had together, and with time, we were able to move past the troubling financial issues early in our marriage. I believed those years were happy. We continued our date nights, movies, dinners out, local weekend travel, and fun times with friends and family, gathering for birthdays or holidays. My siblings were in different parts of the country, but we typically connected with them for family reunions and with both sets of our supportive local parents for Thanksgiving, Easter, and Christmas. We were both actively involved in our children's lives, attending back-to-school nights, open houses, and parent-teacher conferences. I helped with anything academic, medical, or financial. This included homework, school projects, summer camps, themed birthday parties, pool parties, and attending all doctors' appointments for our children.

If our children had late-afternoon athletic events, I would leave work early, go to their events, and return to work as needed, as I had a flexible work schedule—one benefit of being a financial advisor and something I worked extremely hard to obtain. I went to Rachel's dance lessons, Tae Kwon Do classes, piano recitals, and soccer games; I also went to our son John's soccer games, lacrosse events, sports tournaments, and piano recitals, rarely ever missing a single event. I do recall arriving late to one soccer tournament, only to miss my son's first hat trick, three goals in a row in short order! I relished the conversations I had with both children on the way to and from their extracurricular activities. I attended Parent Teacher Association (PTA) meetings and advocated for our children's academic interests every step of the way. I was thrilled to be totally present in their lives. We hosted our children's friends in our home to enjoy our pool, soccer in the backyard, playing on our swing set, frisbee, pitch and catch, softball, badminton, and more.

Traveling and working full-time within a four-state radius in a variety of roles, John was typically home by evening, attending children's activities when he could, making school lunches, doing grocery shopping and laundry, reading bedtime stories, and sharing parenting responsibilities. With my parents, affectionately known to our children as Nana and Granddad, nearby in Schenectady and John's parents, their loving Grandma and Pop Pop, living a block from us, we were extremely fortunate to have their local support and love. When our children were in elementary school, they would get off the school bus at John's parents' home, which was a phenomenal opportunity for our children to spend quality time with their grandparents. They had a wonderful, loving, multi-generational upbringing. We attended many family reunions with my extended family so that our kids could have quality time with their many cousins, visiting resorts in Lake George, South Carolina, Wisconsin, and Maine, as well as my siblings' homes in Minnesota, North Carolina, and Massachusetts. We also traveled to Florida's Clearwater Beach and Disney World with John's parents.

My husband continued to give me the most loving and thoughtful greeting cards with handwritten notes for each birthday, anniversary, Christmas, Easter, and Halloween. Such heartfelt and personal sentiments typically made me shed tears of joy, and I felt secure, believing our marriage was strong and happy. I valued his comments more than material gifts.

CAREER TRANSITIONS

I had reached every professional goal I had set for myself, including becoming a vice president and a mother in the same year. After John found himself in many career transitions when the telecom industry consolidated, I offered him a position on my financial advisory team out of love and support, hoping to give him career stability, given his hard work and ability. My business partner and I had been working incredibly well together for several years, maintaining an extraordinary friendship and business partnership based on trust and hard work. I knew that having my husband on my business team, if not handled delicately and wisely for all interested parties, could potentially pose challenges, but I felt it was important to support him and our family in this significant way, despite the risks. John became part of our team and passed all the required financial advisory exams. I was disappointed when, after working with our business team for only two years, he chose to take a position back in the cable television industry, not mentioning that the position was based in Syracuse, New York, until he was sure he was likely to take the job. The additional expense for his housing would minimize any financial gain the job offered. It also created new uncertainty in our lives with his being away from our children during the week. While he was away, I did my best to support our children's every need with the help of my in-laws and my parents.

John was away while the horrific events of September 11, 2001, were unfolding. I was distraught watching the news all day, as I had done all my professional training on the 103rd floor of the Twin Towers and still had colleagues based in Building 5, who I checked on immediately. Concerned about the effect these terrorist events could have on all our futures, and most importantly, on the emotions of our young children, I picked up Rachel (age 4) from preschool and John (age 8) from Guilderland Elementary School, just to have them close to me. It was heartbreaking to navigate that time without my husband. I struggled with what couples with families working in different cities and with many job transitions experience. Looking back, there were troubling signs, but I didn't see them coming.

FAMILY TRAVEL

I have always felt exhilarated by traveling to many European countries as a distraction over the years. My first trip was to Madrid and Valencia in Spain when I was eight years old. My second trip was to Madrid and northern Spain while I was in high school, to reconnect with our family's foreign exchange student. My third trip was to Seville, Spain, with side trips to England, France, and Italy while attending Union College.

Once John and I had a family of our own and his work was back in town, I felt it was extremely important to introduce our children to international travel. This would be a critical part of their education, as it was mine. I considered the timing of when to introduce international travel to our children.

For me, the perfect timing was at eight years old, so I wanted to come up with a just-right trip for Rachel and our son John. My husband and I had been to Ireland for my brother Mark's wedding, held at Ross Castle in Galway, where his wife Marie's family lived. Aside from that, he had never traveled internationally, so I also wanted to plan something that he could feel comfortable with. I thought Ireland would be the perfect place to start because he had Irish roots.

Our family of four had a wonderful experience exploring Ireland. We went to all the sights in Galway and took a train ride to Dublin, paying tribute to John's heritage. When my husband was in another one of his job transitions, I took our kids to visit my first cousin Aida and her three boys in Valencia, Spain, so that my children could experience a family adventure in Europe with their same-age cousins. We visited the city house of my Aunt Juanita and Uncle Jimmy, my mother's brother, in Valencia and then traveled to the same small beach town of Perillo I had visited when I was eight years old. It was heartwarming to reconnect with all the relatives I had met decades earlier.

All their family members lived within a few miles of each other, a strong Spanish tradition. It was so surreal to see they were all still there and such a profound experience for me to remember my eight-year-old self and to have my children there at around the same age. My soul was full because I had budgeted and saved for the same enriching experiences I'd had as a child.

Each year, I selected a new travel destination for our family.

We went to Italy on a group tour, exploring exquisite Rome, enchanting Florence, magical Venice, and beautiful Lake Como. The next year, we traveled to Ecuador to pay homage to my mother's roots, traveling from Quito to Cuenca through the exciting Avenue of the Volcanoes. We ventured to Reggio di Calabria, Southern Italy, to visit Fuscaldo and Santa Sofia d'Epiro, two tiny villages in the southern boot of Italy that were the hometowns of my father's parents. It was an unforgettable trip, driving straight up into the mountains and being in the clouds without being on an airplane.

What was supposed to be a twenty-minute car ride turned into a very long adventure up and down the mountain that separated my grandparents' hometowns. It was remarkable to think about how they had courted back in their day and later came to this country to settle in Brooklyn, New York. I was elated to reconnect with my Italian heritage and have my children soak in the experience and their relationship to their great-grandparents. I brought my father's memoir *Let It Be a Dance: My Life Story* with me and took a photo of it on the altar of the tiny Greek Orthodox church where my grandparents were married. Then we ventured on to Taormina, Sicily, which was one of my favorite little Italian towns, dripping in exquisite architecture and tiny shops filled with wrought iron, delicate artisan crafts, brightly colored flowers, delicious traditional gelato, and decadent pastries.

Next, we all traveled to Greece, Austria, and the Czech Republic. My husband and I traveled to southern France and Bavaria, Germany, for our thirtieth wedding anniversary. Rachel and I traveled to Belgium, Paris, Switzerland, Portugal, and the Netherlands, as she delighted in European travel just as much as I did. For me, travel was a window to the world, and experiencing it with my family was priceless.

One of my treasured memories of traveling with our children as teenagers was when our son John graduated from high school in 2011. I gave him the choice to have a graduation party or go on an international family trip, and he selected the trip without a second thought. Our son asked if his girlfriend could join us. I hadn't anticipated that request, as his girlfriend had never been on an international trip before, so I wasn't exactly sure how the five of us would fare. We decided as a family to honor his request. We worked with our travel agent Jean, who helped us put together a phenomenal trip to Athens and Santorini in Greece.

We had an amazing adventure, and I was so incredibly pleased that everyone got along well, as international travel can have stressful moments. We enjoyed seeing all the traditional Greek sites, spending a few days in the glorious city of Athens and the rest of our time on the exquisite island of Santorini. We had an amazing housing experience, renting one of the traditional white, plaster homes with a blue rooftop, overlooking the spectacularly blue Aegean Sea during warm summer temperatures. Our vacation could not have been more incredible.

Our son and his girlfriend navigated having quality time together and special time with our family. On our very last day, he asked if we could go to a final shop because he wanted to buy one more thing. At that point, I felt we had managed to get through the entire vacation incredibly well; we were on budget, and I didn't want to jinx anything. Responding to the look on my face, he said, "Mom, it will be OK."

He proceeded to lead us to a little shop in the main section of Santorini, a short journey on the cobblestone street with bright, colorful flowers adorning the way. We walked into a small traditional jewelry shop, and there was an elderly Greek gentleman behind the counter who seemed to recognize our son. John walked over and greeted the shop owner and said, "Could you please show my mother the piece that we were looking at together?"

The shop owner pulled out a small silver necklace with a pendant about the size of a dime. It looked like it was made of pewter with unique black etchings, and it looked antique.

John turned to the shop owner and said, "Can you please explain to my mother how this item works?"

The shop owner, in a very heavy Greek accent, turned to me and said, "You buy this necklace for somebody very special and gently break it down the center, separating it into two necklaces. You give one necklace to this very special someone, and you wear the other necklace yourself."

I thought to myself how sweet it was that our son wanted to buy a uniquely beautiful necklace for his girlfriend, but at that moment, the eighteen-year-old John turned to the fourteen-year-old Rachel and said, "As you know, I am going off to college next year. I want you to know that you are the most special girl in my life. I will wear this necklace going forward, and I want you to have this other necklace to wear so you know I'll always be with you, even when I'm away."

My eyes filled with tears, and I whipped out my credit card as fast as I could. I could not have been prouder of our son at that moment. He was showing deep devotion to his younger sister, who had idolized him her entire life. It reminded me of when our very young son had called 911 because our babysitter had stepped outside our home to make a phone call, and he was protecting his little sister. Thankfully, the story had a happy ending.

As parents, we invested in their brother-sister relationship and allowed them to develop their own sibling bond. They both show empathy and care for each other and place value in their special relationship. This is the most precious gift I can imagine as a parent, and at that moment, I remembered the decision-making process that led to fulfilling my profound desire to have a sibling for my son. I hope they will create their own impact circles and experience the power they have to offer.

CHAPTER FIVE:
Dance

With my professional career well underway and both children settling nicely into their academic and extracurricular activities, I felt it was time for me to find something that I could focus on for my own personal well-being and to be a role model for my children. In 2002, I watched my mother do a ballroom dance quickstep showcase at age seventy-five. She was wearing a beautiful, flowing purple gown with sparkling gemstones, skipping and gliding across the hardwood dance floor with her professional instructor under glimmering crystal chandeliers, and I was hooked! I admired her grace as I watched with her fellow ballroom dancers, all dressed up in their finest attire, cheering her on. I thought, If she can do that at her age, I had better get started now at age forty. I turned to my husband of fifteen years and asked if he would be willing to take ballroom dance lessons with me. To my delight, he said yes.

John and I took ballroom dance lessons together for the next fifteen years. I have been ballroom dancing ever since, following in the footsteps of my parents, who met at the Brooklyn dance where my father was a dance host. They danced together until my dad passed away in 2010 at the age of eighty-six, and my mother continued to dance until she was ninety-four years young. From childhood, I watched my parents do Latin dancing with the carpets rolled up in our living room. One of their first public performances at Union College was an Argentine tango in support of the arts department. They performed in perfect harmony together, deeply connected to the music and each other, just as they did in our home, surrounded by friends and family, whenever there was a reason to gather socially.

I started taking lessons with my mother's instructor and fell in love with ballroom dance and the thought of continuing my parents' legacy. It became a meaningful pursuit, which had a profound impact on the rest of my life. My local Fred Astaire Dance Studio hosted a show at Proctors Theater, and I was totally smitten with the more upscale performances and shifted to taking lessons there. I rotated lessons with a professional instructor and with John so we could both learn at our own pace while receiving professional instruction.

We discovered it took great patience to learn complex figures in ballroom dance and that it's much akin to couples learning to hang wallpaper together. It took a delicate balance of instruction and commitment from us, as it had with my parents. I always admired how my parents navigated their different styles of learning dance and loved each other at the same time. I marveled at their success on and off the dance floor and hoped John and I could achieve the same.

MY OTHER LIFE

After a few years of professional dance instruction, I decided it was time to share my ballroom dance passion in business circles. I still worked predominantly with male colleagues and somehow felt that my ballroom dance hobby would make others take me less seriously in my business career. A member of my PWN, Betsy Feldstein, approached me because she wanted to write a story for our local newspaper, the *Times Union*. The column was called "My Other Life," and it was featured in the business section, highlighting unique hobbies of professionals in our community. It took me a while to embrace the concept, but I finally decided it was time to go public, like a company in the capital markets industry. I did a short phone interview with Betsy and sent her a photo of myself in a beautiful white ball gown that I had designed with a dressmaker who specialized in ballroom dance costumes for showcases and competitions. The elegant image showed me looking over my shoulder, holding both ends of the long ball gown at arm's length.

After the article came out, I attended the Capital Region Chamber of Commerce's economic-forum breakfast and saw the president of the chamber seated three tables away. He mouthed to me, "Nice photo." I grinned. At that moment, I was totally relieved, because if the president of the chamber of commerce was supportive of my enthusiasm for ballroom dance, then it was perfectly fine to have shared that personal, more feminine side of myself in business circles. To my delight, my hobby was a wonderful conversation starter with many community leaders. It became a way to get to know others' hobbies, develop more personal relationships, deepen my network, and develop trust. It was always tricky to balance the personal side of myself with my professional life, but ballroom dancing proved to be very rewarding.

Once my secret was out, sharing my ballroom dance passion in business conversations was an unthreatening way to develop rapport at business networking events, and it became an extension of who I am. I recall beginning to be introduced in business circles as a "beautiful ballroom dancer," which was so odd to me, as I had worked my whole professional career in the wealth management industry without considering that I could be identified as a dancer. I found myself trying to interject information about my true day job into business networking conversations.

One day, when I was driving to work in downtown Albany, I saw two gentlemen I recognized talking to each other. Both were of Italian descent, which was something we all shared. One was the owner of a pizzeria, and the other was a ballroom dancer, but I didn't know what he did professionally. In ballroom dance circles, we rarely talked business, as our focus was on dancing; we connected through a unique art form, which included exercise, health, social connection, and enticing music. As I passed them in my car, they both saw me, so I waved. It was an interesting intersection of my different worlds: business and ballroom. I could imagine one of them saying "Oh, there's Alissa Quinn, my financial advisor," and the other saying "Oh, there's Alissa Quinn, my wonderful ballroom dance friend," as he commonly called me. I said to myself, "I am both," and chuckled. For lunch that day, I went to the pizza shop just to see the owner's reaction, and it was exactly as I had suspected. He knew the other gentleman from the local American Italian Heritage Museum in Albany, and they had discussed who I was, but there was conflict as to who was correct. I then shared my ballroom dance hobby with him, and we both laughed. In time, I grew comfortable being known as both.

BROTHER-SISTER DANCE

When John and Rachel were approximately eleven and seven years old, I thought it would be fun to start sharing my love of dance with them. After all, they came from a ballroom dance tradition started by their grandparents. I began teaching them a basic swing and foxtrot in our kitchen, where there was a hardwood floor. I would put on music and dance a few very simple patterns with them—just enough to give them the gist of each dance.

Around that time, Rachel was asked to be a flower girl at the wedding of one of her beloved babysitters. What a thrill for her! I recalled my own delight in being the flower girl for my dear cousin Gina Sanchez's wedding when she married Vincent Sanchez. On the big day, Rachel wore a beautiful white flower girl dress, had her hair professionally styled in an updo by our favorite hairdresser, and looked adorable. She even rode in the limousine to the church with the wedding party.

At the wedding reception, we were seated together as a family. I will never forget our son John turning to his little sister when the music started playing, putting out his hand, and asking, "Would you like to dance?"

"What will we do?"

"Foxtrot, of course."

Our two young children walked out onto the dance floor and proceeded to do a foxtrot in front of the entire room. I could not stop beaming with pride. When the music shifted to a more upbeat tempo, they switched to swing dancing. They were on the dance floor most of the night, just doing the basic patterns but impressing all the guests with their poise and grace at their young ages. I knew my parents would be thrilled when I shared the news, and they were indeed. It was phenomenal that our son had the self-confidence and ability to lead the steps and dance with his beloved little sister and that she would be willing to dance with him in public. It was a beautiful expression of their incredible brother-sister relationship.

THREE GENERATIONS OF DANCE

had been very active in the Women's Business Council of the Capital Region Chamber, and I was given the Women of Excellence Award in the emerging-executive category in 1993, the same year I became a vice president and a mom. I typically attended most of the Women's Business Council events, including their annual Bold in Business forums, which consisted of a speaker and several breakout workshop sessions. This time, during one of the workshop sessions, the moderator suggested we pair up with someone we did not know for an icebreaker exercise. I listened to the instructions and turned to the woman next to me. We were to share something private about ourselves that we would not ordinarily share in business circles. I went first, leaned in, and whispered, "I just started taking ballroom dance lessons."

She looked up at me and whispered, "I used to compete in Latin dancing in college."

We chuckled, and I said, "If you ever want to get back into ballroom dancing, just let me know. I would be happy to introduce you to the studio where I'm taking lessons."

She said, "Oh no, those days are over."

The next year, I happened to see the same woman at the Bold in Business forum and joked, "Are you ready to get back into ballroom dancing?" Again she said no. For the third year in a row, I saw her at the same forum and persistently inquired, "Are you ready to get back to dancing?" To my surprise and utter delight, she said yes. I shared that there was a social dance on that Friday night, and if she'd like, I would be happy to have her as my guest.

Joan Hayner showed up for the Friday social dance and has been an avid and accomplished student at Fred Astaire Dance Studios ever since. February 14, 2008, Joan sent me an email titled "Something to run by you." Her ten-year-old son Greg had expressed an interest in learning ballroom dance after watching her. Joan knew that my ten-year-old daughter took a ladies' group class with me on occasion. She wondered if Rachel, who had a similar interest in Tae Kwon Do, would like to take ballroom dance lessons with him.

I was thrilled at the thought but knew that my daughter, a tomboy at the time, might not be ready for such a bold step. I figured I would broach the subject gently by telling her it was not my idea; I knew she might be less inclined to consider it if it was. Rachel was initially reluctant, but then surprised me by blurting out, "I'll do it!" Her first foray into dance had been ballet in preschool, and after two classes, she had protested that her costume was too itchy. Rachel enjoyed wearing her beloved brother's hand-me-down shirts, playing soccer, and breaking boards in Tae Kwon Do. She preferred to spend recess with the boys. She was not fond of wearing dresses or doing anything too girly, so I was tickled pink she was willing to give ballroom dance a try.

Joan and I decided to get the kids together socially before their first ballroom dance lesson. We went to Lucky Strike, the bowling alley across the street from the Fred Astaire Dance Studio in Latham. The dance lesson could not have gone better, and their instructor was exceptional with children. Greg and Rachel danced together for the next eight years, learning from a variety of phenomenal instructors, before they both went off to college. They had an amazing dance partnership and partic-ipated in many Fred Astaire Dance Studio showcases.

The third Sunday of each month was USA Dance, a ballroom social dance that I attended with my parents. I took any oppor-tunity to spend quality time with them, doing something we both loved. At one of the dances, we performed a cha-cha showcase with all three generations on the floor at the same time: my parents, my husband John and me, and Rachel and Greg. We delighted the audience of dance friends, who knew how special this was. To this day, the president of the local USA Dance chapter, Barbara Ritschel, reminds me of the tremen-dous joy she felt that night. It was truly enchanting.

After several more years at the Fred Astaire Studio in Latham, my family did another three-generations showcase in the spring of 2014. Rachel and Greg were sixteen and both exceptionally talented for their ages; my mom was eighty-six; I was fifty. My mom danced with the studio's owner, Boris Spitchka, and I danced with my instructor, Serge Nelyubov. We did an Argentine tango, demonstrating the benefits of dance at every stage of life. My mom, Rachel, and I posed for a three-generations photograph in our black sequined dresses with bright red roses. After years of dancing, I created a family website to store our dance photos and videos, and having those precious memories is priceless.

Ballroom dancing would change the trajectory of the Hayner family, as it had mine. Joan went on to compete at the highest national ballroom dance levels, taking her craft extremely seriously, and now manages several Fred Astaire Dance Studios in Maryland, having moved back to her hometown. Her daughter Elizabeth also started taking ballroom dance lessons, became a ballroom dance instructor herself, married a ballroom dance instructor, Grey Masko, and now co-owns a Fred Astaire Dance Studio.

DANCING ABROAD

When our son was a junior at Babson College in Wellesley, Massachusetts, he applied to their international term-abroad program to study global business, which consisted of one month in Russia, one month in China, and one month in India. I was thrilled that he was one of twenty-five students accepted into the elite program. He visited global enterprises in person, touring factories and businesses in all three countries, and comparing styles and economies. It was an enriching and intellectually rigorous program, allowing him to broaden his horizons and perspectives on business and cultures in other parts of the world. He even explored Israel on his own when the term ended, connecting with one of my doctor clients.

I had always encouraged our son to learn the basics of ballroom and Latin dance. To my utter delight, I got the following text message from him while he was away: "Never guess who is salsa dancing in China, Mom!" I squealed with pleasure! Apparently, in China, the women students appreciate partners who can dance! The smile didn't leave my face for a very long time, and it comes right back when I remember that text. Dancing can connect people anywhere in the world. When Rachel and I were vacationing in Switzerland, we came across a group of dancers in a park near Lake Geneva. We joined in the fun, attempting to learn the dance they were doing, which was a spontaneous and culturally enriching experience.

PAPA'S DANCING SHOES

In 2010, before my father passed away peacefully of congestive heart failure in his home at age eighty-six, my son and I had a chance to say a final goodbye. Just prior, John had participated in his high school senior night for Guilderland soccer; he had played competitive soccer since kindergarten, and I had watched almost every game. My father, upon seeing John's soccer jersey and recognizing the school's logo, said, "Dutchmen!" with gusto. We said our farewell to my father, and he passed away early the next morning. This gave us a sacred memory to share together. My father lived a very full life as a beloved college professor, husband, father, grandfather, ballroom dancer, Argentine tango aficionado, classical guitarist, Italian foodie, and jazz music enthusiast.

Shortly after my father's passing, our family convened around the kitchen table to come up with ideas for how to honor his memory and make his memorial service at the Unitarian Universalist Society of Schenectady deeply meaningful. We were extremely fortunate to have such a loving and caring father, and we wanted to make it extraordinarily special. We decided to have a focal point for the ceremony in the rotunda at the church. We agreed to use a few visual props to represent our father: an enlarged photo taken by my brother Carl, our father's prized classical guitar on a stand, and his treasured ballroom dance shoes.

One of my brothers went upstairs to retrieve his treasured guitar, and I went to retrieve my father's ballroom dance shoes. I found my father's practice dance shoes, which were well worn, but I kept looking for his dressy, shiny, black patent-leather ballroom dance shoes, the ones he would wear to elegant affairs. Oddly, I could not find them anywhere. I scoured the entire house. My dad was typically highly organized. He had a large collection of music tapes, VHS tapes, DVDs, and photographs, and everything had a place. I knew exactly where he stored his dressy dance shoes, and they were nowhere to be found. While we were sitting around the table, a startling idea occurred to me. When my dad wrote his autobiography, *Let It Be a Dance*, his last two paragraphs read:

> *I feel most alive when my life is smooth as a foxtrot, exhilarating as a waltz, energetic as the lindy hop, lively as a samba, romantic as a rumba, bouncy as a merengue, racy as a quickstep, pulsating as a mambo, and passionate as a tango.*
>
> *One final thought: As to the possibility that there is an afterlife, I go along with Woody Allen, whose view is "I do not believe in an afterlife, although I am bringing a change of underwear."[1] On the chance there is a hereafter, I plan to take along an extra pair of dancing shoes just in case there's a big-band bash happening above or below.*

I grinned from ear to ear and excitedly announced to my family: "I know what happened to Dad's dance shoes! He took them with him!" We never found his dressy ballroom dance shoes, and I am convinced my dad has them with him for dancing

---

1. Woody Allen, *Getting Even*, (Vintage, 1978).

in Heaven, whenever the mood suits him. I can always feel the power of my father's love, watching from Heaven, especially when I am on the dance floor, dancing to Latin, ballroom, or Argentine tango music. I miss you so dearly, Papa.

CLASSICAL GUITAR DANCE

*M*y father took classical guitar lessons as an adult, and for the last twenty years of his life, they were with his beloved instructor and family friend, Maria Zemantauski. Maria gave a beautiful performance and a touching tribute at our father's memorial service. Years later, I learned Maria was doing her first post-COVID-19 concert at The Hyde Collection in Glens Falls. I decided to attend as an opportunity to reconnect with fond memories of my dad, and I invited a friend to join me. We both wore masks, as the concert was in a small auditorium. The second Maria recognized me in the audience, we had a moment of connection. She knew who I was underneath that black face mask, and I felt she could feel my dad looking down upon us both. At intermission, I went to see her backstage. We hugged and shed a tear, knowing my dad's presence was with us. Maria played her heart out on stage in a phenomenal concert, and my friend and I were moved by her amazing performance. I was certain my dad was smiling down upon us, watching from his seat in Heaven.

The next day, I had a coaching session with world-class choreographer Taliat Tarsinov, who had created all my showcase dances at Fred Astaire Dance Studio for the last eighteen years. My dance instructor, Yurii Astashenya, selected a unique version of the song "Lady in Red" by an artist I had not heard of before. Most showcase songs I have selected have been meaningful. This version of "Lady in Red" was extremely intense. When Taliat did the initial choreography, he felt the song needed a different introduction, an instrumental beginning with flamenco flair. It occurred to me that we could use Maria's instrumental music, and I smiled to think I could forever be connected to my dad with this dance.

I called Maria and shared the concept of using a short piece of her music for our dance intro, and she was delighted. A month later, Tony Dovolani, chief artistic director at Fred Astaire Dance Studio, came for coaching lessons. I shared the story of my father's beloved guitar teacher, and Tony suggested dancing to one of Maria's songs live instead of a recording. Oh, my goodness, I absolutely loved that idea. I picked "Rumba del Rio," a song we could do a strong tango / paso doble to. I called Maria back, shared the concept, and she was all in.

Yurii and I practiced until we were ready for a session with Maria playing live. Maria was remarkable during our practices, adjusting her guitar playing to our need for consistency by staying on the beat as much as possible. She matched each note to our choreography and enhanced our storytelling with her music. It was a very special creative process with the three of us working together for the best possible outcome. I could most certainly feel my dad's presence with us every step of the way. We performed for the USA National Ballroom Dance Week at our local mall, and it was the first time live music had been used in all the years I have been performing for this annual event. I danced my heart out and put everything into that dance, and I no doubt felt my dad was dancing with me. It was strong. It was intense. It was emotional. It was our best performance, well exceeding all our expectations. My dad had been gone from this earth for twelve years, but I felt him smiling down upon me with every part of my being. There is truly never a time when I don't feel his presence on the dance floor or when I'm listening to jazz music or eating anything Italian.

ZOLLER BALLROOM KIDS

ne of the most important contributions I made in local ballroom dance circles was being part of a special children's program called Zoller Ballroom Kids. In 2005, the movie *Mad Hot Ballroom* was released. It was a documentary about how ballroom dance was being taught in inner-city schools in New York City after the horrific events of September 11, 2001, to help ease the plight of families who lost loved ones. My husband and I went to see the movie at our local theater on a Saturday night. The following Monday, a social-worker friend called me and asked if I had seen the movie, as she knew I had been taking ballroom dance lessons. I said I absolutely loved it. She said she loved it too and that the principal of the local inner-city elementary school wanted to explore doing a similar program for their students. Could I help set up a ballroom dance program for their fourth and fifth graders?

I had become familiar with the local ballroom dance community and thought why not? Sure, I would love to help her build a children's ballroom dance program at her local school. We strategized a few ideas on the phone, and I asked her which school she worked at. When she told me that she worked at Zoller Elementary School, I grinned from ear to ear, as it was the elementary school I had attended as a child thirty-two years ago.

Since then, Zoller Elementary School's student population had changed significantly. Zoller's geographical footprint had been redistricted, and 68 percent of students were from families whose income was below the poverty line. Many of the students came from diverse ethnic backgrounds, had limited English proficiency, or were receiving special education services.

Leveraging my contacts in ballroom circles and the business community, I assembled a small committee of caring professionals to join the school's social worker, nurse, principal, and a few teachers. Zoller Ballroom Kids was created! We designed the program with the following goals: increase student self-esteem, teamwork, and tolerance; focus on respect for others; improve physical fitness; increase dance-step skills; introduce dance history; and provide cultural enrichment.

The most important focus was finding the best dance instructors to connect with children of this age group and background. We were extremely fortunate to hire local dance instructors David and Dawn Levesque of Dancin' Time, who were perfect in their roles. They helped the children have fun with a new art form.

We started by showing the children parts of *Mad Hot Ballroom*, then followed this with an informal dance demonstration by their instructors to give them an idea of what they would learn. Next, talented local teenagers from Niskayuna High School gave dance performances, and my parents performed an impromptu cha-cha. The children saw firsthand what ballroom and Latin dance looked like, demonstrated by three different generations. The very next day, the principal of the school had permission slips from forty-two very enthusiastic children.

The dance classes began on January 24, 2006, and continued on Tuesdays and Thursdays immediately after school from 3:15 p.m. to 4:00 p.m. for ten weeks. The classes were filled with tremendous excitement, and it was heartwarming to witness the children in action. When I could duck out of work for a few hours, I was so delighted with what I saw. The children's enthusiasm was infectious, and seeing them moving to the rhythm of the music and connecting socially with each other brought tears of joy to my eyes.

One day, I saw a muscular, robust man of Latin descent on the sideline of the school gymnasium, watching the children dance. The expression on his face drew me to ask him what he thought of the program. Beaming with pride, he said, "That's my son out there. He cannot wait to get to school on Tuesdays and Thursdays because he loves this program so much." He added "My younger son can't wait until next year when he can be in the program." From the way he lit up when talking about his son, it was as if he was talking about football or baseball. He was as proud as he could be. I shared that a local news anchor from Channel 13 was coming to broadcast a story about the program and asked if he would be willing to share his comments on television. He was absolutely delighted to do so. I was curious to know where this man worked because of his athletic physique. He told me he worked at the Schenectady sheriff's office and that his family was from Colombia. He was proud his sons were learning some of the Latin dances from his culture.

The committee, including the school nurse and social worker, worked hard to order and create costumes for a year-end celebration that highlighted the children's progress. I oversaw the fundraising and was thrilled to receive generous contributions from our local USA Dance community through the Ron Curry Foundation, created by a beloved local dance instructor who had passed away a few years earlier. Many of the board members of USA Dance came to watch and support the children's program each year. I connected local business leaders in our community with ballroom-dance-circle friends and a few Zoller Elementary School alumni still residing in the area. Another contributor, who worked in a local prison, commented on her donation card "I am gladly sending you this contribution now, in hopes that it will help keep me from seeing these children later." It was a sobering comment.

We hosted the program for seven years, until 2012. Our year-end celebration in the gymnasium on April 15, 2012, showcased the children's efforts. I was thrilled to welcome so many parents, families, ballroom dancers, and business leaders to share in the special evening. I hoped this program would make a positive impact on these children and the community; based on the feedback we received, it certainly did.

It was a particularly heartfelt evening as we paid tribute to my parents, who had been ballroom dancers in our community for the last fifty years. For me, as a Zoller Elementary School alum, it was a special night. I reminisced as I walked through the halls and danced in that gym, remembering all my teachers. The program would not have been possible without the significant support of many people, and I recognized them that evening. The school gymnasium was filled with hundreds of parents and friends from the ballroom dance community. My soul was full. I had no doubt created an informal impact circle, working with a small committee. I reflected on the quote attributed to Margaret Mead: "Never doubt that a small group of thoughtful, committed citizens can change the world. Indeed, it's the only thing that ever has." This quote inspires individuals to recognize the power of collective action and positive change, just like what happens with an impact circle. It was a huge amount of work, but the rewards were endless.

MALL OF AMERICA

After my father passed away, my mother continued to live a healthy life, until she suddenly became ill while visiting my brother Mark and his family in Minnesota. Our mother had emergency gallbladder surgery and her first experience with hospice services, but she miraculously recovered. She was transferred to an assisted-living residence near my brother and lived there for the rest of her life. While in Minnesota, my mother learned that there was going to be a USA Dance community event in Minneapolis, like the ones she had witnessed me participate in over many years at our local Crossgates and Colonie Center malls. She called to ask if I would come and dance for her so she could see me dance in person one more time! When your ninety-three-year-old mother asks you to dance for her, you dance, even if the event is two plane rides away.

I promptly reached out to my beloved instructor, Florin Vlad of Dance Fire Studio, to ask what he was doing on a Sunday afternoon a few weeks out. To my utter delight, he agreed to fly to Minnesota to make the woman who had been his first Schenectady landlady happy! It didn't take me long to think of something even better: engaging my mother's beloved Argentine tango instructor, David Salvatierra, from Kingston, New York, to dance with her. He also agreed. I flew both instructors out to spend the afternoon delighting my mother. She was elated.

I chuckled when my mother made it clear to me that I needed to make an announcement before her performance to ensure the audience understood her dance would be in lead-follow style and not a choreographed performance like mine. I laughed, but she was dead serious, so I made sure to talk to the announcer. They shared the information with the attentive audience, mentioning my mother's dance background, and she received a remarkably warm Minnesota welcome. My mama and David did a full-blown Argentine tango complete with tricky footwork and lifts they had practiced just thirty minutes before. It brought robust applause from hundreds of onlookers on three levels of the atrium in the Mall of America! Florin and I did a *Swan Lake* medley, using costumes my mother helped sew, including a long, white, bedazzling glove with Swarovski crystals for a swan's neck and face, white feathered wings, and a black feathered cape to show the light and dark sides of the hauntingly beautiful music. My brother Mark and his family came to cheer us on, and I even had a Minneapolis financial advisor friend from my firm surprise us when I told her what we were up to. It was a precious experience for us all.

I posted a video of my ninety-three-year-old mother's Argentine tango performance on my LinkedIn profile to encourage clients to share their passions from one generation to the next. To my amazement, I received over 11,000 impressions on my post with tons of inspirational comments. They were a delight to read.

Shortly thereafter, a ballroom dancer from Minnesota who had seen my LinkedIn post reached out to me. She was writing a book about the benefits of ballroom dance for seniors and wondered if she could interview my mother for one of the chapters. *The Dance of Resilience* by Ember Reichgott Junge captures my mother's dance history beautifully.

CHAPTER SIX:
Cancer

n 2013, I was fifty years old and in excellent health. I had been married for twenty-six years and had two phenomenal children: one a twenty-year-old Babson College business student and the other a sixteen-year-old junior in high school. We had lived in the same home in the town of Guilderland since a few years after we got married. I was a senior vice president and financial advisor for a global wealth management company and had worked in the same building in downtown Albany since 1987. I rarely missed a day of work for any health-related issue, except for the occasional sinus infection or strep throat when the kids were younger. Life was as good as it gets from my perspective. Little did I know my life was about to change forever.

HEALTH IS EVERYTHING

I had my annual gynecological appointment in February 2013, and everything was reported fine. Three months later, in May 2013, I had menstrual spotting for approximately ten days. I called my gynecologist's office to schedule an appointment, and they said that was perfectly normal for a perimenopausal woman of my age and that I did not need an appointment. I waited another week, but when the symptoms persisted, I called the doctor's office and was again told that it was not anything that needed to be addressed and to call them back in a month.

At that point in my life, I had not stayed in a hospital, other than for two healthy pregnancies: one forceps delivery and one normal delivery. I didn't have any medical issues, had never broken a bone, and was not on any prescribed medications.

My gut instincts were telling me that this was something that should be checked by a professional, and my doctor's response did not sit well with me. I knew my own body, and this symptom was not normal for me. I felt I needed to advocate for myself, so I called the office again and politely persisted in getting an appointment.

I went to the appointment on my own. Upon arrival, I sensed I was being treated as a nuisance by the office staff for requesting an appointment so persistently. A technician performed an ultrasound. After the ultrasound, the technician went to retrieve the doctor. The doctor came in to share the results.

The doctor said I had a grapefruit-sized cyst on one of my ovaries. Gasp! How is that even possible? My gynecological exam just three months prior had found no issues. How could something that large have been missed? Or was it possible for something to grow that fast inside of my abdomen without any visible signs or discomfort? Impossible! I could not begin to fathom what I was hearing.

My doctor's on-the-spot reaction was that the cyst was something that needed to be removed surgically and that they would be the one to do the surgery. Really? That was my doctor's immediate reaction? Not "I am so very sorry to share this news with you." Not "I am sorry we gave you such a hard time getting an appointment." Not "So very sorry you were having a symptom, and nobody was paying any attention to you." I experienced no sign of empathy or compassion for news that was terrifying to hear.

As scared as I was at that moment, my professional instincts kicked in. I started asking questions: How many times have you performed this type of surgery? What are the risks of this type of surgery? What options are there for this type of surgery? Can this surgery be done laparoscopically? What are the potential outcomes of this surgery? My mind was racing. I did not hear answers that inspired confidence, and I was feeling extremely uneasy. I sensed I was being told what was going to happen to me instead of being consulted about my options, which is what I had done with my own clients my whole career.

When I politely inquired how many times the doctor had performed this type of surgery, there was no answer. Trusting my gut instincts, and with as much professionalism as I could muster, I broached the topic of getting a second opinion. I was dismayed at the doctor's defensive reaction. This was a doctor I had seen for many years, but in all honesty, typically for less than fifteen minutes a year for an annual exam. This time, when I needed exceptional medical expertise, I felt let down. I asked if there was a local doctor who specialized in this type of surgery. I could see the doctor was reluctant to give me a name. Finally, the doctor shared that I was not likely to be able to get in to see that surgeon and would have to see whichever doctor was available in that practice. I politely persisted in requesting the name of the specialist. I was extremely proud of conducting myself with grace and professionalism but so saddened that my doctor didn't seem to care. That doctor's office never once followed up to check on me to see how I was after learning I had a grapefruit-size ovarian cyst, and I had been a patient for many years. That was the last time I set foot in that practice.

ADVOCATING FOR MYSELF

t was time for me to begin exploring alternative opinions. My whole life, I had created professional networks of executive women who were there to support each other personally and professionally. This time, it was my turn to reach out to them for support and guidance. My first call was to my internist, who was in PWN. She shared the name of the top local surgeon for my needs. I called their office and was told it would take some time to get an appointment with that surgeon as his schedule was booked far in advance. I could see another doctor in the practice if I wanted an earlier appointment. I could hear the voice of my gynecologist ringing in my ear, and I was annoyed. I took a deep breath and strategized, deciding I would just keep using my professional networks to find solutions.

My next call was to another member of PWN. This time, I reached out to an attorney who I knew had excellent connections in the local medical community, as her specialty was defending physicians. I felt she was the go-to expert for anything medical in the Capital Region. I shared the specialist's name from my internist. Upon hearing the name, she immediately said, "Oh, I'll text him now." Really? She was on a texting basis with this surgeon? That meant she knew him well, and I was beginning to feel hopeful. I could see that using my networks might come in handy not only professionally but also personally.

My attorney friend texted the surgeon while on the phone with me at 10:00 p.m. during the workweek. She texted that she had a friend who just heard she had a large ovarian cyst that required surgery, and she asked if he could do my surgery. He responded immediately: Yes, he could do my surgery. Next, my attorney friend specifically asked if the tumor was not cancer, could he still my surgery? I immediately realized that this doctor was a surgical oncologist, performing surgery for women with cancer. I was shocked that she asked that question as no one up until that point ever mentioned my cyst could be cancer. The thought had never entered my mind, and I was stunned. I had been incredibly healthy my whole life. I had no symptoms other than my initial one, and I felt totally fine. The surgical oncologist texted my attorney friend back that he could do the surgery in either case.

I had just finished a four-hour ballroom dance camp with my son, who was kind enough to be my partner for the afternoon. I felt in excellent physical health, was approximately the same size 4 that I had been my whole adult life, and other than menstrual spotting, I felt totally fine.

The next morning, I called the oncologist's office back using the name of my PWN attorney friend and secured an appointment within a few days. I remember thinking So, this is how it is done! Use your networks from now on, and whenever you need to get anything important done, use your networks sooner rather than later. From then on, I navigated the medical system as best I could, leaning on my professional connections, especially when I hit a roadblock, which proved to be quite often as it turned out.

When I went to see the surgical oncologist for an initial examination, he shared that he did not think I had cancer. Whew! What a massive relief. He believed I had a large, complex tumor that he could move cohesively as one unit, which he felt was good news and likely not cancer. He said he would not know for sure until he performed the surgery, as biopsies were not performed in this situation. He explained that he was a laparoscopic-surgery specialist, but that my situation was complicated and would require traditional surgery. I was not too pleased to hear I would have to undergo major surgery, but I was very relieved to hear from this top medical specialist that he did not think I had cancer. At least, that is what he shared with me at the time.

SECOND OPINIONS

My internist in PWN suggested I reach out to the nurse oncologist in PWN for an additional perspective, so I did. The nurse suggested I get a second opinion from a specialist at Memorial Sloan Kettering Cancer Center in New York City to be certain I was getting the best possible treatment, which I agreed was a good idea. I also spoke with another PWN member who had undergone similar surgery with the same specialist at Sloan Kettering. The nurse oncologist helped secure me an appointment. I was hoping to find out if my surgery could be done laparoscopically by going to one of the most renowned medical centers in the country.

I was initially scheduled for an appointment a month or so out at Sloan Kettering and was surprised when their office called me back to get me in earlier. I thought that it must be my professional network at work, but when I asked the scheduler if that was the case, she said my consultation was being moved up due to the seriousness of my ultrasound and bloodwork results. That news was unsettling.

I began researching what a CA-125 blood test was and learned it was one of the determinants of the likelihood of ovarian cancer. My local surgical oncologist shared that he had seen other cases with a high CA-125 that were not cancer, so I was not to worry or jump to any conclusions. I tried very hard not to worry at that time and felt justified in doing so because I was feeling so good physically. I also knew I was in the care of the top specialist in our community. I couldn't possibly have cancer and feel this good, could I? My hope was that I could have a less invasive surgery, laparoscopically, at a prestigious national hospital known for such procedures.

I thought that since I was going to be traveling to Sloan Kettering in NYC for the day, why not make a family trip out of it? The kids were on summer break and could spend the day in the city together, enjoying an additional brother-sister bonding experience, while my husband and I went to get my second opinion. My son and daughter were excited about the opportunity to explore the city on their own. I went into the day believing that I was going to a state-of-the-art medical center hoping to get a better surgical solution. Then I would go home, having spent a great day with my family. In hindsight, that was not the best idea.

It turned out to be one of the worst days of my life. We drove to NYC, dropped the kids off in Times Square, then drove to Sloan Kettering, where my husband and I waited for over two and a half hours in a jam-packed, noisy waiting room that was undergoing serious renovation and construction. When the oncologist became available, I was required to go into the exam room by myself. I said my hope was to have my surgery done laparoscopically. With very poor bedside manner, the physician before me bluntly said, "I don't know what you have been told by your local doctor, but your situation definitely requires traditional surgery due to its significant complexity, and based on your ultrasound and very high CA-125 bloodwork results, it is very likely ovarian cancer." Oh my God! Seriously, this could not be happening. I could not possibly have cancer. Alone in the exam room, I went into a state of shock. I was not expecting that news. It was an extremely long car ride home, and I could see my kids texting each other in the back seat. I cannot even begin to imagine how scared they must have been as we all tried to process this news. Fear started to settle in.

I quickly learned that if I wanted the best possible outcome, I would need to collaborate with trusted medical experts, listen to their professional expertise, look for a team willing to work in partnership with me, and trust my gut instincts about my personal needs. Based on both opinions, which agreed that traditional surgery was warranted, I was scheduled for hysterectomy surgery with my local surgical oncologist on July 9, 2013, approximately two months after my initial ultrasound.

In preparation for surgery, while working full-time, I became hyperfocused on my nutrition, preparing superfood smoothies, lean proteins, and healthy greens. I ate as clean a diet as I could. I kept up my exercise regimen of a two-mile walk each morning, yoga stretches a few days per week, and ballroom dancing several nights per week. I figured that all these healthy choices would help prepare me physically for what my body was going to endure and help me recover from major surgery. I did my absolute best to be mentally prepared too, but honestly, I still could not fathom having cancer. I could not tell if I was beginning to feel a little bloated, which I had read was one of the symptoms of ovarian cancer. Deep down, I did not believe it could be cancer, but maybe it was just hope on my part.

THIS CAN'T BE TRUE

I went into hysterectomy surgery with as positive a mental attitude as I could muster, but I will never forget coming out of surgery and seeing my husband's face. I thought, Oh my God, it *is* cancer. My surgical oncologist came in to see me a short while later and said he was able to remove everything and that everything would be fine. I interpreted that as good news. He said he would come back once he had the pathology results. I thought to myself, If it is good news, why did my husband look like it was not good news? Nothing made sense to me at that point.

I did my best to focus on recovering from surgery, which looking back, was not too bad, as I was walking around within a few days. I vividly recall my son coming to visit me and walking down the hall with me and my IV pole so I could get some exercise. I joked, saying that my IV pole was my new dance partner. I was incredibly grateful that my son had attended the ballroom dance camp with me in June. He did it as a favor to me, and I was giddy about sharing my love of ballroom dance with him. I was thrilled to have spent that quality time together and that he could also be part of the three generations of ballroom dancers in our family.

The next day, my surgical oncologist came to see me in the hospital. He said, "OK, so here's the plan. You will have three months of chemotherapy, followed by a daily round of radiation for six weeks, followed by three more rounds of chemotherapy." I thought, What happened to "I got it all out" and "It is going to be fine"? Shock, fear, and despair were surging, because no matter how much I had mentally prepared for the possibility of this news, I honestly still felt blindsided. Chemotherapy and radiation had never been mentioned prior to that conversation. I had incorrectly interpreted the meaning of the surgeon's ability to remove everything, thinking it meant no other treatment would be necessary. I was honestly not emotionally or mentally prepared for the reality of chemotherapy.

I later learned that ovarian cancer is considered the silent killer because so few women seek medical attention for symptoms that can be construed as normal for women in perimenopause. I thought to myself, Thank goodness I chose to advocate for myself so persistently, or I might not have had such a positive outcome. I was proud of myself for being assertive, requesting to be seen and heard. Catching cancer early can mean the difference between life and death. Once I got a grip on myself, I knew I needed to wrap my head around this news and prepare physically and mentally for the next phase of treatment. Once I was home from the hospital, I needed to continue using my professional networking skills to ensure I had the best medical plan going forward.

A few days after my surgery, Rachel did a ballroom dance showcase at our local Fred Astaire Dance Studio with her instructor. I was truly heartbroken not to be there in person to cheer her on because we had been joined at the hip for all our dance lessons and performances over the last six years. I watched a video of her showcase from my Apple iPhone, beaming with pride at the way she got through her routine as strong as ever, not missing a single step of a very advanced cha-cha routine. She danced to Jennifer Lopez's "Let's Get Loud," which I found in my father's favorite Latin music collection, making it even more meaningful. Every time I watch that video on my family-dance website, I well up with tears of joy and pride. It brings back such a flood of emotions about all I was going through and how strong my daughter was to be able to get through that performance. Besides attending all of Rachel's dance performances and soccer games, I had been focused on helping with her comprehensive college search, using the same College Advisor of New York coach we had used with our son. As Rachel's college experience was something I had been planning and saving for since before she was born, I was determined to be there for her for what I hoped and prayed would be a very long time to come.

I needed to focus on my next stage of treatment. I set up an email distribution list so I could correspond with a small team of local professionals, family members, and friends in a systematic way. Initially, I kept my cancer news to a small, informal impact circle of meaningful support. I chose my circle wisely. I also received an excellent suggestion from my sister, who told me to be specific about what I needed every step of the way so I could receive the help I genuinely wanted. I remember thinking that all I wanted were cards, supportive emails, and meals for my family. I did not want to be visited in person until I was up to it psychologically.

My mother was living with her sister and brother-in-law in Long Island at that time. I know she was concerned about not being nearby to help because she had always been a loving caregiver to our family, looking after her elderly mother and uncle. I assured her that I was truly managing well and getting most of the assistance I needed from my husband and mother-in-law. Recuperating from abdominal surgery was not as difficult as I had anticipated. I started attending my beloved ballroom dance lessons as soon as I was cleared to do so by my doctor, allowing for physical activity and help with emotional processing. Ballroom dancing most definitely helped distract me from my cancer news, and it helped me continue my fitness regimen.

PERSONAL HEALTH TEAM

My medical team came from the unique connections in my life. Anticipating my upcoming chemotherapy treatments, I shared my cancer news with the co-owner of the Fred Astaire Dance Studio. I genuinely believed that I was not likely to continue doing ballroom dance lessons while undergoing chemotherapy for six months. In my mind, I prepared to work remotely as needed, and I was thankful I had the technology to do so. I would not miss a beat with client needs. At the dance studio that day, a fellow dance student heard about my health news and said that if I ever needed a second opinion on anything oncology-related, her husband might be able to help. I had no idea that her husband's medical specialty was cancer, even though we had danced in the same studio for many years.

I immediately reached out to him to ask his opinion on my treatment plan of three months of chemotherapy, six weeks of radiation, and three more months of chemotherapy. After reviewing my medical data, he shared that he understood why chemotherapy was recommended because it acted like an insurance policy against the cancer recurring, but he did not understand why radiation was being recommended. He said that if I were his wife, mother, or sister, he would recommend that I get another opinion before undergoing any treatment plan. He gave me the names of two top specialists in the US, one at Massachusetts General Hospital and the other at Johns Hopkins Hospital. I was extremely grateful that he knew the right experts for my situation. I added him to my small email distribution list of local medical professionals, friends, and family.

I felt it was prudent to get a second, and possibly a third, medical opinion so I could live knowing that I did everything in my power to have the best possible outcome. The next step was to get my medical slides to the two nationally recognized specialists. I called the local lab where I had my surgery to request the transfer. I was willing to do any treatment necessary to save my life, but I also did not want to do anything that wasn't required, as I knew some treatment options could have adverse side effects over the course of my lifetime.

That is when I met with my second case of significant medical resistance. The lab manager who had my slides immediately said they do not send slides for second opinions without medical insurance coverage. I probed further, explaining that I had an extraordinarily complicated case and needed to get my slides to two top specialists, as it could change my course of treatment. She insisted it was not an option because it would not be covered by my insurance.

I called my medical insurance company to request approval for second and third opinions. Dozens of phone calls to my insurance company ensued, as well as hours and hours of follow-up research with no progress. At every attempt to get my pathology slides to the specialists through traditional channels, I was thwarted by roadblocks. I was losing hope and knew the clock was ticking in terms of when my prescribed medical treatment plan was scheduled to commence.

IMPACT CIRCLE INFLUENCE

I called upon my professional impact circles once again. I needed a different approach, as I was not having any success getting a second opinion, let alone a third. I knew getting both opinions would be critical in case I needed a tiebreaker. My wise impact circle members suggested I reach out to the specialists on my own. As a result, I wrote personal letters to both specialists with a plea for them to help assess my treatment plan and included my family's holiday photo card.

I was pleasantly surprised to get an immediate call from the specialist at Mass General. He said he got my lovely card and was happy to help. He would need the pathology slides from my local hospital. I said I was having difficulty getting additional opinions covered by my insurance, and the lab would not release my slides without it. I asked him point-blank how much it would cost for his expert medical opinion, thinking it would be an enormous amount. At that juncture, I was pretty much ready to pay anything to help save my life or avoid unnecessary treatment. He said his consultation fee was $250, which I considered to be an extremely modest amount, considering what was at stake. I was stunned, to say the least, and I was so relieved that I could get a second opinion. At the same time, I was furious with the local medical lab for not letting me know that self-payment was an option in the first place. I had spent literally dozens of hours making phone calls to the insurance company, the hospital lab, and medical professionals, all while still recovering from major surgery, caring for my family, working full-time remotely, and managing my sanity.

I called the hospital lab, requested they send my slides to Mass General, and said I would be paying for the second opinion myself. I called the lab every day to get an update on the status of my slides, which had not yet arrived at Mass General.

Incredibly, I was told that my medical slides could not be located because there had been a chemical spill in the lab and my slides were missing. I was in disbelief and beyond upset. I calmly, professionally, and assertively said I needed those slides to be sent to Mass General immediately, or I would be there in person to pick them up. The lab administrator said I could not do that as it was against hospital policy for slides to be released to patients. I was stressed beyond belief, as I was getting down to the wire on seeking advice before my treatment started. I tried to keep my composure and said my slides needed to be found *today*. I was livid, as I knew my life was literally at stake.

My next call was to my local surgical oncologist with a plea for his intervention. Later in the day, I got a call from the lab stating that they had located my pathology slides, and they would be sent directly to Mass General. Once that assessment was completed, Mass General would send the slides directly to Johns Hopkins. Whew! Finally, progress.

Ultimately, I got two additional opinions. However, as anticipated, each physician provided a different interpretation of the same complex data, which continued to make my treatment plan uncertain. With this new information, my surgical oncologist convened a tumor board to analyze all the data and opinions. Who knew there was such a thing? They came back with the recommendation of chemotherapy only. Sweet success! All my hard work, research, and persistence had paid off, and I was at peace. Psychologically, it was a huge victory for me because I had relied on my professional skill set and had not given up on my gut instincts. I hoped to live a very long, vibrant life after my treatment plan.

Looking back, I now realize how the monumental resistance that came from the hospital lab caused colossal unnecessary stress. Being diagnosed with cancer was tough enough, physically and emotionally, but battling to get additional medical opinions for my unique cancer was maddening and preventable. I was fighting for my life on two levels. Thankfully, I was also extremely fortunate to have people in the medical community who did an amazing job helping me achieve the best possible outcome, including my oncology surgeon and staff.

I wanted to be certain that when I looked back on my decision-making process, I would know I had done everything possible for my personal well-being for the rest of my life. It was a huge relief that I could enter the next phase of treatment with a strong positive mental attitude, which I knew would be important for the best possible outcome. Using my professional impact circles made a huge difference in the outcome of my cancer treatment, mental and emotional health, and the rest of my life! Leaning on my informal medical impact circle proved to be quite pivotal in my treatment trajectory.

HEALTHY APPEARANCE

Knowing I would lose all my hair was honestly one of my biggest fears as I prepared for chemotherapy. I truly never felt that I would die from cancer, and I never allowed that thought to enter my psyche. I just had a strong core belief that I was meant to live a long, healthy life, and that is all I ever let myself think. However, the thought of losing my hair was truly terrifying. My frugal mother used to take my sister and me to a local training salon where haircuts were less expensive. After having a pixie haircut in high school, I protested and have worn my hair shoulder length since college. I knew that when I had my own career, my appearance was not something I would have a limited budget for.

I went on a mission to see if I could find a way to look the same as usual while going through chemotherapy so I could focus on my physical health and well-being. I researched my local options and found a hair salon that specialized in wig fittings. I made an appointment and reached out to my best friend and business partner to see if she would be willing to go with me. Unfortunately, she was going to be out of town. I could not sleep, as I was completely restless from worry about losing my hair. I ended up texting my dance friend Joan Hayner in the middle of the night and was surprised to get an immediate response from her at that hour. She said she would be honored to go with me.

Joan and I attended the wig-fitting appointment. The stylist looked as if she had her own cancer challenges, but she never shared as much, so I didn't inquire. I knew how private I was being with my own news and respected her wish to do the same. The caring stylist helped me find the best option, but the wig that most closely matched my hairstyle cost $700. This was much more than I had anticipated. However, I knew that looking like myself was going to be an extremely important part of my overall well-being during my cancer treatments. I figured I could order other wigs online much less expensively, but I felt strongly about supporting this local stylist, who was so thoughtful, professional, and discreet.

I was extremely emotional about the whole process as my personal and professional image was extraordinarily important to me. When the wig arrived, I called on another friend in my Executive Network to pick it up with me. I shared that I would only come out with the wig on if I felt comfortable enough to show her. If not, we would just leave. I put the wig on, tucking all my long black hair inside the cap, and chose not to say anything when I came out.

My friend Kathy Rowe, who was extremely supportive, kind, and caring, took her cue from me. We left, and once outside of the store, I asked, "So what do you think of my hair?" She was confused, and I was so happy that she thought it was my own hair, not my new wig. That was an important first litmus test. I was truly relieved because if she hadn't noticed I was wearing a wig, chances were others wouldn't either.

Subsequently, I purchased five more wigs from a much less expensive online provider. When the wigs arrived, they had big, bushy, long black hair. I decided to bring them one by one to my long-time and compassionate hairdresser Barbara Baker, who kindly and professionally cut them to look like my normal hair.

At each appointment, I put a wig on my head and held on to it as tightly as I could while she cut each one as she would normally cut my own hair. I truly looked just like myself. This meant that with a total of six wigs, I could carry on with all the activities of my life as usual. I used two wigs for my rigorous daily walks and dance lessons, during which I perspired, kept two for work, and had my hairdresser do two updos for my ballroom dance showcases.

No one had to know about my cancer journey, which was so important to me at the time. My hairdresser became a trusted and treasured friend, which was a positive outcome in my cancer journey.

My next focus was preparing mentally, physically, and emotionally for the next five and a half months of chemotherapy treatments. I did as much research as I could. I concocted superfood shakes, and I walked daily in my neighborhood or on my basement treadmill, going a little farther each day until I was up to my typical two miles from before my surgery.

DEEPER CONNECTIONS

was not allowed to drive for a few weeks after my surgery, and we did not have ride-share options like Uber or Lyft in 2013. To get myself through the next phase of treatment, I felt it would be prudent to seek outside help to ensure my family and close friends did not become depleted by helping me. John and my mother-in-law both provided meal preparation and rides to medical appointments, which was very helpful while I recovered from surgery, but I didn't want to exhaust them. In the 1990s, I had taken a Myers-Briggs personality assessment with PWN and learned that I was uncomfortable asking for help. At that time, I was the one typically helping others, and I viewed asking for help as a sign of weakness. I did not want to be a burden on my family, so I composed an email to send to my suburban neighborhood's distribution list. Without mentioning anything about my cancer journey—I absolutely was not ready to do that yet—I said I had recently undergone surgery and asked if anyone might be available to drive me to doctor's appointments and give my family some respite. I was reluctant to expose my vulnerability, but I hit the Send button and got so many exceedingly kind responses that I burst into tears. So many people offered to help, including some I had never even met, and this deepened my relationships with my neighbors, another positive outcome.

I would be done with my chemotherapy treatments after Thanksgiving, which was significant to me because I had been attending an annual national conference recognizing top women in wealth management across our industry, since 2008. I always looked forward to attending, and I knew that this year, it could be a source of support and healing after the trauma I had been through. I could envision myself healing emotionally by sharing my story with this incredible group of women. I was also looking forward to my annual ballroom dance showcase with the Fred Astaire Dance Studio in January 2014. As a result of my self-advocacy and with help from my impact circles, I would be able to attend both. This was very gratifying on all levels.

CHOCOLATES AND LICORICE

efore I started my chemotherapy, which would be once every three weeks for five and a half months, I coordinated a list of dear women friends to accompany me. For my first treatment on August 12, 2013, my chemo buddy picked me up at my home and drove me to my doctor's office. She was a former nurse, so I knew I was in excellent hands. I packed a bag with snacks, lunch, and a bag of chocolates for giving out—a tradition I started for whenever I went to a medical appointment of any kind. I brought a private selection of my Million Dollar Chocolate Bars, individually wrapped Lindt Dark Chocolate Truffles, or Lindt Dark Chocolate Squares to give to anyone I saw: the clinicians who drew my blood at the local lab, the technicians who did my scans, and the receptionists wherever I checked in. I figured it certainly could not hurt to be nice to people who I would see on a consistent basis. I would hand them a Million Dollar Chocolate Bar and say, "Thanks a million for taking good care of me today!" I was typically met with a warm thank-you and a big smile. One time when I walked in to get my blood drawn at a local lab, the receptionist announced to the whole waiting room "It's the Million-Dollar-Chocolate-Bar lady!" It was my turn to smile, and I handed her another bar.

When I walked into the infusion room at my doctor's office with my chemo buddy, the edge of the room was lined with reclining vinyl chairs connected to IV poles. It was a sterile environment with a big counter and one nurse. I was puzzled when the nurse looked annoyed to see me and my former-nurse friend, saying with an unpleasant tone in her voice "What are you doing here? You are not supposed to be here." I was taken by surprise, as I was reasonably sure I was supposed to be there, but I was most certainly nervous, and with my poor sense of direction, I could have been mistaken.

I sheepishly said, "I was told to come here." She asked if I had a purple sheet. I said yes and gave it to her.

She looked at it and said, "Oh. Go ahead and sit down."

"Anywhere?"

"Yes."

I was the first patient in the room, so I had my pick of chairs. I selected the one closest to a window in an attempt to see sunlight.

My chemo buddy and former-nurse friend just looked at me and then whispered, "Well, that's not the best way for a nurse to handle herself. That would never be tolerated under my care."

I was heartened to know that I was not the only one to feel that I was not being treated with compassion. I truly appreciated having such a dear friend with me at that moment. As a former nurse, she knew what acceptable professional behavior was. That behavior was clearly not empathetic, especially for my first day of chemotherapy, as I was scared enough on my own.

Next, the chemotherapy nurse handed me an American Cancer Society catalog and told me to pick a wig, which I would get for free. She followed up by announcing that it was not worth purchasing anything else. She could not have been more insensitive in the way she shared the information, and she didn't understand anything about me or my lifestyle. Those wigs were the key to my living a normal life during and after chemotherapy; it would take many months after my treatments ended for my hair to grow all the way back to its normal length. I never selected a wig from that catalog.

I tried to shake this off, settling into my reclining chair. I was told about the chemotherapy drugs I was about to get infused with as the nurse hooked me up to the IV poles. There would be a combination of anti-nausea drugs to combat the chemo drugs and a Benadryl-like drug to avoid an allergic reaction, quite the cocktail of medicines. I was told I might be sleepy from the Benadryl and assumed that would likely be the case based on my prior reactions. I chatted with my friend until I fell asleep for a bit, woke up, chatted again while we had our lunch, and then asked my friend to give the two chemo nurses in the room at that time the chocolate selections I had brought for the day. My friend and I were surprised again with the less than appreciative thank-you from the first nurse, especially compared to the incredibly positive reactions I had gotten from gifting chocolate in the past. We were in the infusion room from roughly 10:00 a.m. to 4:00 p.m., which went by relatively quickly because I was chatting with my dear friend. My first chemotherapy treatment was officially done! My friend drove me home, and I thought, OK, that was not so bad. I had made it through the day, physically and emotionally.

Next came the difficult part. I was warned that I would definitely feel worse the next day and for the next several days. That was most certainly the case. Getting the combination of chemo-therapy drugs felt like the worst flu you can possibly imagine. I was extremely achy from head to toe in addition to being incredibly nauseous—not a pleasant combination. Worse yet, I had to get Neulasta shots in the days following chemo to keep my white blood cell count in the proper range, which was low to begin with. The side effect of those shots was horrific bone pain on top of the extreme body aches and nausea for a trifecta of feeling dreadful. All my treatments were on Mondays, so the next four days were horrifically difficult to endure, but remarkably, by each Saturday, I began to slowly emerge and feel like myself again.

I worked from my bed with my laptop computer, returning client emails all week, and I was back in the office the following Monday, ready to meet with clients for all review appointments. I continued to manage my financial advisory practice with my business team—my financial advisor–business partner and Susan Brown, our senior wealth strategy associate—who were extremely supportive throughout my entire cancer journey. Susan was a mother who was focused on her own work-life balance, so I was fortunate to have two women on my business team who understood the challenge of balancing work and life. Susan had been a strong part of my business team for four years and my financial advisor–business partner for over sixteen years. I tried to keep my life as normal as possible and protect my income, focusing all my energy on taking care of myself, my family, and my clients. Based on all the positive medical feedback and my strong core faith, I honestly believed I was going to be fine.

In my office, I only shared my health news with my immediate business team, my boss, a former manager, and one other financial advisor friend. I went to each of my six chemotherapy sessions with a treasured friend. Each time, at my request, my chemo buddies would buy me lunch from a local bagel shop: a sesame bagel with muenster cheese, lettuce, tomato, and mayonnaise, plus Sun Chips and lemonade. This was the comfort food I needed to get through the intensity of the experience. My dear friends picked me up at my house, drove me to my doctor's office, and stayed by my side for the day. We chatted for hours about anything on our minds. I slept, we ate, and we chatted some more. Going through the treatments was never physically painful, just emotionally intense. I tried keeping a positive attitude, choosing to believe that the medicine in the hanging bags on my infusion poles was going to prevent me from ever getting cancer again. It would allow me to live a beautiful, long life with my family, attending all milestone events in my children's lives. I thanked each chemo buddy for being with me every step of my cancer journey with a big bag of Lindt Dark Chocolate Truffles. I was filled with gratitude for such incredible women friends.

At my second chemo session, I dropped off my traditional bag of chocolate truffles with the same nurse who had said I wasn't supposed to be there on my first day. This time she said, "You shouldn't be bringing in chocolates because I don't like chocolate, and I just give them to my husband, and he doesn't need them." That was an interesting reaction. I always try to remind myself that I never know what other people are going through, so I just chose to be as pleasant as I could be. Later in the day, I saw the very same nurse munching on something behind her big medical counter. I could not tell what it was, so I decided to get up to use the restroom and glanced over nonchalantly to get a closer look. Ah-ha! It was red licorice. Not only am I a dark chocolate lover, but one of my favorite sweet treats, in addition to Skittles, Swedish Fish, and Peanut M&M's, is red licorice. I love all kinds of red licorice: the traditional cherry or strawberry flavor; the sour, filled cherry-and-lemon kind; and the pull-and-peel cherry variety. That evening, I went to my local CVS drugstore, and I bought every type of red licorice they had before the severe pain of chemo set in.

On my next chemo visit, I gently placed the variety of red licorices on the nurse's counter and walked to my vinyl recliner. The nurse opened the bag, looked up, and said, "You are my new best friend!" From that day on, I brought in red licorice for her and dark chocolates for a second nurse until my chemotherapy treatments were done. After each treatment, I felt about the same each week—horrific for four days, but thankfully not worse as the treatments went along, which I had read could be the case. The worst pain continued to come from the Neulasta shots, which caused severe bone and muscle pain. Next to the nausea, the shots were the most difficult part. I cringe when I think back on that unique combination of pain and nausea.

When my hair began to fall out, I made the decision to cut it myself at home and begin wearing my wigs. I closed my eyes and began cutting, choosing never to look at myself in the mirror without my hair throughout my entire cancer experience. I never wanted to have a physical or mental picture of myself without my hair in my own brain, as I am such a visual person. I truly never looked once, because I felt I would never be able to unsee myself that way. I even colored my hair with my eyes closed once my treatments were done—quite a feat!

I also chose to use makeup to enhance my appearance, which included filling in my eyebrows and eyelashes when those began to fall out. Through my ballroom dance journey, I knew a variety of makeup strategies, and it certainly helped to have a few appearance tips at my disposal for projecting a healthy image.

Emotionally, the worst chemo week was the one scheduled for the week of Thanksgiving 2013. I was scheduled for chemo on Monday of that week and knew that by Thanksgiving Day, I would still be in substantial distress. I asked my surgical oncologist if I could postpone chemotherapy treatment that week and do it the following week, so I could have Thanksgiving dinner with my family. He politely said no and shared the importance of keeping to my exact schedule for the best possible outcome. Brokenhearted, I had my Thanksgiving dinner in bed while my family ate at our dining room table. Psychologically, this was a struggle, and it's the only time I gave in to fear and shed tears over how difficult this process was for me and my family.

FAMILY SUPPORT

y husband and mother-in-law helped provide support while I underwent treatments, as Rachel was focused on college planning in her junior year of high school and our son John was away at college. I did my best to be as little a burden on anyone as possible.

One of the most treasured gifts I received during my cancer journey was a container of Sanders Dark Chocolate Sea Salt Caramels from my brother Mark and sister-in-law Marie. The precious part of the gift was a personalized prescription label made to look official with dosage instructions, which I didn't see at first, as I was too busy eating the canister's contents. Marie asked if I had seen the label, so I pulled out the container and read "Take two caramels, three times per day, for five months. Finish the entire container as prescribed." I tear up every time I think about that label, sent to me with so much love and followed by replacement canisters. To this day, Sanders Dark Chocolate Sea Salt Caramels are my favorite chocolate treats. I recently discovered they make phenomenal firepit s'mores if you stick one inside a toasted marshmallow. Mayela and I experimented with this as we sat poolside around my firepit one delightful summer evening when she and her husband Stephen were in town.

My relationship with Mayela deepened during my cancer treatment. She thoughtfully sent me weekly cards, which I had said would be appreciated, and she took true care to connect with me often and with love. My niece Maya participated in a cancer-fundraising event with her soccer team, donning a pink jersey with "Aunt Alissa" on the back. I also received many cards and calls of support from my extended family. Aunts, uncles, and cousins continued to provide a foundation of love and care, which has been present my entire life. I tear up every time I think about the profound blessing of how supportive my siblings, their spouses, and my extended family were during my cancer experience.

HEALTHY, WEALTHY, AND WISE

In the first week of December 2013, I completed my chemotherapy regimen. I felt incredibly fortunate to get through all my treatments with no major setbacks or complications. Although that week marked the end of my physical treatments, I knew the emotional scars and challenges would take much longer to heal from.

I was thrilled to be able to attend a national conference for the top women advisors in the US, and I could only go because I had avoided radiation treatment through my own persistence. I called my main contact and shared my idea of giving a presentation called "Healthy, Wealthy, and Wise Through Challenging Times." This described the goal I had set for myself at the beginning of my cancer diagnosis. I wanted to inspire other women with their own challenges, whether related to health, the loss of a loved one, divorce, or another life transition. He embraced my idea right from the start and connected me with his team to make it happen. I was most definitely nervous about doing the presentation, but I truly felt a calling to do it. If I could just help one other person in the audience, my effort would be worthwhile.

After delivering my impassioned presentation, I got a standing ovation from the caring and thoughtful audience—an overwhelmingly positive reaction. I was so very touched by their response that I could not help but tear up, but I managed to keep it together. Many women came up to me afterward to thank me for sharing my story and offer tips for how to get through life when it becomes challenging. I felt a true release of emotion, knowing that I was following my heart by listening to an inner voice that encouraged me to share my authentic self with others, including the vulnerable side, which I had not typically shared in business circles of that magnitude. It was indeed an important step in my emotional healing, and having a meaningful impact on my audience brought me true inner peace and gratitude.

I will never forget one woman who immediately came up to me after my presentation and shared a very personal, distressing health issue she was dealing with. She had not told anyone—not even her young-adult children or her extended family. She shared that my presentation had given her the courage to reach out to others for help without viewing it as a sign of weakness. We chatted, hugged each other, shared tears of hope, and began an unbreakable connection. She kept in touch with me for the next several months as she slowly let her family and friends in on her pain. As a result, healing came more readily. I could see firsthand the power of sharing my story and strategies.

CHAPTER SEVEN:
Recovery

I recall contemplating, early on, what I was supposed to do once I was on the other side of this cancer experience. All I kept hearing, from a higher power, was this: "Share. You are good at sharing. Talk about your cancer experience to help others and share your journey. Share your strategy of how you got through to the other side, and attempt to do so with grace and dignity." That is what I heard. Use your voice. Share your story. Doing so at the conference was a good start. But I felt it was the perfect time to create my next impact circle, a healing circle for executive women touched by cancer.

Thankfully, with my wigs and makeup to keep my personal image intact, I had kept my cancer journey private until I was ready to share on my own terms. I simply continued my normal work at the office, attended networking events in public, took dance lessons, and did showcase performances. I carried on with my life as normally as possible, feeling thankful to my family, closest friends, business team, hairdresser, and my dream team of holistic and complementary therapists who allowed me to focus on my overall well-being and healing: my massage therapist, acupuncturist, craniosacral specialist, and chiropractor.

PASSION, PURPOSE, AND LEGACY

A few months after my chemotherapy was complete, I decided it was time to share my cancer journey more publicly. John and I attended the local chapter of the American Cancer Society's gala at the Hall of Springs in Saratoga Springs, New York, a formal black-tie affair. It was a major fundraising event with a live auction, where the auctioneer encouraged donations "in honor of" or "in memory of" or "in support of" someone affected by cancer. My mind started racing, thinking this could be the right time to share my news with my local business community, as there was a large audience in attendance. The more I considered the idea, the more I was truly petrified, but I had been keeping this secret for far too long. I felt like I had been silencing my authentic self, and I needed to use my voice to continue my emotional healing journey. I jokingly thought to myself that the room's acoustics were so poor that most of the hundreds of people in the room would not be able to hear me anyway. When the auctioneer, a dear family friend, came to our table, I raised my paddle and simply said, "My donation is in support of me." Once the words were out of my mouth, the other guests at my table whipped their heads around with looks of shock on their faces. It opened a meaningful conversation, and my secret was finally out.

I looked directly across the room and saw a woman I knew professionally who was a revered and iconic executive in our community. She and her husband owned a well-known, respected supermarket chain. I somehow rose from my chair and started walking directly toward her to share an idea that had been percolating. It was about starting my healing circle for executive women touched by cancer. Jane Golub had openly shared her breast-cancer journey in business circles, so I figured she would be an excellent person to run my idea by. En route, I was approached by another woman who said she had heard the news I shared and that she had also recently finished treatments for ovarian cancer. We chatted briefly and learned that we had shared the same surgical oncologist and had been in chemotherapy treatments at the same time, even in the same infusion room, which was quite a coincidence, or "God wink," as I like to refer to it. She had finished her chemotherapy treatments a few weeks before I finished mine, but I recalled seeing her there a few times. She looked a little different, as she had been wearing a wig during her treatments and was not wearing one that evening. I learned she was a psychiatrist in private practice. At that moment, I took the liberty of sharing that I was putting together a group of women executives touched by cancer to be a professional support network for one another. I asked if she had an interest in learning more, and she said yes. We agreed to connect for a cup of tea to discuss the idea further.

I kept walking toward my supermarket-executive friend on my mission to see what she thought of the idea. I was greeted warmly by Jane. I told her I had been very reluctant to share my ovarian cancer news publicly due to my profession, and I had chosen to share it for the first time this evening with my monetary pledge. Her husband turned to me and gave me a big bear hug, which I certainly was not anticipating. I told her about my idea and that I was thinking we could have a monthly private dinner for sharing our stories confidentially, connecting with other professional women who had experienced cancer, and helping support other recently diagnosed women. We could serve as role models, hoping to inspire others going through similar journeys. To my utter delight, she immediately said, "I'm in!" Supermarket mogul Jane Golub loved my idea. I was amazed, in part because she was such an iconic figure in the Capital Region but also because I knew she had a busy schedule, attending many philanthropic and networking events, just as I did.

Over the next few weeks, I attended several not-for-profit fundraising and business networking events, including the Women's Employment and Resource Center's First Impressions, Second Chances reception at The Crossings of Colonie. I overheard a few professional women I knew talking about their cancer journeys. I politely entered the conversation and shared my cancer news with them. They were quite stunned. I then asked them if they would like to join a healing circle I was forming for professional women touched by cancer. The reactions were all an immediate yes. I reached out to a few other professionals in our community who I knew had been impacted by cancer, and I set up a first dinner meeting. I had thought about what to call our group and came up with Passion and Purpose, chuckling to myself about the abbreviation PAP with its connection to early detection cancer screening for women. The name stuck, and our Passion and Purpose healing circle was born. This was my third formal impact circle.

Here is the introductory letter I shared with potential members.

Dear Ladies,

I am reaching out on a personal level to share an idea. As some of you may know, I had a health issue over this past year, one that I kept fairly private. I have found that personal healing journeys can take a variety of paths, and no one way is right for everyone. I am just beginning to be more public about my journey in hopes that I might be able to help others along the way.

As a professional with a practice to run, I felt that I had some unique issues to address.

- *How and when do I share my news with coworkers and/or clients?*
- *How and when do I use my professional networks and connections for my healing journey?*
- *Why did this happen to me, and how can I turn this experience into something positive for others?*
- *What difference can I make for other high-level executive women who have had similar questions or experiences?*
- *How can I be a resource to other businesswomen who are newly diagnosed?*

My idea is to put together a caring and compassionate forum of other high-level businesswomen who may wish to explore these issues, be resources to each other, and be willing to help other newly diagnosed professional women.

I would like to gather women who might appreciate connecting on occasion for encouragement, wisdom, and shared experiences while remaining at the top of our professional careers, physically and emotionally, during and after our health-care journeys.

This is not meant to replace any resources or services currently available in our community, but rather to be an independent group of highly caring and compassionate women executives who have experienced cancer and are willing to make a difference for others, and in the process, continue their own healing journey.

I got positive responses from all the executive women I reached out to. In our first few dinner meetings, we got to know each other more meaningfully and focused on establishing a mission statement and goals for our group. As executive women touched by cancer, we focused on triumphing over adversity, individually and collectively. We shared our stories with others who were faced with similar life challenges, reflecting upon our journeys and inspiring each other with our courage, strength, dignity, grace, and grit. Sharing adverse challenges allowed us to find unique ways of coping, healing, being inspired, and deepening our relationships. That was the spirit in which we shared our health-care journeys.

We knew that how we reacted to adverse experiences could determine the course our lives took. Choosing positive paths gave us the potential for learning, self-awareness, personal growth, reflection, and silver linings. We appreciated the simple, positive things in our lives, recognizing what we already had and living our best lives going forward. We also explored the idea of advocacy as part of the mission of our Passion and Purpose impact circle; we wanted to help ease the medical and emotional journey not only for ourselves but also for other women who would be diagnosed in the future.

UNTHINKABLE LOSSES

The Passion and Purpose impact circle grieved the loss of four members. Our first loss came early on with the passing of a member who came to us with stage IV breast cancer. She shared her prognosis freely, and we witnessed a woman navigate the late stages of terminal cancer with incredible grace and dignity. I remember sending her doughnuts from a new shop in Albany, Cider Belly Doughnuts, which left the doors open in the summertime and let the sweet, intoxicating smell waft down the street to my office. Her husband called to thank me and let me know how much they both enjoyed them. I later held a holiday party in my home, and we honored her memory by lighting candles and sharing memories. I read this passage I wrote in November 2018.

It cannot be…

It cannot be… heart-wrenching news of one of our healing-circle sisters. It cannot be… she joined us just so recently, only to leave us too soon.

It cannot be… the fear we all feel, thinking it could be me.

We break bread, open our hearts, support each other, enveloped in our common bond. We heal, we learn, we grow, we thrive, we love, we grieve.

We choose to gather here on earth and know we will be reunited in Heaven above, as we are healing-circle sisters, forever bound.

You joined our circle for just a short while but made an indelible mark we hold forever in our souls.

It is to be… for all of us when it is to be. So, let us use our precious days here on earth wisely, doing what we each hold dear, spending time with our families and friends in harmony with the universe and each other.

We are blessed to have one another along our journeys, making the most of our precious gift of life and giving thanks for every moment. We are Passion and Purpose healing-circle sisters.

Our second loss was also a member who came to us with late-stage breast cancer. Our healing-circle holiday party, planned well in advance, was coincidentally on the same day as her memorial service. We went to her wake and then to my home to grieve as healing-circle members. We again lit candles; this time they were for both our fallen members. "We miss and honor our second sister who has passed and are heartbroken that we are sending another. Our tiniest solace is that you will be together in our hearts, through friendship eternally."

Our third loss was one of our founding members, our beloved Jane Golub, who did in-store marketing for her supermarket chain and continued to work right up until her unexpected passing in 2019. She and her husband were on a business trip in California when Jane fell ill unexpectedly and passed away a few short weeks later. Jane had just attended our monthly dinner meeting and was incredibly supportive of a book idea I had shared for each of us to contribute a chapter about our cancer journeys. As Jane was our distinguished matriarch and a long-standing community leader and friend, we felt this loss immensely.

I was honored to be asked by her husband to be a pallbearer at Jane's memorial service at Gates of Heaven in Schenectady. It was the first time I had ever been asked to be a pallbearer. It was heartwarming to think how much our group must have meant to her. After the memorial service, I went to the cemetery and took part in a traditional Jewish service, which was an overwhelming experience. Jane was such an icon in our community and a dear friend to all of us in our healing circle that the emotion was tremendous. It was made easier by the bonds of friendship I had with the other pallbearers. I attended a follow-up reception at Jane's home, where I had been the previous summer for a lovely garden event for business leaders in our community. I'll never forget how Jane always treated me as a professional, continually looking to connect me with potential clients and showing meaningful support.

Exhausted with grief, I felt it was time to engage a professional to help PAP navigate our sorrow. I consulted with my dear friend, healing-circle member, and clinical social worker, Liz Dunn, who I used to babysit for when her children were infants. Liz would be out of town for a medical appointment of her own, so I consulted with another professional about how best to lead a tribute discussion in Jane's honor at our next healing-circle dinner meeting. I simply had everyone in our circle share their fondest memories of our treasured member. We toasted Jane with her favorite chardonnay, and we chose to give ourselves time to come up with a meaningful gift to honor her memory.

A few months later, when Jane's husband and daughter were ready, we invited them to join us for a special healing-circle dinner. We each shared memories of the impact Jane had on our lives, and it was truly an unforgettable evening. We presented her husband and daughter with a gift of two hundred trees, which had been planted in a grove in Israel in Jane's honor, as she was known as "the tree lady" in her Jewish Federation. It was a night none of us was likely to forget. I also announced that we would officially change the name of our healing circle from Passion and Purpose to Passion, Purpose, and Legacy (or PPL) in Jane's honor.

The fourth loss was that of our cherished member Petia Kassarova, a cellist and music teacher who was referred to me by a friend in ballroom dance circles. My dance friend's husband, a doctor and avid ballroom dancer, was significant in connecting me with the top oncologists in the country when I needed them. I felt including Petia in PPL was a perfect opportunity to pay his kindness forward.

I had developed an immediate and close personal friendship with Petia and discovered we shared the same oncologist. When Petia received serious news of her diagnosis, she called to see if I could spend some time with her, doing anything to distract her from her grim journey ahead. She suggested we go to the local mall and do some retail therapy. I was bereft to hear her news but honored to accompany her and that she felt comfortable speaking freely with me. During our Colonie Center mall excursion, I received an unexpected call from R.J. Shook, Head of SHOOK Research, sharing that I had been selected for a prestigious advisors list. I was elated to be included. R.J. congratulated me, and we had an incredibly meaningful conversation. We just seemed to click in a deeply significant way, which was quite astonishing for a first discussion. I was struck that R.J. genuinely wanted to know about me as a person and about the impact that I wanted to make on the world. I shared stories about how I worked with clients and how I had built my client base over my entire career, one relationship at a time. It was a memorable discussion and one that I could not have anticipated. After the conversation ended, I shared what had transpired with Petia, and it was a very special, private moment to share with her.

Heartbreakingly, Petia passed away a short time later, which was another devastating loss for our PPL healing-circle sisters. Petia was an exquisite cellist, born in Bulgaria, who came to the US with her husband to share their love of music. In her honor, we created a music scholarship at the local community college where she taught. The scholarship would be awarded to a talented young musician, which we felt was a lovely tribute to our beloved Petia.

After Petia passed, my conversation with R.J. Shook lingered in my mind, as I simply couldn't put my finger on why we connected so authentically. I decided to explore their website to see if I could learn more about this research organization. I was pleasantly surprised to discover that R.J. was a Babson College graduate, like my children. Then I watched a video of him on stage at a previous conference, where he shared a story about his mother's battle with breast cancer. She passed away when he was seventeen years old, on the night of his junior prom. In that moment, I realized that our unique bond was likely based on the work I had done with my PPL circle. I surmised R.J. may have read about this passion project of mine in my application.

Forming PPL, my third formal impact circle, provided me with the phenomenal gift of dozens of meaningful friendships. This is one of my greatest joys in life. With every new dinner meeting, I walk away more enriched and more proud, knowing that I have connected incredible, like-minded women who genuinely and deeply care about each other. Despite our heart-wrenching losses, we savor the joys of good health, and we meaningfully celebrate each time we are together.

HEALING-CIRCLE INFLUENCE

PPL is most definitely an example of how one plus one is much more than two. The power of the collective wisdom of this extraordinary group of women exemplifies the power of impact circles. When I asked our healing-circle members to share what PPL meant to them, they sent me the following responses:

- *"PPL led to me finding a group of amazing women, where I can receive help and offer help. Alissa created a place for women who lead to lead in a new way—lead each other in sometimes very private life struggles—and we lead by example most often. I think of the women in this group every single day. It is absolutely true that no matter what you are going through, you can also help someone else. I love this group because even though it deals with matters of life and death, it's also a place filled with laughter and love."*

- *"After being cancer-free for a few years, I joined this group as a way to pay it forward and meet and cancer-coach those who are going through it for the first time. I recently had a recurrence of cancer, and this caring and knowledgeable group rushed to my side with tips, advice, and love. They are all my sheroes."*

- *"PPL has been a source of grounding and support that comes from truly knowing one another's shared experiences. I feel the affection and caring concern of an extended family. PPL is women helping women—strong women with a wide variety of professional accomplishments who have all been touched by cancer. It's a shared experience that brings a special closeness."*

- *"PPL is women empowering other women. Exemplary and accomplished women thriving through the shared experience of cancer and focused on creating belonging, hope, and unconditional love and support. You all mean the world to me, and I am grateful to be a part of this amazing group."*

- *"Strong women bonding together ... lifting and holding each other up under stressful times ... knowing we care, and sharing and understanding what is needed to get through the ordeal. I don't know what I would do without all of your support. I feel blessed."*

- *"I came to this group a mere three weeks after being diagnosed. I was still numb and in shock from the news. I was scared and felt overwhelmed. I had no idea what I was going to do. After one meeting with all these amazing women sharing individual stories, I was welcomed and immediately felt safe and secure. I was provided with so much knowledge to conquer this diagnosis. I left feeling empowered, knowing I had a group of loving warrior women invested in me, my health, and my journey. I am eternally grateful to be a part of this group. I could not have gotten through this without you."*

- *"A sisterhood of love, compassion, and strength. A safe place to be who we are."*

- *"I joined PPL after being treated successfully for my second breast cancer with a second mastectomy. Walking into this room of such accomplished women of a very wide age range (thirty to seventy-plus years) who welcomed me with open arms felt so safe, and they were so accepting of me. It was a breath of fresh air to be in this circle, and I could even partake of the incredible, delicious food, including chocolate, without feeling guilty. I am very grateful for Alissa's invitation."*

- *"It is incredibly reassuring to know that I have a group of women who are there to support me emotionally and mentally through an almost endless number of issues."*

- *"It was terrifying being invited to join a group I never intended to need. I found emotional support and information to empower me to make decisions about my care and answer questions I may not have had otherwise. I will always and forever be grateful for their friendship and support."*

- *"Our network of PPL friends is a collaboration of like-minded women who are passionate about helping others and being there for each other in a time of need. It is a network of friends with whom we can share our secrets without judgment, our fears without pity, our tears without shame, and our successes without envy. We empower each other and help each other to thrive and live purposeful lives. Together we laugh, love, and inspire each other. I would be lost without my friends and am grateful for them every day."*

While leading our healing circle, and more grateful than ever for my life, I have found myself additionally focused on helping others, including my family, clients, impact circle members, and community. Forming and leading our healing circle has given me the opportunity to fulfill part of my life's mission, which is to impact our members, their loved ones, and the world. I feel an enormous sense of pride in choosing to listen to the voice inside my soul that encouraged me to share my cancer struggles, pushing through my own personal fears about trusting others with such deeply personal information. In the end, it has been very rewarding to know that something meaningful has come of my cancer journey.

DANCING THROUGH THE STORM

While I was getting my energy back after chemotherapy, I learned of an organization called Get Your Rack Back, founded by a local breast-cancer survivor who was raising money for other survivors. She was hosting an event to be held at a local hotel in Troy. I inquired whether they would have a dance floor. Much to my delight, the organizer said yes, so I offered to do a ballroom dance performance with my outstanding instructor Serge Nelyubov for her spring fundraising evening. It was the first opportunity for me to combine my love of ballroom dance with my desire to give back to the community in a unique and meaningful way. When we arrived at the event, Serge and I were both surprised to see that the dance floor was outside, lying on top of the grass. This was a first for both of us. In ballroom circles, we are typically very careful with the specialty dance shoes we wear because they have suede on the bottom, and we only use them on hardwood surfaces. We walked on the grass to get to the floating dance floor, which was significantly smaller than we had anticipated, but we made the best of it, chuckling to ourselves.

The second cancer-fundraising dance performance I did was with another excellent instructor from Fred Astaire Dance Studio, Grey Masko. Liz Dunn, a PPL member, asked me to perform for the Schenectady Cancer Foundation, an organization she supported that was headed by a prominent local oncologist. After I was through with my cancer treatments, I started thinking about song selections for new showcase routines, and I chose meaningful songs to perform to as part of my healing process. The first song I chose was "The Prayer." I used the Josh Groban / Celine Dion version, which is hauntingly beautiful. Grey and I performed that showcase with a variety of theatrical lifts, where I literally felt like I was flying—such an amazing feeling after all that I had been through. The next two showcase songs were Michael Bublé's "Feeling Good" and Il Divo's "The Power of Love." All reflected deep emotions, and I was truly grateful to be alive and to be able to dance.

The next year, I performed a follow-up showcase for the Schenectady Cancer Foundation. This time, I was psychologically ready to disclose my cancer news to what I knew would be a supportive audience. After chemotherapy, it took approximately a year and a half for my hair to grow back to shoulder length. I wore my customized wigs daily and used my updo wigs during my dance performances. The most terrifying part of doing my showcases was worrying about one of my wigs flying off during my performance. I used little hairnets and tons of bobby pins to secure my wig in place, but it did not stop me from worrying, especially during the energetic lifts in our routines, where I was twirling and swooshing around with significant centripetal force. Grey Masko shared that in one of his prior comedic showcase performances, he had worn a woman's wig that came off by accident. This was my biggest fear! Thankfully, that never happened to me.

USA DANCE COMMUNITY

My next performance was at the USA Dance's Sunday social held at the Polish Community Center in Albany. I danced to "The Prayer" one more time. I still had not shared my cancer news with the broader ballroom dance community at that point. At the end of my performance, I was overcome with emotion and felt I was going to burst if I did not tell someone there. I don't know why I selected this person, but toward the end of the evening, I walked over to a kindhearted woman I knew socially from attending the monthly dance with my parents. I asked her if she had a moment to chat.

She said, "Yes, of course."

"I've been reluctant to share this news, as it has simply been too difficult for me to do so, but I'm finally realizing I need to share my news more broadly. The reason I chose to do this performance to the song 'The Prayer' is that I recently had surgery and completed five and a half months of chemotherapy for ovarian cancer. It looks like I am going to be OK."

She just looked at me in disbelief, as I had been dancing there monthly and no one had any idea of what I was going through. I told her I was wearing a wig, and I was completely relieved it had not come flying off during my performance. She hugged me tightly. As it turns out, she was a nurse and as compassionate as could be. We shared a special bond from that moment on.

VISIONS OF STRENGTH

I was heartened when PPL was honored with a Visions of Strength community award at a fundraising event for a local cancer center. The mission of the foundation was to provide funds for complimentary services for cancer patients, including integrative health-care treatments, transportation to medical appointments, hair accessories, and healing touch and massage therapies. PPL members were particularly proud to be a part of this mission, as we knew firsthand how significant these services could be for a cancer patient's health and well-being, along with traditional medicine. This public exposure gave PPL a chance to raise awareness of who we were and how we might help others. In my acceptance speech in front of a large crowd, I said, "We celebrate this evening's survivors and thrivers of our Passion, Purpose, and Legacy healing circle. These women are extraordinarily brave, strong, intelligent, thoughtful, and caring business professionals. Each one has a powerful story behind her. We stand ready to welcome professional women who might benefit from our collective, indomitable spirit."

Offstage, two women approached me, wanting to learn more. One was a survivor who was being celebrated on stage that evening, and the other was the leader of the breast-cancer not-for-profit at whose event Serge and I had danced previously—a full-circle moment. As PPL kept growing, we began to consider what an ideal size would be for us. When we grew to fifteen members, an ideal size for sharing our private journeys, it was time to look for a leader for a second chapter so we could keep our conversations intimate. I attended a business friend's Galentine's party and met Carole Heaney, who had recently launched a business called In the Spirit of Healing, a consulting practice for those affected by cancer. I was so impressed with our conversation that the next day, I called and suggested the idea of her coleading a second chapter of PPL. We cofacilitated dinner meetings for the second chapter, where I fell in love with every new member. At one point, we had twenty-five members split between the two circles, but ultimately, we merged back into one circle.

I contacted the editor in chief of *HERLIFE Magazine*, Angela Beddoe, to share our healing-circle story in hopes it might resonate with her readers and potentially attract other executive women touched by cancer. Her team set up a photo shoot at Yaddo Gardens in Saratoga Springs. We had our hair and makeup done, and a few members were interviewed. We were honored to be featured as their June 2016 cover story. Each time I met a potential new member, I would share the article to give them a sense of who we were, in addition to a wonderful professional video created by one of our members highlighting the mission of our group. Our healing circle celebrated our tenth anniversary in 2024, thankfully with no further losses.

NEW LENS

Since my cancer diagnosis, I have attempted to live my life differently. With every choice I make, I pause to reflect on how to react to life's challenges. Admittedly, I have not mastered this process yet. Post-cancer, however, I have tried to give myself a little more grace to truly reflect on the definition of a crisis, emergency, or challenge. I find myself making different choices, focusing on core values and priorities more than I did before.

I have always been a huge fan of Stephen Covey's *First Things First*, a book that I read early in my professional career. Covey highlights the importance of keeping your top priorities front and center. I find that I am doing that even more now. I have always taken my career very seriously, but recently, I have tried to make a distinct shift toward also living life to its fullest: traveling more often to Europe, taking more ballroom dance and Argentine tango lessons, attending more culturally enriching events, visiting extended family more often, and advocating for myself more. I also connect to my spiritual self more often than I used to, praying to God and the universe more frequently to help and guide me.

I can definitively say that I am extremely appreciative of more of life's small moments: a peaceful walk in my neighborhood, a conversation with a family member or girlfriend, a colorful flower in my path, a creature in nature, the sound of a waterfall or the ocean at my feet, soothing music, the smell of home cooking, lingering with a book or watching a movie or television show, sitting quietly on my back porch overlooking natural beauty, and treating myself to my favorite comfort foods. This includes a big bowl of popcorn, ice cream sundaes, or a small bag of my favorite red licorice. I have found that I am genuinely enjoying these experiences more than I ever did before.

When I travel to Europe, I am reminded of how much I absolutely love the architecture, cuisine, music, dance, people, and flowers. I have expanded my love of art, particularly European art. I am truly in a trance-like state when I am in the presence of artistic genius, especially when it connects me to my heritage and my parents. I have found myself doing more creative projects, including my cherished flower arranging and home decorating, in addition to deepening my passion for dance with both Fred Astaire Dance Studio and Dance Fire Studio and attending Argentine tango events.

I have always prided myself on living life with meaning. I try to be more in tune with making time to just be, rather than do all the time, as I heard a simple phrase that reminds me we are human beings, not "human doings." I have admittedly lived my life at warp speed at times but now hope to be more focused on finding joy in the ordinary. I attempt to live my best life, keeping my priorities straight.

CHAPTER EIGHT:
Divorce

was invited to attend a national conference in late February 2020 in Las Vegas, Nevada. It was the pinnacle of my professional career. This was for all top advisors in the US. There were approximately one thousand financial advisors from firms across the industry. As I have experienced throughout my entire career, the majority of advisors present were male.

As spouses were included, my husband and I arrived a day early to do some sightseeing. We had not been to that part of the country before, and we attended two Las Vegas aerial water shows, which were spectacular. We had never experienced anything like the unique combination of sensational acrobats, phenomenal gymnasts, circus performers, synchronized swimmers, and ballroom dancers, all flying in the air and diving into deep water tanks ... and all in high heels. Mind blown! We walked the Las Vegas Strip together and saw many of the famous hotels, including the Venetian and the Bellagio. They had a surprisingly European flair, which was such an unexpected delight. We were not keen on visiting any casinos, so we explored parts of the Grand Canyon and the Hoover Dam instead. While attendees were in training sessions for two days, focused on the financial market and best practices, spouses and significant others were offered a variety of leisure activities to participate in.

CHANGED WORLD

D uring the last day of the business-training portion of the conference, we heard breaking news of a rare virus with its first case in the US. All participants began checking their cell phones. Upon arriving home on the first day of March 2020, we learned COVID-19 was sweeping the world, and our lives changed forever. John and I, like much of the country, were required to work from home. As the global economy was in crisis, I needed to hunker down with work, supporting my clients not just financially but also emotionally, as the impact COVID-19 was having on their lives was vast. Client families were experiencing unforeseen challenges with unemployment, parents were working remotely, children were learning from home, and in some cases, people were caring for aging parents. All of this caused monumental challenges for the individuals, couples, businesses, and families we served.

My colleagues and I were witnessing the highest stress levels of our lifetimes. We were being thought of as financial first responders, which was territory we had certainly never experienced before. Emotions such as fear were running high, and we were being called upon to help calm nerves due to financial uncertainty and to assist with the turmoil in our clients' lives.

My business team and I learned how to use video-conferencing technologies like Skype, Zoom, and Microsoft Teams to conduct client review meetings remotely. It was extraordinarily stressful to engage in critical conversations all over the country with noises in the background such as barking dogs, lawn services, and neighborhood distractions. I did my best under the circumstances, but it was tremendously challenging.

To have a productive and suitably quiet home workspace, I created what I called a serenity room in our basement, a new makeshift remote office. Although our two miniature long-haired dachshunds were thrilled to have us both on the home front, they also felt they needed to protect us from potential intruders, including the mail carrier, children in our neighborhood, cars, and anyone walking by. I transformed our basement craft room into a serene office area, using a soothing, soft-blush palette and decorating with a European-style theme, all inspired by one painting I found in a local craft store. It was of a woman in an open-back dress that looked like a beautiful oil painting from one of the French Impressionist masters. I draped seven beautiful, flowing fabric shower curtains around the room, with one covering my treadmill, which got daily use during the winter months. I decorated the room with soft lighting, soothing candles, artistic accessories, silk flower arrangements, and European-style artwork.

I did all my interior decorating on a very low budget. My design-on-a-dime flair is something I have always prided myself on and something my mother always had. I had already created a welcoming and attractive home environment, filled with my own handiwork, by spotting bargains, sewing my own curtains, reupholstering our dining room chairs, and accessorizing with unique lanterns, tassels, and inexpensive embellishments. My mother taught me to cook, sew, crochet, knit, embroider, and needlepoint as a young child, so it was nice to use some of those skills later in life, especially to create this important home office.

I found that using my creative skills was a stress-relieving outlet during COVID-19, especially as ballroom dancing was restricted to Zoom lessons. This was not nearly the same soul-enriching experience as dancing in person. Two years prior, John had stopped ballroom dancing. We did a showcase performance together at the Fred Astaire January Showcase at the Albany Marriott in 2018 that did not go as well as our practices, due to heavy stage lights in our eyes. We repeated the performance at the end of the event, which went just fine, but John did not appear to find the same joy in dancing that I felt.

I, like the rest of the world, had no idea COVID-19 would last for years. I also had no clue what the repercussions would be for the world at large, let alone for my marriage. From my perspective, the phrase that summed up our remote work was not "working from home" but "living at work." We would all need psychotherapists and other mental health professionals to help us address the impact this would have on the rest of our lives.

One silver lining of the pandemic was the ability to see clients via video conferencing as opposed to just hearing their voices over the phone. I had not physically seen some clients in over thirty years, as I had started those client relationships in 1987. Several clients had moved to other parts of the country, so up until that point, we had only communicated via phone and email. My clients' challenges continued to grow: job losses, career transitions, adult children moving back home and sometimes adult children needing financial resources, depleted emergency cash reserves, physical transitions from big cities to suburban locations, childcare challenges with children and grandchildren, and remote work. All required empathic consultations, wealth management expertise, and financial guidance.

As difficult a time as the pandemic was for me professionally, I took enormous pride in attempting to make a positive impact. I helped my client families live their best lives, despite these unanticipated trials. I calmly created and reviewed financial plans with them, had lengthy conversations about adjusting plans as needed, and kept everyone on track to meet their financial goals, regardless of the upheaval in the world and financial markets. Working remotely was exhausting, mentally and physically, but I felt amazingly rewarded, knowing I could be there for client families in such a significant way. The pandemic allowed for a deepening of client relationships as I helped them navigate a world in crisis.

In June 2020, John and I celebrated our thirty-third wedding anniversary by going out to dinner at one of our favorite local Italian restaurants around the corner from our home. I received another beautiful, loving anniversary card and red roses, which John had given me virtually every year for the thirty-three years we had been married, and even once when we were high school sweethearts, leaving a dozen red roses in my school locker. Over the years, John had always given me the most heartfelt, meaningful, thoughtful, sentimental cards anyone could possibly imagine. I have saved and treasured every single one since we were married in 1987, typically shedding a few tears of joy on each wedding anniversary, and this one was no different. To this day, I still have two very large satchels with hundreds of greeting cards he gave me, all with extremely loving handwritten sentiments. I always marveled at every holiday, birthday, anniversary, Christmas, Valentine's Day, and Easter card he gave me, which is why what was to come was so shocking to me.

In September 2020, when the pandemic and the financial markets began to moderate, John and I went on a vacation to Maine. We enjoyed a great week in Ogunquit, Portland, and Kennebunkport, seeing all the sights and enjoying tons of fresh seafood, including lobster, clams, and mussels. We wore our masks on the Marginal Way, a beautiful ocean walkway with calming water vistas, and we found a lovely colonial inn that had the most exquisite, warm, luscious blueberry pie—the best I have ever had. I couldn't believe it was that good, but it was a wondrous experience for our palates, especially when topped with vanilla ice cream. We had a great getaway, a nice mental and physical break from our remote work, and a welcome change of scenery. Shortly after our vacation, we were finally allowed back to work in our respective offices, which was a massive relief for me.

I was thrilled to be back in my new office, which had moved from downtown Albany, where I had worked for the last thirty-four years, to a wonderful office park only fifteen minutes from my home. This reduced my commute time by ten minutes each way and provided a more convenient location with easy access to complimentary parking for clients. I was delighted to have a quiet and beautiful professional workspace for connecting with clients and coworkers, and I was very thankful to be back to some sense of normalcy in a COVID-19-challenged world.

SHOCK

On October 26, 2020, a little over a month after our lovely Maine vacation, I got home from work, and John said that he wanted to talk with me. We sat down in our living room. This beautiful space was filled with soothing pastel tones, soft throw blankets, Queen Anne-style upholstered chairs, original artwork from Artforms, a wonderful art gallery in Guilderland, meaningful sculptures and statues by my mother and grandfather Poppy, an Ecuadorian oil painting by my mother's cousin, warm-colored Asian rugs, my homemade flower arrangements, and a wrought-iron-and-glass table John and I had selected together when we moved into our home over thirty years ago. It was elegantly decorated.

John said, "I'm sorry to do this, but I'd like to talk with you about getting a divorce." To say I was shocked, beyond shocked, was an understatement. What had blindsided me was that up to that day, John had never shared any discontent with me about our marriage that I can honestly remember. I truly believed that John and I had an enduring commitment to our life together and our children's well-being. The thought of divorce had never remotely entered my mind; the wedding vows I had taken on June 27, 1987, were sacred to me and never to be broken, despite the challenges we had experienced early in our marriage with his job transitions and our different values around money.

Not knowing what to feel in that moment, I simply suggested we consider engaging in couples counseling. I could never have imagined not being able to work through any issues he was feeling about our marriage. I believed, with proper counseling and commitment, we could get through whatever he was unhappy with.

My mind began racing. Was our marriage perfect? No. But I can honestly say I did not know of any couple with a perfect marriage or even a marriage I perceived as better than what we had, except for my parents, who I admired immensely for their deep love and dedication to each other. Did John and I agree on everything? No. Did we have similar personalities? No. We were both independent individuals, but I always thought we were stronger together. We had what I believed to be a beautiful life: a family with two phenomenal children, all of us in excellent health, and all of us with full-time jobs. I have always been a happy person, and to be alive post-cancer with two amazing young-adult children, my wonderful siblings and their spouses, my beloved mother and mother-in-law who were both alive, and wonderful extended family and friends meant I was living a life I was extremely grateful for.

We immediately engaged in couples therapy with a highly regarded psychologist. It was an extremely intense process. As excruciating as it was, I was fully determined to do everything in my power to save our marriage. Divorce was not remotely a consideration from my perspective. Several weeks into counseling, I was devastated when I answered the doorbell before heading to work and a man asked my name and handed me an envelope. I opened it and burst into tears, shaking uncontrollably. I had just been served divorce papers. How could this possibly be happening? John and I had only been in couples therapy for a few weeks. I immediately called John at work, and he denied knowing this was going to happen.

We continued couples therapy over many months with official divorce proceedings as part of the backdrop. I learned there was something called a pause that temporarily delayed divorce proceedings, which could be used while undergoing counseling. This meant we were not legally forced into a strict timeline of actions. As the initiator of divorce proceedings, John controlled the pause. It was horrific having a legal threat hanging over my head throughout our marriage counseling. John had full legal power and control over the pause from month to month. I had no choice but to have the pause extended at his discretion if I wanted to continue to attempt to save our marriage.

SILENCE

The power of impact circles was never more evident than when I was without them. At the start of couples therapy, John requested that I not share our divorce proceedings with anyone, which for me, was one of the most hurtful parts of the process. I was asked to pretend that absolutely nothing untoward was going on in our marriage in front of our children, my mother, my siblings, my mother-in-law, dear friends, or my impact circles. For over three decades, I had built deep meaningful relationships with my impact circle women friends, and I felt totally inauthentic not sharing this devastating journey with them. I felt completely isolated at an extraordinarily destructive time, a time that they could have been there for me, as I had been for them. Our psychotherapist advised that I could have a few close confidants, but generally, I felt like I was being silenced by someone I had trusted and loved. I believed marriage counseling was the only way I could attempt to save my marriage, and keeping silent felt like a condition of counseling. This request simply felt cruel.

I went through a year of holidays with my family and friends pretending that everything was fine in my personal life: Thanksgiving, Christmas, Valentine's Day (the day we were engaged), and Easter. It was crushing me inside. My physical and mental well-being were taking an enormous toll. My blood pressure was high for the first time in my life. I had never had a cardiologist until a few years prior, when Mark had significant heart issues and all siblings were encouraged to find a heart doctor. Attending the American Heart Association's Go Red for Women luncheon annually provided me with a wonderful connection to an exceptional cardiologist. When my cardiologist asked what was going on with me emotionally, I did not feel free to communicate with her, which was literally heartbreaking; the one thing my cardiologist was there to help me with was my heart, and I felt that I couldn't share the truth that it was shattered. I knew I was a strong woman, but I was reaching my breaking point, and I was fearful my cancer would return.

After almost a year of therapy, I specifically asked John if he felt we were making positive progress in our intense couples counseling because I never knew where I stood from month to month. He said, "Absolutely, yes." Believing we were finally turning a positive corner, I scheduled a vacation for the two of us to Newport, Rhode Island, hoping we could continue to make positive strides in our marriage. I booked a hotel and a few excursions for a respite and change of scenery. As excruciating as couples counseling was, I never allowed myself to believe that we would not navigate this storm, no matter how difficult it was. I felt that working on a marriage was just that:

hard work. I have worked extremely hard my whole professional life, never expecting it, or marriage, to be easy. Although I anticipated this storm would be extremely difficult, I somehow believed that with my dedication, and so much at stake, we would make it through.

The day before we were supposed to head to Rhode Island on vacation, just a few days after John had shared that we were making positive progress in our counseling, he chose not to extend the pause on our divorce proceedings. At that point, my husband became unrecognizable as the person I had known, been committed to, and loved for thirty-three years. Our marriage was over.

I got in the car and drove to Boston to share this devastating news with my children in person, as I was no longer willing to withhold this very significant information from them. Afterwards, sobbing uncontrollably, I kept on driving to Newport by myself, as I had already arranged and paid for the time away. I used the opportunity to attempt to process what had just transpired in my life. I was numb.

COMING TO TERMS

What occurred over the next year were intense legal proceedings and complete emotional upheaval in my life. My experience during the legal proceedings was, astonishingly, worse than my cancer journey. I had never experienced grief of this magnitude, and on any given day I was filled with feelings of anger, betrayal, sadness, and despair. It felt cruel of John not to move out until our divorce was final, as I knew many spouses who did otherwise for the sake of the couples' stress levels. Several years prior, feeling secure in our marriage, I had provided my husband and our two young-adult children with a comprehensive financial-planning document. It delineated all financial assets, estate-planning wishes, the locations of important documents, and important contacts and passwords in case anything should happen to me. There were over one hundred pages of detailed personal information that I had trusted would remain confidential and safe with my spouse. This is the level of trust I once had, but it had been eviscerated.

HUMAN PIÑATA

fter hearing my plight, a business friend suggested I consult with an independent divorce attorney to ensure I was doing everything in my power to advocate for myself, as I had during my cancer journey. A consultation confirmed that I was in fact doing everything I could to protect myself legally. He said, "It sounds like you are being treated like a human piñata, getting whacked and whacked and whacked and whacked and being forced to give away all of your candy." It was a strong image, yet it was precisely how I felt.

During the legal proceedings, I was required to provide over a thousand financial documents, which required countless hours to collect, and my firm was subpoenaed to verify them, which they did in full support. I wanted to handle myself with grace and dignity and was proud I did so, despite the anguish I felt.

CREATIVITY THERAPY

o attempt to distract myself from all that I was navigating emotionally, I did my daily walks, yoga stretches, weekly ballroom dance lessons, and a meditation practice to calm my worried mind. I also increased my activity in creative projects.

In a treasured local home décor shop, I saw a blush-colored bedspread that I fell in love with. I found matching pillows, a throw blanket, scented candles, and complementary

European artwork. Within an hour, I had an entire shopping cart full of items with a French-bistro motif and thought, I guess I'm redecorating the main bedroom, which has had the same dark green and maroon décor for thirty years. I finished buying items for the makeover, including silk flowers to make two new floral arrangements. Next, I tackled redecorating the two upstairs bathrooms. I wanted a change in my main bathroom from the same dark-ivy green and maroon to my new soft, muted-blush, cream, and taupe palette. I reached out to half a dozen contractors to replace my ceramic bathroom tiles with very little response. One contractor suggested that if all I wanted was a color change, I could use vinyl tile stickers. His quote would be ridiculously high to remove all the green tile around the walk-in shower, jacuzzi tub, and floors. I ordered enough stickers for the whole bathroom, and in one weekend, I transformed the entire look of the bathroom, creating my own little European sanctuary on a very low budget. I had the painter use the same color from my "serenity basement" and kept the same muted tones throughout the house.

SETTLEMENT

After an arduous two and a half years, divorce papers were signed, and astonishingly, John moved in with his mother a block from our home. Upon settlement, I was legally required to give away a large portion of the funds I had saved over my entire professional career and pay spousal maintenance to a spouse who had not sacrificed any part of his career to stay home with our children, despite his many job transitions. Additionally, I was forced to pay legal bills for a divorce I did not initiate, as I was considered the "monied spouse," based on my financial success. It was even mandatory for me to pay for life insurance on my own life, because if I died before paying all required spousal maintenance, my ex-spouse would be entitled to it in full. As a spiritual person, I performed my actions in God's eyes and handled myself with grace and dignity every step of the way. In the end, I was proud of how I conducted myself, advocating within the law for my own financial future and that of my children. Ultimately, I knew I would be fine, as I was a strong woman with a solid educational foundation and the means and ability to thrive independently.

Initially, I honestly believed that if I followed the legal process with a good attorney, there would ultimately be fairness. I did not find that to hold true. Paralleling my experience, a dear friend was going through an amicable divorce she had initiated, where her spouse compassionately moved out and they split assets fairly. It was a loving partnership that simply dissolved. That was not my experience. I knew it was just about money, which was not how I defined myself. In the end, it was just very sad.

SILVER LININGS

I had two amazing children. My focus going forward would be to allow them time and space to grieve the loss of their parents' marriage. I would be there for them no matter what life had in store. My deepest love has always been for my family; these two phenomenal human beings were the most important silver lining of my marriage.

Next, I created a new second-floor home office, moving myself out of the basement, hiring the same painter to remove outdated wallpaper in our guest room, and transforming it into an elegant workplace. I used the same soft, soothing tones of blush, taupe, and cream and added Buddhas, candles, a sofa settee, lush throw blankets, travel photos, a chandelier, and meaningful sculptures. I was able to enjoy all the rooms of my serenity home!

Right before COVID-19 hit, I had adored the flower arrangements of a fellow dancer and florist friend, Carolyn Valenti, and asked if she could teach me the basics of flower arranging. I drove an hour to her home in the Berkshires of Massachusetts during an unexpected snowstorm, determined not to let the weather derail my desire to learn something new. She graciously purchased dozens of flowers and spent three hours with me. She had meticulously selected a gorgeous array of flowers and taught me to make a variety of arrangements. I was so thrilled to test out my new skills the minute I got home. That started a new love affair with flower arranging. I began making fresh flower arrangements and then silk flower arrangements for my home or as gifts for dear friends. I made them for members of my healing circle undergoing treatment or other friends in need.

When I was finally free to confide in and lean on a few close friends during my divorce proceedings, those relationships deepened significantly. My financial advisor–business partner of twenty-five years and EN member Pat Bucklin, former executive director of the New York State Bar Association, were both phenomenal confidants, and I was incredibly blessed to have their extraordinary support during the most difficult chapter of my life. They were right by my side every step of the way with their wisdom, sage perspectives, love, and support. This was a huge life blessing.

The power of impact circles was never stronger than when I was finally able to share my divorce news with them. It allowed for a deepening of relationships in an extraordinarily profound way. I also deepened the relationships within my informal impact circles. We shared the beauty and sorrow of life. My neighbors were the ones who saw me without my makeup, being my raw, vulnerable, and authentic self, and were willing to walk with me before or after work or chat over a fence. I have lived in my neighborhood for close to thirty years and hit the jackpot with having wonderful neighbors.

When I shared my difficult divorce news more widely with family and friends, I did so in person over a cup of tea or a meal as much as possible. It was truly wonderful to have an extraordinary support system. The support and love I received were overwhelmingly positive. Friends cried along with me, shared in my pain, and consistently said that I could genuinely call them anytime, day or night. I was emotionally drained after each conversation, but it ultimately led to slow healing. Another silver lining of my divorce was the deepening of so many significant relationships in my impact circles and in my life.

I chose to move forward by putting my time and energy into self-care, making sure I remained physically, emotionally, and mentally healthy. Here, going forward, I would continue to choose joy. I knew my own actions would provide for my personal well-being, my livelihood, and my lifestyle. I drew up a completely random list of future positives, and surprisingly, they were plentiful! Freedom lay ahead.

CHAPTER NINE:
Transitions

eciding where to spend Thanksgiving 2022 turned out to be very important. I chose to spend it with my mother, aged ninety-four, and my brother Mark's family. Our mother had been dancing Argentine tango twice a week and enjoying life. Mayela and I Zoomed with her weekly on Thursday evenings but had to adjust this to accommodate our mother's third Argentine tango class on Thursday nights. Nothing made us happier than knowing that our mom was thriving and up to dancing an extra night per week while living in a wonderful assisted-living residence in Minnesota, near her four local grandchildren.

Mom started to tell us that she was having some pain in her side and had made an appointment with a cardiologist, thinking her pain was heart related. She postponed getting her third COVID-19 shot until after her appointment. My sister and I encouraged her to get her booster shot, because I would not feel comfortable visiting her if that meant putting her at risk in any way. She promptly agreed.

THANKSGIVING

arrived in Minnetonka the day before Thanksgiving and visited my mom at her assisted-living residence. She was proud to show off her beautiful, art-inspired apartment. It was decorated in her colorful Japanese-style motif and filled with her exquisite sculptures, serene Chinese brush paintings, and treasured family photos. I had made my mother a scrapbook of her Schenectady Japanese garden and home of fifty years, which she proudly displayed on her cocktail table. My mom was delighted to reconnect me with her friends, especially one friend my mother enjoyed talking with who was over one hundred years old. That friend's daughter was also visiting, so we all chatted and celebrated their marvelous long lives and loving families.

The following day, I picked up my mom to celebrate Thanksgiving with Mark, his wife Marie, and their children Mario, Rory, Sophia, and Rose. As is traditional in their household, they had a tablecloth on which everyone could write what they were grateful for. I always acknowledge my family, good health, and catching up with my engaging nieces and nephews and witnessing their incredible musical talents.

As my sixtieth birthday was the following week, I asked Marie if it would be OK to celebrate that milestone with them. She made a reservation for her family's favorite Italian restaurant. We had a fabulous dinner, and my mom was happy to treat us all, which was not an insignificant gesture. I adoringly referred to my mom as "feisty and frugal." Everyone shared their favorite stories about me, which were quite endearing. I especially loved hearing from my nieces and nephews about their joy in spending time at my home, swimming in my pool, playing soccer, bocce, and badminton in our backyard, as well as doing arts and crafts in our basement. Nothing made me happier than seeing the next generation of cousins enjoying priceless time with our family.

In anticipation of my visit, my mother had found us a ballroom dance to attend. She was very proud of her dancing daughter and happy to show me off to her local community. This warmed my heart and was a perfect birthday gift. We went to the Duende Dance Studio, fifteen minutes from my brother's home. As if the host could read our minds, she walked over and said, "There are many experienced male dance leaders in attendance, and it is perfectly acceptable, and actually encouraged, for women to ask men to dance." This was music to our ears. I asked an instructor to do the first foxtrot with me. From there, I ended up dancing for practically two hours straight, until I was dripping with perspiration. My mom did many dances throughout the evening and was proud to video her daughter dancing with excellent leaders in between. She stored precious memories on her iPad, which she navigated well, savoring treasured experiences to revisit. The highlight of the evening was when my mom and I danced an amazing, energetic mambo together, bringing us back to our roll-up-the-carpets-and-dance days with the same magical, joyful, priceless feeling of dancing with family. We were beaming with happiness, truly dancing the night away, and our hearts and souls were filled with pure satisfaction.

SIXTIETH MILESTONE

ack home, attempting to distract myself from the heartache I was still navigating, I decided to throw myself a sixtieth birthday bash in my festively decorated home. Since 2008, I had attended a national conference for the top women advisors, which always fell around my birthday. Instead, I decided to forgo the event and surround myself with supportive family and friends, feeling grateful to my brother Carl, my sister-in-law Jeanine, my sister Mayela, and my brother-in-law Stephen for making trips from Massachusetts and North Carolina to celebrate with me. It turned out to be a lovely celebration with over fifty caring guests.

When each of my guests arrived, I had them wear a name tag displaying their first name and their favorite holiday food. I went around the room, asking guests to share why they picked that holiday food. There was usually a lighthearted family story that went along with the choice, which made for touching conversations.

I stood on my first-floor staircase and thanked my beloved guests for being there with me during this past year of personal challenges. I recognized important people in my life and publicly acknowledged Rachel as my new business partner. I beamed with pride. I had not told her I was going to do that, and my voice was shaking because I felt so raw and broken inside. She came up on the stairs with me, wrapped her arm around my waist, and stood by my side. I was grateful for a meaningful way to mark the occasion, as any birthday post-cancer is one to celebrate.

MAMA'S LAST DANCE

Just one week after Thanksgiving, my sister and I noticed our mother had a bad cough. I asked, "Mama, what did the nurse's station say about your cough?" Mom replied that she was taking an herbal remedy, which was typically her first course of action. She was generally reluctant to trust traditional medical interventions, due in large part to her childhood. My sister and I strongly encouraged her to go to the nurse's station and report back.

The next day, concerned, I texted my mom to inquire about her cough. There was no response to my text, which is not entirely unusual, but I would typically hear from her within a few hours. Instead, I received a call from the nurse to say my mom was experiencing shortness of breath and had been taken by ambulance to the local hospital. I called Mark, and he said she did not sound great, but she did not appear to be in immediate danger. Later that day, we were notified that she had a lung infection and was being treated with antibiotics for pneumonia. Evidently, it had been her lungs, not her heart, causing pain on her side. The nurse later reported an additional infection beyond the lungs. Our mother wished to be released from the hospital as quickly as possible, as she felt she couldn't rest there, so she was discharged with a combination of antibiotics.

Our mother had suffered from pneumonia before, so we hoped that the antibiotics would allow her to recover as she had in the past. The following day, feeling a little better, she attended a social event at her assisted-living residence that she did not want to miss, which included dancers. That was an encouraging sign. She said she enjoyed watching the dancers very much. The next day, Mark invited her to dinner at his home, but she declined.

On December 10, 2022, exactly two weeks after I had danced energetically with my mother in Minnesota, she sent me the following email to share with the rest of our family.

My last days

My time has come: The pneumonia took my breath away!!!! However, it was a life well lived in harmony with the earth, brethren, family, and friends. I will keep you all in my core. You were the ones to make me what I am, and I am very thankful and proud. Errors I have made, but never misdeeds, for which I ask to be forgiven. Dancing and its music were the art forms I most enjoyed, and they sustained me all these years; they were passions of mine. I loved the visual arts as much as the written word; sculpting, painting, and gardening seemed like a combination of those. Sharing these passions of mine was my way of giving back to the community at large.

I shared the email with my siblings, and we began a triage strategy to address our mother's medical and psychological needs. We understood our mother had been released from the hospital with an expectation of recovery. It was puzzling for us that she felt these were her last days.

I called my mother immediately and asked why she felt that way, and she sounded depressed. My mother would experience blue periods during the cold winter months, and more so when she was not feeling well, but this time, she really sounded downtrodden. I called the nurse's office at her assisted-living residence to inquire about getting her psychological support because we were detecting a disconnect between what the doctors were saying and what our mom was feeling. The nurses confirmed our concerns, reporting that medically she was improving daily, but she was not doing well emotionally.

I called to let my mother know I would be performing a showcase at Dance Fire Studio in Niskayuna with my instructor Florin Vlad in her honor, and she perked up. She asked me to send her a video, which I did, so we could dissect every part, step by step. The next morning, I got an email from her in response: "Very lively, very beautiful. I could cry knowing that soon I will not be around to experience these feats." My mom felt like she was dying, despite the medical reports saying otherwise. My heart broke.

Then my mother unexpectedly shared that at my suggestion, she had begun listening to the audiobook *Signs* by Laura Lynne Jackson. The book held such incredible meaning for me about connecting with my father after he passed. Little did I know, my timing could not have been more profound.

By December 14, 2022, it was all hands on deck, and all four siblings decided on a plan of action that included Carl getting on a plane to help Mark assess the situation firsthand. We were all having a hard time understanding our mother on the phone. Carl felt that although she was rail thin and weak, she appeared to have the ability to recover. He would report daily on her condition. We spent the next few days trying to assess how we could support her psychologically as well as physically.

I was having flashbacks to 2018 when our mother had landed in hospice for the first time. At that juncture, she had unexpectedly taken ill after visiting Mark. She had emergency gall-bladder surgery and experienced complications; her surgeon said that one of her internal organs had been perforated during surgery. She was not expected to survive. Our mother received her last rites, called all her family and friends, and said her goodbyes. I shared my dearest memories with my mama, which I read to her over the phone. We attempted to provide her with the best palliative care and had her transferred to a state-of-the-art hospice residence nearby.

I flew out to see my mother to say my final goodbyes in person and was told that the cost of her hospice care would not be covered under her long-term care policy. They had never reimbursed any patient for the cost of care previously, but with my advocacy and persistence, she was reimbursed 100 percent at $500 per day. I was relieved. I had researched the policy years ago and engaged an independent long-term care specialist to ensure my parents would have the best options during their elder years. Within a matter of weeks, with exceptional medical care and hospice oversight, she miraculously improved and was then transferred to an assisted-living residence in Minnetonka, where she recovered fully, cheating death a second time.

Four years later, we didn't know if the odds were in her favor again. I had carefully saved my favorite memories of my mom in a draft email, stored on my cell phone, never knowing when they might come in handy. Upon receiving my mom's heartbreaking email in which she believed she was dying, I decided to send the email just in case.

I am grateful

Dear Mom,

Whether it is your time to pass on now or in the future, I lovingly share the following with you. We have had a lifetime of beautiful memories together, and I want to share that I am truly grateful you were my mom and that I will hold all the positive memories in my heart, forgiving the challenging ones. Here are just a few of my fondest memories.

The first birthday I can remember where Mark and Carl gave me a toy accordion and a pink jewelry kit, which you must have purchased for them to give to me.

Having my own room at our first home on Frantone Lane in Colonie.

Leading my little girlfriends to the Farmer in the Dell to buy candy, including BB Bats lollipops at four years old, even though I got scolded when you found out.

Getting caught for taking two cents out of your wallet to buy a freeze pop with my girlfriends while walking home from Zoller Elementary School. I already had two cents and needed an additional two cents. When you caught me, you took away my two cents, which was an important life lesson.

Having tea and toast with you and Abuelita at our kitchen table, simple but memorable.

Being proud of all my school academic achievements.

Teaching me to sew, cook, knit, crochet, and needlepoint, just as your mother taught you.

Teaching me how to cook all your favorite family recipes, including Italian red sauce, chicken soup, roasted peppers, chicken cacciatore, lasagna, chili con carne, tacos, ceviche, shrimp toast, lemon cake, coffee cake, crescent cookies, tapioca, rice pudding, and more.

Taking our family to Spain when I was eight years old, which sparked my love of travel to Europe.

Letting me paint with you on occasion in your home silk-screening job, where I could fill in the blanks and even do some of the outlines.

Letting me go to folk dancing with you on Friday nights at the YWCA, just so I could spend time with you and Dad, which began my love of dance.

Bringing me to gymnastics and piano lessons and watching all my piano recitals.

Letting me quit taking piano lessons when they became too stressful.

Allowing me to live on campus at Union College, where I could learn and grow.

Coming to watch my first Tae Kwon Do belt testing, where I got the highest ranking in a class of twenty-five boys and five girls.

Allowing me to go to Seville, Spain, with travel to England, France, and Italy—a life-changing experience.

Coming to my college graduation and celebrating at the Van Dyck Restaurant in Schenectady with family.

Being a loving Nana to our young children, Johnnie and Rachel, and remembering their birthdays and special occasions.

Coming to the Zoller Ballroom Kids year-end celebrations, where we could make a meaningful impact on children in our community by introducing them to ballroom dance.

Going to Sunday school at the Unitarian church, main church services, and holidays thereafter.

Enjoying my entrance into ballroom dance and Argentine tango, and coming to all my dance showcases.

Doing our three-generations cha-cha with you and Dad, Rachel and Greg, and John and me at the Polish Community Center followed by our three-generations Argentine tango at Fred Astaire.

Spending virtually every holiday with you over fifty-six years while you were in Schenectady: Christmas, Thanksgiving, Easter, Mother's Day, and seeing you most weeks for ballroom dances.

Being proud of all the things I have accomplished in my personal life and professional career, and attending my business award ceremonies.

Doing our dance performances at the Mall of America when you were ninety-three years young and getting over eleven thousand likes on your Argentine tango video performance on my LinkedIn profile.

You finding us a ballroom dance to attend for my sixtieth birthday celebration, dancing the night away together, and videotaping me with lovely leaders in your Minneapolis dance community, who were incredibly welcoming.

Visiting the Minneapolis Institute of Art (MIA) with you and Mark to see the Botticelli exhibit, and unexpectedly seeing many Buddhas, one of my connections to Dad, in the Asian exhibit.

I am grateful for all the significant time we shared and will remember the warmest memories in my heart.

I believe we will always be connected in the universe, just as I am connected with Dad, so please send me signs. I will watch and listen for Argentine tango connections or anything else you want to send me signs for so we are always connected!

All my love, Alissa

Her immediate response via email was "You forgot two. Tucking you in bed on winter days, I would smoosh you all, rub your feet, or even blow my hot breath into your toes. And the other one, taking you begrudgingly to art museums. But once you were there, you all enjoyed the programs."

I chuckled and thought to myself, Well, she is still with it! If she can come up with that response and email in this manner, maybe it is not her time yet.

I got another email from my mom later in the day that read "Last night I got my first sign: My mother was just getting the bed ready for the night. I slept with for her many years. So, she is inviting me to join her." That was the last email I got from my mother.

It was phenomenal that my mama had listened to *Signs* immediately before she passed, embraced its message, and was beginning to receive her own signs. This was marvelous as far as I was concerned. I continued to call my mother daily, while she could still manage a phone call, and we spoke twice daily for a few days. Then, my mom called me to just check in while I happened to be at a Fred Astaire Dance Studio lesson. I took the call, and we spoke briefly, always ending the conversation with an "I love you."

Within a few days, Carl reported that our mother was declining physically. I called Mayela, a clinical social worker and former hospice worker, and inquired whether it was time to engage in hospice care again. She confirmed it was. In short order, hospice professionals engaged in medical oversight, music therapy, massage therapy, spiritual support, psychological support, and medicine management, providing extraordinary comprehensive and compassionate care.

On Tuesday, December 20, Carl reported that our mother could no longer communicate well verbally—he couldn't understand any of her words. My heart sank. I received daily updates from the hospice nurse, and I inquired how long they thought she might live. They said up to weeks, not months. The next day, after a garbled conversation with my mom and based on my own assessment, I did not anticipate her surviving long in this state. I suggested to my siblings that it was time to engage in additional 24/7, long-term care. As a family, we chose to increase the number of hours of long-term care she was receiving to round the clock. We quickly put together a team of care providers on short notice and were grateful for all the coverage, especially right before the Christmas holiday.

On Wednesday, December 21, I was sitting in bed watching television at 10:00 p.m. when my cell phone rang. I looked at the number, and it was my mother's. I thought, this is the call. It must be hospice, or her long-term care provider, calling me on my mother's phone to share the news of her passing. Instead, it was my mother. I could not understand a word she was trying to say, and I started sobbing quietly on the phone. I did my very best to listen and understand anything my mama was trying to say, but I simply could not understand a word. I asked if anyone was there with her, as I knew we had just engaged 24/7 companion care. That is when the caregiver Susan replied, "Your mom wanted to call you." I kept silently weeping and did my best to listen. I could hear my mother's breathing was labored, and there were long pauses of silence.

I used the pauses to gently share that I was there with her, that I loved her, that all of us four kids were with her in spirit, and that my father was ready and waiting for her, as was her mother. I said we were all fine and that I would be fine because I knew she worried about me going through my divorce. My heart broke as I attempted to share anything I could think of that could bring her peace and help her let go. The caregiver helped her sip water during our conversation, and I attempted to compose myself, be patient, listen, and say whatever came to mind. It was one of the most heart-wrenching experiences of my life.

After forty minutes on the phone with my mama, she somehow communicated to the caregiver that she wanted her to get her silver Argentine tango shoes out of the closet and then her favorite Argentine tango dress. I was uncontrollably shedding tears on the other end of the phone. At that moment, I knew what to do.

I pulled out my iPad, which was on the nightstand next to my bed, and opened the Pandora music app to start stream-ing Argentine tango music! I had my iPhone in my right ear and my iPad in my left, and then I connected the two so my mama could hear the Argentine tango music playing. The caregiver said that my mom held the phone to her chest and had a serene smile on her face. My mom and I listened to the Argentine tango music together for another twenty minutes until it finally soothed us both. Susan got back on the phone and said that my mom was ready to rest for the evening. I said "I love you, Mama. Rest now." I knew that was the last time I would speak with my mom.

Two days later, on December 23, I received a text from Carl: "Mom is at peace" at 9:56 a.m. Mountain Time, 10:56 a.m. Eastern Time, 12/23/22. It has been just over three weeks since my mom and I had danced blissfully together in Minnesota; it was Mama's last dance. Our mama was at peace, having danced here on earth right up until the end. Now she was no doubt reconnecting with my papa and her mother in Heaven. I believe she was dancing in Heaven with our father, who had patiently waited for her for thirteen years.

I was extremely grateful that our mom let go and passed peacefully the day before Christmas Eve, as I had spent most Christmas Eves with her and hoped she would not pass on that day or Christmas Day. I had such incredibly happy memories of each of those days with her, so I wished to have a separate day of remembrance for her passing. On Christmas Eve, our family would typically have a dinner of chicken cacciatore, rice pilaf, zeppole, asparagus, shrimp cocktail, rice pudding or tapioca pudding, and crescent cookies. Then we would open stockings filled with lighthearted, practical things from my dad, including tape, scissors, crayons, and other craft items. My favorite was LifeSavers Storybooks, which my daughter just gifted me this Christmas, in addition to an LP player with Frank Sinatra and Louis Armstrong albums, in remembrance of my father, which had me in sweet tears. As children, we would typically receive one present from our parents. We had magical Christmas Eves, and I wanted desperately to keep those memories independent from her passing. I felt that was the last gift she gave her children, and it was indeed a gift of love.

CARING SIBLINGS

In the days after our mother's passing, my siblings and I worked together to follow up on everything that needed to be attended to: writing her obituary, providing care packages for all our mother's caregivers and the nursing staff, cleaning out her assisted-living residence, and estate-planning follow-up. Two memorial ceremonies were planned to honor our mother's beautiful life, the first in Minnetonka, Minnesota, and the second at the Unitarian Universalist Society of Schenectady in the spring of 2023. This would allow our family to connect in a meaningful way.

As my siblings and I began grieving, we gave each other space and time to mourn in our own ways. Mayela, with her years of hospice expertise, had many profound insights that were extremely helpful. I have been blessed to have loving relationships with my siblings my whole life. Each parent's passing brought us even closer together, which I know is not always the case.

The most treasured gift I have ever received came from Mayela, who called me on Christmas Day, two days after our mother's passing, to read this passage to me over the phone.

The Coming

Dad and Mom knew you were coming, and maybe so did Carl and Mark. I don't know. I wasn't there on December 2, 1962. But on that day, you were coming, whether or not Mom or Dad were ready, or the rest of the world for that matter. I don't know if you came out kicking and screaming or with a little squeak, but soon thereafter, everything in the world changed, and no one saw it coming. A baby girl graced the planet like so many others, but this one was different. Of course, she liked to talk and dressed in pretty clothes and was smart like many babies, but unlike so many baby girls, this one had a mind of her own and was a force of nature no one saw coming. This girl knew what she wanted and had one of the keys to life: She knew how to get there. With determination and a plan, she demonstrated that no one could stop her from becoming who she was and is. She demonstrated that she would not be bullied, stood up for others, fought for her fair share, and dared to enter a hemisphere generally designated for boys from the moment she graduated from high school and through careers that directed her toward greatness and beyond the ever-elusive glass ceiling.

She was not afraid to roar, wearing a belt in a karate studio, but she *knew that on the dance floor and when mingling with the boys, some steps needed to be quick, some slow, some repeated, and that sometimes you need to step forward and backward, all in a matter of seconds. She learned that sometimes it's important to execute a routine after constant hours of practice, doing the same thing over and over, and other times to simply let the music direct your feet. She knew that this was another key to life, on and off the dance floor, in and out of the office, in conversation with others or in silence.*

So, this girl saw lots of things coming because, some may say, she was born that way, and others may say she learned it the hard way. She adjusted her posture in those challenging times and did her best not to miss a step or beat. But she was not a perfect child, and she could not see everything coming.

Cancer came and tried to drain the joy and strength from this girl. It was a battle that some wondered if she could win, and she dared not imagine her defeat. And I would wager that she could not see herself coming out stronger from such a hardship, but that was exactly what was coming. She wore her new scar with honor and picked up a whole new repertoire of moves and skills when it was all said and done.

But then disappointment came and tried to poke new holes in her polished armor. Disappointment is tricky because it comes in all shapes and sizes. Sometimes it comes from dreams being dashed, friendships ending, life experiences, the loss of a loved one or beloved pet, from goals yet to be achieved, or from those closest to us, or family members who do things we do not always understand, agree with, or condone. Cancer was conquered, but disappointment left scars deeper than cancer did. Cancer became an afterthought, whereas disappointment has overstayed its welcome.

Divorce was coming. Despite the many things this girl could see coming, she never saw this coming and was crushed by the weight of it, until she used all her strength to lift the weight of it off her. She learned to carry the weight like a hiker carries a large pack and practiced how to step in order to maintain balance. And, just like a hiker starts out as a novice, one becomes stronger with every step in the journey on the path. And so did she. So, this time, when something "bad" was coming, she could see it.

Death came for her mother, just as it had come for her father. But, because she had grown stronger, death did not knock her to the ground with its crushing weight. It still came at her, but she stood strong as she has done so many times in her life and faced it head on, simply adding the weight to her back. I bet she didn't see that coming. She didn't see it coming as she has grown accustomed to being so strong, so resilient, so practiced, so determined that she forgets who she has become.

I see who you have become and look forward to seeing how else you will power through life. You are loved, and you are not alone. If you ever need anything, just call me, and know that I am coming.

~Mayela Calabria Harris, December 25, 2022

I would say I have never been prouder to be a Calabria sister than while navigating the passing of both of our parents. My siblings and their spouses were phenomenal humans every step of the way. We each rose to the occasion of supporting one another as humanly and beautifully as possible. I love and appreciate them all deeply.

POLKA-DOT MILONGA

As a special way to honor my mother, I came up with the idea of attempting to learn Argentine tango the proper way. I inquired about taking tango lessons with one of my mother's instructors, David Salvatierra. I made a physical, emotional, financial, and time commitment to take this goal of learning authentic Argentine tango seriously and to do my best.

I got the idea of hosting an Argentine polka-dot milonga, a dance tribute to my mother, from the Minneapolis Argentine Tango Society, which held a similar dance tribute to her with guests donning polka dots of all kinds. This was a nod to my mother's favorite Argentine tango dress, which was white with black polka dots. It was a heartwarming concept that made me grin from ear to ear. In preparation for the evening, I took a few lessons with David Salvatierra, the same instructor who had flown to Minneapolis to dance with my mom the year before. I drove to Kingston, an hour away, and we practiced in lead-follow style, just as David had done with my mother.

We held a memorial Argentine tango dance on Saturday, March 25, 2023, at Dance Fire Studio in Saratoga Springs, New York, with the wonderful support of Kevin Magee, organizer at the Albany Tango Society and a long-standing friend of my parents. I decorated the dance studio in polka dots and brought many polka-dot garments I had, including dresses, tops, scarves, and even a few men's ties and bow ties. Everyone showed up wearing polka dots of some type or picked something from my collection, which made for a very fun and festive evening. Somehow, polka dots were a lighthearted representation of joy, something I knew my mother would love!

I ordered many dresses with polka dots online, but not one of them was what I was hoping for. I wanted a drop-dead-gorgeous polka-dot Argentine tango dress that swirled and swayed in all the right parts of the dance. When nothing suitable arrived in the mail, I took matters into my own hands and ordered one-inch black vinyl polka-dot stickers, brought them to my local tailor, and asked if she could decorate my fancy, white-sequined Argentine tango dress. I picked up the dress a few days later, pleasantly surprised by what a lovely job she did.

When guests began arriving, I came out of the dressing room in my special new, shiny white-sequined dress with black polka dots. It was a nod to my mother's polka-dot dress, which I had displayed on a mannequin. I giggled with delight as there was a literal gasp of support when I walked out. My dear friends could not have been more complimentary about how the dress looked. I turned and looked in the mirror with a huge grin on my face. It was indeed a spectacular dress. I received tons of compliments all night, as I had my matching reversible polka-dot shawl, one side black with white polka dots and the other side white with black polka dots. I reversed the shawl a few times and got pictures of what looked like several different outfit changes, using a bit of my own creativity.

To lighten the mood in preparation for my lead-follow Argentine tango tribute dance, I told the room full of guests that the polka dots were vinyl stickers. Everyone burst into laughter! I proceeded to explain that I had recently started taking dance lessons with my mother's instructor David in hopes of learning proper Argentine tango, and that I was a work in progress: a ballroom dancer beginning to learn tango.

Typically, when I perform a showcase dance, it is fully choreographed. I know every step and how each step matches the music. Doing a lead-follow tango dance was more challenging for me, as I barely remembered the dance because I was quite nervous. I did my best to channel my mother and feel her grace with me at that moment, just relaxing, breathing, and following my instructor. We had a couple of very intricate patterns, and based on the enthusiastic audience response, it went very well. I received many wonderful compliments and a gracious outpouring of love from all my mother's friends. They came to pay their respects to her, and in so doing, they also supported me. It was quite a profound experience all the way around. Many friends told me how much they loved my dancing, but more notably, how they were touched by what I had said about my mom. I recounted many priceless memories as a loving tribute to her.

I had hired my friend, professional photographer Joan Heffler, who captured the essence of a very precious evening. I have several treasured photographs from that night, depicting my shining joy, despite all the emotional pain I was going through. It is a testament to my grit that while I was dancing, my spouse was in the process of moving out of our home of thirty years. I came home that evening, and he was gone. The timing could not have been more profound.

JAPANESE MAPLE

My siblings and I waited to have a memorial service until the spring of 2023, when we would have the best opportunity to reunite our family. It had been four years since we celebrated our mother's ninetieth birthday with a fabulous dance party at Dance Fire Studio in Niskayuna with ninety guests. We thought about how to honor our mother's beautiful, long life as we grieved.

Fittingly, we had our mother's Memorial Celebration of Life ceremony on Mother's Day weekend. Mark, amazingly, showed up a day earlier than expected and asked how he could help. What a lovely gesture. I replied, "I want to plant a tree for Mama."

He replied, "Let's plant a tree!"

I was overjoyed, as I believed our mom would be deeply moved by the idea. When we initially discussed it, there were many obstacles to planting: possible bad weather, getting a proper tree specimen, appropriate tree placement, accurate planting, muscle power, tree transportation, planting equipment, cost, where to plant the tree, and coordination with our Unitarian Universalist church. However, my PPL healing circle lovingly gifted funds toward purchasing a memorial tree for my mother, which was a genuinely heartwarming gesture, and I just felt compelled to plant one.

I was very busy getting my home ready to host a catered dinner for forty guests after the service, finalizing and practicing my mother's eulogy, coordinating out-of-town guest hotel accommodations and last-minute family updates, overseeing the church program, making flower arrangements, and coordinating lawn services, sprinkler repairs, swimming pool cleaning services, and pool-heater repairs. It was a bustling week, and I had plenty on my plate, but I believed our mother would really love having a tree planted in her honor in a meaningful, spiritual location.

I had driven to a few garden nurseries and attempted to find a way I could plant a tree. Unfortunately, the proper-sized tree would be too heavy for me to transport on my own, let alone attempt to plant. I researched a couple of local tree-planting services, but none were cost-effective or available on short notice. So, when Mark arrived, it felt like he was a knight in shining armor. We met at my office, had an unexpected financial-planning session, and then we went to the nursery, where I looked at Japanese maples with the assistance of horticulturalists. Mark and I arrived just in time to get a clear understanding of options, costs, and strategies for tree planting for long-term survival before the nursery closed.

We needed to get consensus from our other siblings because the idea had originally been met with some hesitation, but they were all on board. Next, we called the reverend at the church to see if we could logistically plant a tree there before the church service. To my delight, although we had initially agreed to hold off on tree planting, the reverend heard my plea and agreed to see if we could get it done. I was heartened when she called and provided a timeline that fit perfectly into our schedule.

Next, I needed to find a shovel and spade for the actual planting. I reached out to a neighbor across the street who provided me with both. I collected gardening gloves and safety goggles, which I was laughed at for providing, but I had pushed hard to get this accomplished, and I wanted to make sure we avoided any injuries. I loaded my car with three large silk flower arrangements I had made, my mother's polka-dot Argentine tango dress on a dress form, her silver Argentine tango shoes, a guest book I had purchased for the occasion, and a decorative wicker basket for sympathy cards. Mark followed me to the nursery across town, where we purchased a hearty Japanese maple with plant food. On the way to the church, I suggested we stop to see his high school friend who owned Homestyle Pizzeria, recently renovated as Ritz on Union, and who was providing catering for our reunion dinner the next day. It was fabulous to see the two childhood friends together again. Then we were off to plant a tree!

Serendipitously, Mayela and her husband Stephen met us at the church to help us plant the tree, which turned out to be a very emotional tribute. The reverend and the groundskeeper met us to help decide on the best location. We chose to plant the tree next to the sculpture by Robert Blood called *Sanctuary*, which my mother had commissioned as head of the Visual Arts Committee of the Unitarian Universalist Society of Schenectady. I was at peace and truly believed that not only was my mom pleased with the tribute but that my dad was also grinning from ear to ear. I believed my parents were dancing in Heaven together, witnessing how their caring children worked together to do something so thoughtful. I felt at peace, knowing my perseverance meant our guests would see our mother's serenity tree in person at her memorial service the next day.

To celebrate our feat, we went to Civitello's Italian Pastry Shoppe for their famous lemon ice. This was a treasured family tradition, and Civitello's had recently celebrated their one-hundredth anniversary. We reveled in our treats and caught up with the owners, who hadn't seen Mark for many years. My soul was full.

Mayela asked me to make a fresh flower arrangement for the prominent church mantel as well as the silk arrangements. On my way home, I popped into Market 32, remembering my dear friend Jane. I felt her warm-hearted presence as I carefully selected a large variety of white flowers for a vivid bouquet. I went home and channeled my mother's creative energy to assemble a special arrangement, using a beautiful large Venetian vase I had for the occasion. I was pleased with the outcome.

It was an extremely busy time with full-time work as a financial advisor and business-team leader, addressing client emails, calls, and inquiries while trying to pace myself for my mother's memorial service. I needed mental preparation for my eulogy, serenity for my Argentine tango dance performance, and energy for the church reception and the family gathering at my home. It was a lot to navigate mentally, physically, logistically, and emotionally.

REMEMBERING MAMA

I pulled out the letter I had written to my mother several years prior, saved on my phone, and read to her once it was evident she was ready to let go and join my father and her mother in Heaven. I used it in my eulogy, adding a few cherished childhood memories, her last emails, and how she wanted to be remembered. My eulogy was an organic flow of feelings and storytelling with a natural sense of her life and her last few weeks. I had recorded my mother's life story a few years earlier, making sure to capture it before it was too late, on the car ride back from Carl's surprise sixtieth birthday party in Boston. His wife Jeanine chartered a sailing vessel from Boston Harbor, and family and friends joined in the festivities. My mom continued to lament not having written her life story yet, unlike my father. I suggested we try recording her story instead.

I started by asking her to share her life story. She started sharing but soon became agitated, as the words didn't flow as easily as she had hoped. She was feeling uneasy, knowing I was recording her on my iPhone. After a few minutes, she became increasingly frustrated and did not want to continue. I was surprised by that, but I was not willing to give up the chance, so I gently encouraged her to continue by trying a different approach. Instead of asking her to recount her story on her own, I prompted her with a series of questions: "So tell me about the Gardener? Who was he?" And to my surprise, my mom relaxed and began to answer my questions. The answer made for a fascinating story about what could have led to a completely different trajectory for the whole family. I inquired about what happened next for each part of her story. Three hours later, with a bit of my prodding, I was delighted to have captured her whole life story. Although my mother was quite annoyed with my first approach, to our credit, we had a lovely drive home and made a priceless keepsake recording. I later found someone to transcribe her story. When I shared it with my mom, she immediately felt compelled to fine-tune it to her satisfaction. In a few months, she finally got it in a form she was comfortable with. Hooray! Again, my persistence was rewarded.

I shared my mother's fine-tuned transcript with the two incredibly caring reverends at our church, and they created a beautiful eulogy to honor her with levity, humor, and historical context. I had encouraged my mom to share how she felt about some of the significant events in her early life, which she did: her typhoid fever, her first engagement to another man, and how her parents' divorce impacted her and her siblings. So many guests shared how moved they were after hearing more about our mother's story.

TANGO TRIBUTE

*M*ayela inquired whether I would be open to dancing at my mother's service. I had been contemplating what type of ballroom dance performance I could offer locally, in honor of my mother, at one of the social dances I used to attend with my parents, but I never considered performing at the church service. After a bit of reflection, I recalled my mom performing an Argentine tango at the church a few years earlier. I checked my family-dance website and uncovered a video of my mom dancing with a local instructor, David Deluise, right in the center of our church. I had videotaped it around Valentine's Day when the church hosted a talent-sharing event in 2018.

I knew what I could do in that space. I could do an Argentine tango to honor my mother! I drove approximately two and a half hours each way roughly every three weeks, from February to May 2023, taking lessons with Luis Ramirez and Analia Carreno, exquisite instructors from Argentina, who taught lessons in Maywood, New Jersey. I was up for the challenge, as I knew my mom and dad would be smiling down from Heaven, knowing I was attempting to learn proper Argentine tango.

I asked the instructors to choreograph a three-part medley so I could learn the three different types of Argentine tango: vals, milonga, and tango. When I saw the choreography, all I could think was do they actually think I can do that? It was extremely intimidating, but I would certainly give it my all in honor of my mama. The lessons went well, and I could handle a good portion of the choreography but not all of it. I assumed my instructors would drop the parts I couldn't do well as we got closer to performance time. In the end, they kept more in than I anticipated but were patient with me when I struggled to learn such intricate figures.

MAMA'S LIFE CELEBRATION

he task at hand was delivering my eulogy with the right balance of emotion, storytelling, and reverence while getting through it in the allotted eight-minute time frame. I practiced reading it many times to avoid falling apart. I considered how I might be a blubbering mess when I got up to read it in church. I knew some level of emotion would be acceptable, but I couldn't get through my practice runs without a huge release of emotion, and I was not ready for public delivery yet.

My siblings and I had planning sessions with the two compassionate and wise reverends. Everyone weighed in on what would make the service significant for them. It was evident that with four independently minded individuals, we would find a way to honor our mother in our own unique ways. We agreed on the structure, flow of speakers, music, slide shows before and during the service, readings, eulogies, reflections, and my tango tribute dance performance.

When planning my performance, I learned that we would be dancing on a rug in the center of the church in the round. I vividly remember seeing, as a child, a yin-yang symbol underneath the rug, so I anticipated that we would just roll up the carpet and dance. Unfortunately, I discovered that if we removed the rug, it significantly impacted the acoustics of the church, resulting in a loud echo. I considered renting a dance floor to put over the rug, but that would be extremely costly, and I don't think my mother would have approved from up above. I rewatched my mother's Argentine tango performance and saw that she had performed on the carpet. If she could do it, I could do it!

I called David Deluise and asked him how they had danced on the carpet, and he replied, "Duct tape!" I laughed out loud. Really? Something so simple could be so effective? It wasn't perfect, but it was more cost-effective than renting a dance floor and certainly better than disrupting the acoustics of the church for the rest of the ceremony. So, duct tape it was! I purchased a few different varieties and selected a clear option to put on the soles of my Argentine tango dance shoes. It would allow the ball of my foot to glide over the carpet and still allow me to use my heels to stop, which was especially important with a very fast-paced ending.

I experimented with a variety of outfits suitable for a church setting that would still nod to my mom's favorite white Argentine tango dress with black polka dots. I figured I could use a black Argentine tango dress and add white vinyl stickers to it. I knew I wouldn't have enough time to change outfits between delivering my eulogy and dancing, so I hunted through my clothes closets—yes, I have several—to find my black-and-white polka-dot wrap. It was perfect, just as it had been for my mama's polka-dot milonga! I could keep that wrap on while greeting guests and doing my eulogy reflection, removing it when I was ready for my Argentine tango performance.

On the morning of the service, Luis and Analia arrived early so we could practice for a bit and test out the duct tape. Soon, "Für Elise" was being played on the piano, guests flowed into the sacred space of our family church, sympathy cards were placed in my wicker basket, kind words were shared, family and friends from near and far embraced, and the light scent of the fresh flower arrangement I made for the mantel filled the room. Grandchildren gathered to light the ceremonial church chalice, Carl played two phenomenal slide shows of cherished photographs, and the two reverends presented their eulogy with care, compassion, and humor. Each of the siblings shared their own unique experiences: Carl described the last ten days of life with his mother, Mark related how clever she was mechanically when they strategized on woodworking projects in Minnesota, and Mayela shared an incredibly creative story, highlighting her exceptional writing talent, which included a poignant analogy with the movie *Scent of a Woman* and its Argentine tango scene with Al Pacino.

I was relieved that my eulogy went extremely well, and I delivered it with just the right amount of emotion and humor. I shared the heart-wrenching story of my last conversation with my mother when I played Argentine tango music via Pandora, bringing us both peace before she passed. I also told everyone that my white polka dots on my black Argentine tango dress were vinyl stickers, just as I had a month earlier, which provided some levity.

Our cousin Edward Coddington read a touching tribute written by his father Robert, who couldn't attend in person due to health issues. Ed delivered his father's words with humor and heartfelt emotion after a fiercely determined, unassisted walk up several stairs to the church podium—he had suffered a debilitating stroke the year before. The humanity we witnessed in that sacred space was palpable throughout the church. Ed was followed by his two older sisters, Anita Gesky and Jacqueline DiCarlo, who referred to their tita (aunt) with beautiful, loving kindness. Jacki spoke of her gratitude for the transformative experience of living with our family when she attended college and fortuitously meeting her husband, Anthony. Lastly, Rory Calabria, Mark and Marie's son, represented the grandchildren by speaking with wisdom beyond his years about the collective strength and love of our family, bringing the service full circle.

At tango-performance time, with duct tape on my shoes and polka-dot stickers on my dress, I was ready! I removed my black-and-white polka-dot wrap and smiled when I noticed Luis was wearing a handsome black-and-white polka-dot ascot. The music started, and I channeled my mother's calm energy from up above, following Luis and letting my muscle memory take over. I made it through the three-part performance in the blink of an eye. The ending was super-fast, but there was robust applause after each section. I was relieved it went well and delighted with how much I had grown as an Argentine-tango dancer. I could feel my mama's pride. Luis and I ended with a gentle bow to the photo of my mother, displayed elegantly on an easel alongside her dress and shoes.

My siblings' spouses extinguished the chalice, allowing for a serene closure to the service. I asked my ex-husband whether he intended to attend my mother's memorial service, having known her for forty-three years, but he declined. It was an official way for guests to know that we were no longer married, in addition to the wording in my mother's obituary. This was an emotional trigger for me, but I focused on all the positives that lay ahead in my life. My mother was a dear blessing to me, and I hoped and prayed for a beautiful, long life like hers.

CHAPTER TEN:
Signs

My father, on rare occasions, had shared with me his experiences of the metaphysical world and cosmic realm when I was younger. He identified certain experiences with the term "synchronicity" when he felt that something was not just a coincidence in the universe. After consulting with a spiritual guide, he shared his belief in potential past lives he felt he'd had, which I did not know what to make of at the time. I did not understand concepts of that magnitude when I was younger, but I came to embrace a connection to my father after he passed, based on my own personal experiences. Looking back, I feel that my father was reluctant to share too much about his experiences because being a college professor carried gravitas, and perhaps he thought I was not ready to embrace ideas about the universe at that time.

The concept of receiving signs from loved ones who have passed was first introduced to me in a book written by a neighbor and attorney, Kristen Carter Rowe, called *The Most Undeniable Things*. It's a story about her connection to her mother through the smell of lilacs. I remember not being able to put that book down until deep into the night and sobbing at the profound connection in the tale. Never in my wildest dreams would I have expected to experience such a profound connection with my own loved ones decades later after they had passed.

As I began to come to grips with my own strange metaphysical experiences, I shared my unique encounters with a few professional women, including my dentist Kendra Zappia, who recommended the books *Signs* by Laura Lynne Jackson and *The Universe Has Your Back* by Gabrielle Bernstein. The more I shared, the more deeply I connected with women in my impact circles, as several told me about their experiences connecting with loved ones who had passed. This was not the type of thing I would normally share with my professional connections, but with a strong foundation of trust already in place, it undoubtedly became a further bonding experience beyond my imagination.

CARDINALS

The first meaningful exchange I had in terms of a metaphysical connection was immediately after the passing of Petia Kassarova who had been in my healing impact circle. I was sitting on my side patio on a beautiful, warm summer morning eating breakfast when, out of the blue, I heard the loudest squawking of birds behind me. It was unusual because the noise felt like it was trying to get my attention and did not stop until I turned around to see what all the commotion was about. I tried to locate where the squawking was coming from. Then, out of nowhere, I saw a bright red cardinal flying out of the arborvitaes, which I could not recall seeing in the thirty years of living in my home.

At first, I didn't think much of it. Then, when I went to swim laps in my backyard pool, as I often do for exercise during the summer months, I saw the cardinal again. I typically start swimming breaststroke to warm up my muscles and then shift to sidestroke on each side. When I did my first sidestroke, there was the bright red bird again, and when I flipped over to the other side, the cardinal was following me. It didn't dawn on me until later that a friend in my healing impact circle had shared with me that cardinals can be a connection to someone who has passed. In that moment, it felt like a sign from Petia, who had just passed away, trying to connect with me—a profound moment that helped me feel my beloved friend was at peace. We had a loving friendship, and I was devastated that she did not recover from ovarian cancer as I did. It was such a scary situation, as we shared the same oncologist, and her fate could have been mine. However, I felt a sense of peace seeing the cardinal, as if she was letting me know that she had crossed over into Heaven.

A year later, another woman in my healing impact circle, Carole Heaney, published a children's book called *The Cardinal's Gift.* It was a true story of how a cardinal offered hope to a grieving family struggling to adjust to loss. There was no doubt that she'd had a profound experience with cardinals connecting her to her loved ones, just as I had.

After both of my parents had passed, I began to consistently see cardinals—both male and female—in my yard or while out on my neighborhood walks, especially anytime I was having a particularly difficult day. That started what I felt was a deep connection to my parents and to the women in PPL. This was a completely unanticipated outcome of my impact circles and extremely thought-provoking.

Mayela frequently teases me when I point out signs I experience, but she, a tennis player like my mother, called me on our mother's birthday to let me know that when she walked to the service line, a cardinal had landed on the net above the box she was preparing to serve into. She admitted that she'd said "Happy birthday, Mom," out loud, and after the bird alighted, proceeded to serve an ace. She remains skeptical but keeps an open mind, as her hospice work has provided countless experiences that she says were difficult to "scientifically" explain.

DANCING LIGHTS

During the summer evenings of 2022, I sought solace in my backyard among my beloved flower gardens, as a form of healing therapy. I started noticing that the solar light strand on one of my garden trellises would blink in weird ways. I checked the settings to ensure they were on the "stay lit" option, but each night when I went outside, it felt like the lights were trying to get my attention. Each night, the light formations were different. Sometimes the lights twinkled slowly and glowed softly like a rumba; other times, they were peppy and light like a cha-cha. Sometimes they sped up and were intense like a tango or whimsical and bright like a quickstep. I named them the dancing lights.

Then, one night, the twinkling lights took my breath away. I immediately felt the metaphysical presence of my dad. I sensed that his spirit was trying to get my attention. Not a day goes by when I don't think of him, especially on the dance floor, but those magical dancing lights allowed me to feel his presence in a profound way. I felt he was trying to let me know that as difficult as this time was—going through an unanticipated divorce since 2020—everything would be OK. I was allowed to release my fear and sadness to the universe and grieve my loss, but I could also emerge triumphantly by choosing joy going forward. I could feel victimized, or I could choose empowerment. I spent plenty of time with sorrow, heartache, and anger, attempting to process all the stages of grief. Seeing the dancing lights felt like a sign from my dad to find joy again, knowing he would be right there by my side. I sat under the blinking lights and felt his huge hug wrap tightly around me. I sobbed. And then I dusted myself off, got up, and chose to release my sadness to the universe and embrace joy. The dancing lights were there to help me see a positive path forward. My dad would always be with me in my heart, as would my incredible family and friends.

Thank you, universe, for having my back. I am getting ready for the next chapter of my life.

Each subsequent night, I would quietly go out to my back porch to see if the garden trellis lights were still dancing, which I believed to be the presence of my dad's spirit. Astonishingly, many nights, the lights danced. Each time, I shed a tear, feeling a deep connection to my dad. He was still by my side. I could not explain it in any way other than that I firmly believed his spirit was with me always, and in my mind, the blinking lights were a sign. I was in complete awe as the lights danced for me for well over a year. When I took down my fall harvest decorations and put up my Christmas holiday decorations, I wondered if removing the autumn flower swags and replacing them with red winterberry swags would somehow disrupt the connection I felt with my dad through the blinking lights. To my amazement and utter delight, they were still there! I wept again, realizing I would still feel such a strong connection to him. My logical, pragmatic engineer's brain was giving way to an illogical presence I could feel and see! The lights were a visual representation that I could not account for in my mind but could feel in my soul. I continued to take videos every few nights just to have proof for myself and others who might think I was going crazy. I felt it was undeniable what sign the universe was giving me—a treasured connection to my beloved father.

The dancing lights also continued after my mom's passing. Every night when I arrived home after a busy day at work, I quietly opened the back door to my enclosed back porch to peek and see if the dancing lights were still there. When I opened the door, the lights were typically very dimly lit. I would stand quietly for a few seconds, and miraculously, the lights would start to twinkle. To my amazement and delight, the lights kept dancing, following a unique pattern each evening. It was the most profound, illuminating, and enchanting experience I had have ever had. Each time I saw the lights dancing, I burst into tears and felt the deep presence of both of my parents, especially while I was going through such a deeply painful divorce. I believe my parents were with me in a very significant way. My soul was nourished with delight. I knew I would be OK going forward, no matter how many times I was tested. With their presence, I would thrive.

I like to believe that we can be connected to our loved ones once they pass. I have felt an undeniable connection to my parents, an unbreakable bond, and that they have been with me always, and our souls will continue to be connected forever.

WARNING LIGHTS

I thought I was ready to move on, but the pain kept coming. To squelch any skepticism about my dancing lights, Laura Lynne Jackson, author of *Signs*, suggests her readers select another sign to connect with loved ones who have passed. On a warm summer evening, while I was sitting on my chaise longue after swimming rigorous laps in my pool, I asked the universe for a different sign, just to see what would happen. What came next was astonishing—more undeniable proof of my connection to the universe and truly remarkable. Within a few minutes, out of a darkened sky, I saw my neighbor's four pool lamppost lights turn on and start blinking intensely, deliberately, and quickly for well over a minute. I have lived next door to the same neighbors for over thirty years, since before we had our children, all close in age. We installed swimming pools around the same time, as a beautiful way to spend time with family and friends during the summer while our children were young. I wondered if there was an electrical issue with my neighbor's lamppost lights? Could there be someone in their home turning the lights on and off in a consistent, steady fashion? No one appeared to be home, or they had retired for the evening, as their house was dark except for the wildly blinking lamppost lights. What was disconcerting was that these lights, rather than twinkling, felt like warning lights of some kind in the way they flashed intensely, quickly, brightly, and steadily. It reminded me of the television show I used to watch as a child *Lost in Space*, where the robot says, "Danger, Will Robinson!" foreshadowing peril. I videotaped these eerie lights to have proof. They were truly unbelievable. It felt like a very clear sign that the dancing lights were not a fluke. I really didn't know what to make of them, but they seemed to be a warning of some kind. Perhaps the worst was not over yet, as I was still in the throes of hurtful divorce proceedings. I felt that the outcome of this divorce would not be fair, which proved to be true.

I hadn't shared my divorce news with my neighbor yet, as we hadn't seen each other for a while, and I wanted to find the right time to share such difficult news in person. When I finally got a chance to catch up with my neighbor on her back deck, I told her about my divorce. I also showed her the video of her intensely flashing lamppost lights, and she was in shock. She couldn't account for such a thing! No one was home at that time. Coincidentally, her maiden name was Robinson, which was another connection to the *Lost in Space* show and another connection to the universe.

As a follow-up, I read a book called *Ask Your Guides* by Sonia Choquette, which I was initially skeptical about, as it delved into the realm of connecting with angels, archangels, ministries of angels, and other guides from the universe. At the time, I was in such personal pain and grief due to the continued intensity of the legal proceedings that I decided I would again reach out to the universe for answers to things that did not make any sense to me here on earth.

I learned to tap into the energy of the universe and began developing a sense of peace and calm, trusting everything would truly be OK. I knew I still had to get through the next stage of intense divorce proceedings, but I had a new sense of belonging to the universe and felt that the universe had my back, as author Gabrielle Bernstein suggested. Perhaps this connection to the universe could serve as another silver lining that would emerge from my unrelenting divorce experience. The first time I met with my divorce attorney, I drove out of the parking lot and saw the largest rainbow I had ever seen. Could that be a sign?

BUDDHAS

After becoming immersed in books related to the energy of the universe, I started looking for other ways to connect with my father. Laura Lynne Jackson encouraged her readers to continue to ask for different signs to confirm their skepticism. I decided to test her theory once again. I came up with the symbol of the Buddha, as my father and mother always enjoyed Asian décor around them, including their extensive Japanese garden, Chinese brush paintings, and a few Buddhas in my father's study.

The next day, while I was walking in my neighborhood, I passed by a home I had walked by for dozens of years, and I noticed a brand-new statue of the Buddha in their front garden bed. I knew the previous owners had moved out a few years earlier, but this was the first time I noticed the Buddha statue on my daily walk. That evening, I was at Fred Astaire Dance Studio in Latham for a dance lesson and shared the story of the dancing lights with one of the studio owners, along with my belief that the lights were a connection to my father. His immediate reaction was to share a story of why he believed in connections to the universe. He shared that when he had first come to this country from Ukraine, he and his wife were driving up from New York City to their new home in Latham and by happenstance, they stopped at a Buddhist monastery in Carmel, New York, called Chuang Yen Monastery. He said they stopped there on a whim. He decided it wouldn't hurt to pray to a statue of the Buddha, asking to make a living with their new business. He said that at that moment, the sun shone directly on the Buddha's face, and he became a believer. I never mentioned the Buddha connection to him, just the dancing lights. That was my second Buddha reference that same day. Incidentally, the Fred Astaire Dance Studio in Latham celebrated their twenty-fifth business anniversary, confirmation of their long-standing success, which the owner had asked for from the Buddha.

The following weekend, when I went to visit my mother for Thanksgiving 2022, Mark suggested that we attend the traveling Botticelli exhibit at the Minneapolis Institute of Art (MIA) with my mom, who had visited the exhibit the week prior with Mark's family and thought I would enjoy it. As I adore Italian Renaissance art with my passion for European travel, I was thrilled to do that. I absolutely loved the Botticelli exhibit. On my way to connect with Mark and my mother, I serendipitously went through an adjoining hall called the Sacred Arts of Buddhism and Shinto, which included twelve Buddha statues, seventy-five silk-screened Buddha prints, and sixteen metal Buddhas, for a total of one hundred and three Buddhas. My dad was surely with me. Hello, Papa!

POLKA DOTS

After my mother listened to the book *Signs,* she suggested our personal signs would be related to her passion for Argentine tango. My symbol for my mother was always polka dots because of her favorite tango dress. Since her passing, I have seen polka dots everywhere: dresses, skirts, tops, pants, socks, shoes, jackets, pocketbooks, umbrellas, mugs, dishes, pens, and accessories. I feel that I see polka dots whenever I need a sign from my mom to keep us connected. I see polka dots often and just grin. Hello, Mama!

Another profound connection to polka dots came after the unexpected passing of a friend my age, who I knew from the Unitarian Universalist Society of Schenectady and from the Dance Fire Studio in Niskayuna. Betsy Tyler was a gentle soul who danced for many years in our community. I saw her husband, the former executive director of Joseph's House & Shelter, at the Easter church service in 2024, and we had a lovely chat. Shortly thereafter, I attended the Dance Fire Spring Showcase, and Betsy asked me to double-check her makeup and eyelashes before performing. In ballroom dance circles, we embrace stage makeup to enhance our showcase videos. Betsy performed a beautiful West Coast swing dance with her instructor, Andrei Bires. I was delighted to cheer Betsy on and videotape her performance so she could have an extra copy.

Nine days later, I was devastated to hear of Betsy's unexpected passing from a heart issue that was being monitored. Betsy had been an ardent volunteer, rescuing cats for a not-for-profit organization called Kitten Angels, in addition to fulfilling her professional role as a psychotherapist. Betsy had just reached out to me to set up a financial consultation in my office but had to reschedule due to a conflict. I was honored to offer professional guidance, but sadly, we never had that appointment. When I heard the horrific news, I immediately pictured Betsy dancing in Heaven with my mother, as she had known both my parents from church for many years. It was unique that Betsy, my parents, and I shared two things in common: a love for our Unitarian church and ballroom dance.

When I arrived at Betsy's wake at Daly Funeral Home, I paid my respects to Betsy's husband, who greeted me with a gentle hug and the story of Betsy's unexpected passing. When I went to greet Betsy's daughter, I could not believe my eyes. She was wearing a flowing outfit with black-and-white polka dots from head to toe—not attire you would typically see at a wake. I felt it was another sign that indeed Betsy and my mother were dancing in Heaven together. Her daughter had absolutely no idea of my connection to polka dots through my mother, so I shared my simple story, which brought us both to tears.

In the line of friends waiting to pay their respects to Betsy's family, there were many dancers from our ballroom community, and I hugged each of them. When I saw Barbara Ritschel, matriarch of our ballroom dance community and president of USA Dance for decades, I whispered, "Wait until you see what Betsy's daughter is wearing." She looked at me. I said, "You will understand it's a sign that Betsy is dancing in Heaven with my mother."

Barbara held her hand to her heart and said, "She must be wearing polka dots."

I nodded, and we shed a few more tears. Barbara has always been an incredible supporter of our local ballroom dance community, including our Zoller Ballroom Kids program.

Not surprisingly, on my morning neighborhood walk the next day, I saw not two, but three red cardinals, which I felt was another sign that Betsy was dancing in Heaven with both my parents. I typically see one or two cardinals at a time—one initially represented Petia, two came to represent my father and mother, and this time there was a third, which I felt was Betsy. Betsy was not in any of my formal impact circles, but she was a dear member of my informal dance impact circle. My instructor Florin Vlad was also one of Betsy's instructors, and he said Betsy had shared that she missed her sister dearly, who had also passed way too soon. They were now reunited.

FOXES

I received an announcement from a treasured member of PPL, Diane Cameron Pascone, saying that Laura Lynne Jackson was offering a weekend workshop at the Omega Institute in Rhinebeck. I secured the last room at a local hotel, as approximately a thousand guests were descending on the small town to attend this popular event. I believed that was synchronicity in action.

I spent an extraordinary weekend at the Omega Institute with participants from nine countries and forty states. When we entered the main conference room, where around 90 percent of the attendees were women, we were each asked to randomly select a goody bag. Mine contained a sticker of a book, which made me chuckle, as that certainly connected me to my father, who had spent many years writing his memoir. Seeing author Laura Lynne Jackson on stage for the first time, I thought, She looks like a very ordinary person—an English teacher from Long Island with her two young-adult daughters assisting her. I was not sure what to expect from this metaphysical writer, known as a psychic medium.

In the huge conference center, I saw many polka dots, the sign for my mom. One guest handed me a colorful, mesh, polka-dot case and said I was meant to have it, as someone on the subway there had just given it to her for no reason. I saw plenty of Buddhas, the sign for my dad, which was not surprising at the Omega Institute, which is a place of serenity and the sacred arts. What I was astonished to see was a Buddha with holes cut out that looked like polka dots! A Buddha with polka dots. What are the chances of that? I chuckled as Laura Lynne

Jackson said you could ask for any sign, no matter how unlikely it might be. A polka-dotted Buddha certainly fit the category of unexpected.

Laura Lynne next suggested we ask for new signs for loved ones who had passed and specifically select an animal and a song for each. I immediately thought of a fox for my dad, as he was known affectionately as the Silver Fox at Union College and had a sign proudly displayed on his home-office door, handwritten by my mother using a calligraphy pen. I then spotted a large handmade quilt of a fox in the back of the conference room. I couldn't think of an animal for my mom at that moment.

Next, we were asked to think of a song that reminded us of a loved one who had passed. On a huge screen in the front of the room, Laura Lynne showed a list of fifteen songs that she felt were meaningful to the participants. She only played one song, "Hallelujah," which was the song I had just danced to as a tribute to my mother. That was certainly no coincidence. The fourth song on the list was "Let It Be" by the Beatles. It took me a second, and then I grinned from ear to ear, as the title of my father's memoir was *Let It Be a Dance*. That was surely another sign.

Over the course of the weekend, I witnessed dozens of connections among the hundreds of guests. I couldn't even process how significant they were as I watched them unfold firsthand. The last sign I saw was unbelievable. As we were concluding the conference after an entire weekend of profound sign connections, a woman suggested to the audience that we look out the side floor-to-ceiling windows, as there was a fox trotting along on the grass. I took a photo and video of the clever fox. In the video I captured on my iPhone, it was clearly a reddish fox, but when I took a photo of the video to capture a still image, it was indeed a silver fox. Hello again, Papa! I also thought of the connection to our ballroom dance, as a foxtrot is one of the smooth and international dances my father and I did together.

The Christmas after my mother's passing, I met Mayela and Stephen in Asheville, North Carolina, to visit the Biltmore House, which was spectacularly decorated for the holidays. My sister encouraged me to come and tour it. I shared with them the stories of my sign connections from my experience at the Omega Institute, and shortly thereafter, we popped into a highly recommended local hotel with a beautiful floor-to-ceiling fireplace, and I shook my head when I saw a large, stuffed silver fox over the mantel.

At a networking event for the Forum for Executive Women (FEW) at the Saratoga Racecourse, I grinned again when I saw the organizer of the event was wearing a silver fox necklace. She told me it represented her connection to her mother. While on business in Boston, I had an impromptu dinner with my brother Carl, his wife Jeanine, and their son Nico and marveled when I saw Carl's screensaver was a beautiful photograph he had taken of a very regal silver fox, no doubt understanding the reference to our father.

TURTLES

The morning after I returned home from the Omega Institute weekend, for some strange reason, *tortuga*, Spanish for "turtle," popped into my head as an animal connection to my mom. She had grown up in Ecuador and visited the Galapagos Islands, where many species of turtles live. A minute later, I read an email from Carl in which he referred to himself being known as "turtle man" to a young friend, and I smiled.

When I traveled to Northern Italy and Romania on two separate trips, I saw numerous signs and connections to my beloved parents, which I now refer to as "the magic of the universe," as I can find no other rational explanation for all these things in my path. I would not have known about the Laura Lynne Jackson workshop had it not been for my willingness to share the experiences I was having around connecting to my parents with my impact circles.

It is interesting to note that when I returned from my international trips, the dancing lights on my garden trellis stopped for a bit both times. When I got back from Northern Italy, where I had explored my parents' honeymoon travels, it was fascinating that my backyard trellis dancing lights had stopped blinking. However, two very small lights at the base of my trellis continued to flicker. Then I discovered that deer had chewed through the wires. I'd like to believe that the two tiny twinkling lights represented my parents.

When I returned from my Romanian adventure, the dancing trellis lights completely stopped, so I wondered if I was well on my path to healing and no longer needed them. A few months later, on the day that would have been my father's one-hundredth birthday, September 23, 2024, Mark celebrated by making one of my father's favorite Italian pasta dishes. That night, when I got home from my PPL dinner, which fell on my father's birthday and was also my parents' wedding anniversary, my neighbors' pool lights were going bonkers, blinking like the dancing lights. It was as though they were saying "We haven't forgotten you, Papa and Mama, dancing together in Heaven!" I guess I still need heartwarming messages from my parents, wherever they present themselves.

My signs continue to be everywhere. My logical brain has no basis for understanding how this could possibly be happening, all these signs: polka dots and turtles for my mama, Buddhas and foxes for my father, the dancing lights on my backyard garden trellis for my parents, and cardinals for my parents and friends who have passed. All I know is that I am incredibly grateful and blessed to have this deep, loving, and beautiful relationship of what I believe is a continued connection to my departed parents and friends, who are missed so significantly. On my last round of book edits, the overhead light in my bedroom started blinking with joy! I feel that my parents are pleased with my tribute to them.

CHAPTER ELEVEN:
Partnerships

always felt it was important to expose our children to opportunities for personal and professional growth. Over the years, I took both children to many business networking events to provide a foundation for their future careers and life endeavors. My son accompanied me to work on many occasions, did a summer internship with my business team, and attended several educational programs at the Fort Orange Club, a city club in downtown Albany I have been a member of since 1995. This included listening to business leaders speak on a variety of topics. One business lunch allowed him to hear an IBM executive talk about the future of computer technology, which my son included in his college essay years later, making an important connection between his academic and career paths as he attended Babson College, a prominent entrepreneurial college focused on business, in Wellesley, Massachusetts, twenty minutes outside of Boston. My son later witnessed global business innovation during his term abroad in Russia, India, and China. This intrepid international travel was based on his family experiences. Rachel also attended many professional networking events with me. The first was when she was in a baby car seat, joining me at my first formal impact circle, PWN, in a member's home and at countless business events thereafter.

ROLE MODELING

achel always felt her brother was a huge mentor to her and by her side her whole life, including when he suggested that Babson College could be the best fit for her academic interests as well as his. Immediately after she graduated with her business, entrepreneurial, and marketing degree, I asked her to come to our firm's business council recognition event, as my husband was not available to join me. On this trip, Rachel had the opportunity to meet a high-level woman executive who was genuinely interested in learning how to attract and hire more young professional women in the financial services industry. The executive pulled me aside and shared how impressed she was with my daughter and that she would really like to hear more from her about how to attract more women financial advisors to our firm.

At first, I thought she was simply being courteous to me in complimenting my daughter. However, later that afternoon, I received an email inviting Rachel and me to attend a private dinner to discuss the topic. At the time, Rachel was twenty-two years old and just beginning her career in sales and market-ing at a software company outside Boston. The executive from the Midwest hosted a small, private dinner, which included the longest-tenured financial advisor at our firm with forty-five years of service, his wife, a political analyst, another high-level woman financial advisor, Rachel, and me. This savvy leader initiated a thought-provoking conversation to strategize how to attract more young women to financial advisory roles. She immediately turned to the youngest member of the group, Rachel, for her thoughts and ideas. Knowing that she would be included in this dinner, Rachel had given the matter consider-able thought and was well prepared to answer authentically. Rachel shared her perspective on some of the challenges she perceived our industry faced and was not shy in voicing her concerns in a professional manner. Simply put, Rachel commu-nicated that she felt our industry had room for improvement in reputation, diversity of thought, gender, and race. It was an honest and productive discussion. I had the privilege of seeing Rachel use the professional communication skills she had acquired at Babson College as well as the many summer internships she had in business and finance, including at our firm. Everyone around the table had a chance to share their perspectives, but honestly, Rachel's insights were spot on. I recognize I am biased as her mother, but it was a proud-mama moment and later served as a monumental experience for her future career.

After the council trip, the firm's executive put together a task force of women from a variety of advanced positions in our company to continue brainstorming. I was honored to be among the chosen few. Our mission was to present a proposal to management on how to increase gender diversity in financial advisor roles in our firm. This had remained low over the course of my career since 1987. Our task force met for monthly discussions over the next year, identifying challenges in attracting and retaining women financial advisors and providing strategies for improving long-standing career paths. Many other professional industries have made significant strides in balancing gender representation, including medicine, law, and engineering, but the financial services industry has not made similar strides. The task force identified reasons for the imbalance and potential solutions for improvement, which were later instrumental in benefiting Rachel's future career—a full-circle moment.

CATERPILLAR METAMORPHOSIS

At age twenty-four, after Rachel graduated from Babson College, she was promoted from her initial role as sales and marketing associate to senior manager of sales and marketing, and then to director of sales and marketing. This was an impressive first few years in the working world. However, after working exceptionally long hours, flying on nine flights within a few weeks, crisscrossing the country for sales presentations—all while navigating a company merger—Rachel found herself with little work-life balance and began experiencing symptoms of mental, physical, and emotional exhaustion. Feeling the need to advocate for her own well-being, she chose to take a short leave of absence from her job. I trusted my daughter's assessment of the situation and supported her choice, despite having reservations about the potential outcome. For my generation, a leave of absence was atypical, but there were also no expectations of working around the clock to the point of burnout. My priority was to support Rachel's overall mental and emotional well-being. I later learned she had been working from 7:30 a.m. to well after midnight daily, an unhealthy and unsustainable pace.

Rachel used her short time away from work to learn and grow by exploring her passions. She traveled and volunteered for causes she cared deeply about, which her professional role had not allowed time for. She volunteered for several not-for-profit organizations in the Boston area through Boston Cares, which encouraged volunteers to submit their goals, availability, and specific interests on a weekly basis. Rachel discovered she was most fulfilled when volunteering at the American Red Cross Food Pantry in Boston, bagging groceries for up to 1,200 families on any given morning.

Rachel called me with frequent updates, sharing her excitement when she met other professionals while volunteering. She emerged from her work fog in a matter of weeks, beaming with enthusiasm as she connected with other volunteers who were drawn to her passion for making a difference. Rachel was becoming a butterfly. She unexpectedly found herself talking about potential new career paths, networking with executives in various industries, and even going to a few job interviews, simply to ensure that her current job, where she had excellent mentors, was still the best fit for her skill set and passions. She went to yoga classes daily, focused on healthier lifestyle habits, and listened to self-improvement audiobooks. I had given Rachel a few Brené Brown books and Meg Jay's *The Defining Decade* when she graduated from college, hoping they might resonate with her at some point in her career. Now was that time. She was listening to positive influences and had the time to absorb their meaning.

Rachel also used this time to travel and see friends she hadn't connected with since her Babson days to nourish her soul. With her temporarily open schedule, I asked her if she would like to join Mayela and me on a trip to Avignon and Lyon, France. To our delight, she said yes. At that point, I was greatly in need of a change of scenery, and European travel was a source of deep enrichment and enchantment for me. Mayela, knowing the emotional challenges Rachel and I were navigating, chose to engage us in deep conversations over exquisite gastronomic delights in darling French bistros. We had decadent meals with tearful and uncomfortable conversations, interspersed with magical adventures. We explored all the gems of each city: phenomenal culinary delights, incredible architecture, exquisite churches, impressive museums, serene countryside, fun shopping escapades, and quaint towns. We were all taking healing steps in our own lives. Despite the complicated conversations, the three of us had an extraordinary experience on our first adventure traveling together. It was a meaningful example of how my family impact circle made a significant difference in my life, my daughter's life, and my sister's life. Mayela knew that her expertise as a social worker was just what this mother-daughter duo needed, and she took a calculated risk. Those conversations were the start of a huge turning point for us both.

WOMEN'S SUMMIT

The week after our adventures in France, I was invited to attend a national conference, a first annual event being held in Palm Beach, Florida. As the conference coincided with Rachel's twenty-fifth birthday, I invited her to join me. I explained that she could spend her birthday with her girlfriends in Boston or join me in a warmer climate at a luxury beach hotel, where I would be attending business training. Once she checked out the hotel online and saw the palm trees, pool, spa, and other amenities, she smirked and said, "I will be happy to join you!" I was thrilled. I knew it could help with Rachel's continued rejuvenation and reconnect her with business associates she had met at prior conferences.

I also knew Rachel could meet the executive who had sought her input about attracting women financial advisors to our industry. This was a role model Rachel admired and respected immensely. I let her know that if she wanted to reconnect, I could make that happen. Rachel was most enthusiastic about that possibility. Prior to the conference, I asked if Rachel could join us at our private company dinner on the second night of the conference, as that would be Rachel's twenty-fifth birthday, and they were delighted to honor my request.

A few days before the industry conference, I received an email informing me that I was one of nine women selected to deliver a best-practice presentation to an audience of four-hundred and fifty top women advisors. I was honored. I spent hours fine-tuning my submitted idea, crafting every word for maximum impact. I wanted my delivery to be exceptional. I practiced repeatedly in front of a mirror to make sure that my presentation would come in under the allotted two minutes. The best-practice presentations were a contest, and the winner would receive national media coverage. That idea was daunting, but nevertheless, I simply wanted a positive outcome and to make my firm proud of my participation in such a prestigious event. I changed my flight to a day earlier, just in case there were any travel snafus, which were common due to the pandemic at that time, and just to put my mind at rest. I wanted to deliver my presentation in the best way possible.

I booked a room for the extra night at a lower-priced hotel in the vicinity, mindful of my business budget. Upon arrival at my Palm Beach hotel, I continued practicing my presentation and felt prepared to deliver my speech. It reminded me of my first public-speaking contest in 1983, which had readied me for this event. The next day, I headed over to the resort where the business training conference was being held. I dressed for the outdoor cocktail reception, and upon arrival, I immediately connected with R.J. Shook, the head of the entire conference. R.J. mentioned that the CEO of the Susan G. Komen Foundation, focused on breast-cancer research, was at the conference and asked if I would like to meet her. I said, "Absolutely, I would love to meet her," as our healing impact circle had grown to twenty-five executive women touched by cancer.

The next afternoon, I coincidentally saw R.J. again, this time in the hallway of the hotel. I had been exploring the hotel to see where I would be speaking and to familiarize myself with the setting. It was early afternoon, and R.J. asked me if I'd had lunch. I typically have lunch at noon, and it occurred to me that because I was so nervous about preparing for my presentation, I had forgotten to eat lunch—a very rare occurrence for me. Upon hearing that, R.J. escorted me up to a corporate dining room on the top floor of the Palm Beach resort hotel, a room with a delectable spread of food to rival any I had experienced before. There were two service providers to see to any need I might have. That was certainly one of those "pinch me" moments in my professional career, allowing me the peace and preparation time I needed to be ready for my speech in front of four-hundred and fifty peers. R.J. wished me luck. He was not a judge, but we both chuckled, and I said, "I will do my best."

After lunch, I was headed back to the presentation room when I saw the female executive I was hoping to connect Rachel with from our firm coming in the door with shopping bags in her hands, looking a bit frazzled. She said her luggage had not arrived, and she had gone shopping for business clothing. I immediately asked if she needed anything else. She said she was looking for a pair of professional shoes. I went up to my room to double-check my options and texted her photos just in case she hadn't found another pair, but thankfully she had. We both needed to be on stage within a matter of minutes, so we met in the presentation room.

In the meantime, Rachel texted that her flight was late, and she might miss my big presentation, which I was disappointed to hear. I texted her back and let her know that, should she by any chance be able to make it, she could view the presentation in an overflow room, where they had big-screen monitors. Five minutes before going on the big stage, I looked up and saw the most beautiful sight ever: my daughter in the back of the room, waving to me, trying to get my attention. She had texted me several times: "Look up, look up, look up, I am here!" To prepare for the presentation, I had put my phone away. Seeing my daughter was available to witness a significant professional moment in my career flooded my heart with emotions, giving me every ounce of courage I needed to simply do my best.

Because I had been going through such an intense personal time, I had to compartmentalize my emotions and focus on the task at hand. I presented my two-minute speech in front of a very significant crowd, with hundreds in attendance, enunciating every word and using the presentation skills that had prepared me for that moment after thirty-five years in the business world. My idea-sharing went great. I was honored to represent my firm and, more importantly, make my daughter and myself proud, which was my goal. I remembered my public-speaking course through the BPW, and I used every tip that my instructor Judi Clements had taught me, the most important one being: practice, practice, practice. Incidentally, the topic of my best idea was the power of impact circles.

After I walked off stage, Liz Shook, cofounder of SHOOK Research and R.J.'s wife, said, "That was excellent!" and my heart pounded with pride. Immediately, dozens of women approached me and shared that I had done an outstanding job, that they loved my idea, and that they thought I should win. I got incredible feedback and encouragement through-out the conference, which my daughter witnessed, making it infinitely more special. Although I did not win the competition, I knew I had done a great job and was proud of my effort. I did exactly what I have encouraged in my children: Do your best.

BUTTERFLY WINGS

mmediately after the best-idea sharing ended, I connected Rachel with the executive she had met at our prior conference. I witnessed my daughter, articulate, charming, and intelligent, engaged in a professional conver-sation with someone she admired enormously, and the two of them appeared to connect on a meaningful level. Fortuitously, the executive introduced Rachel to a mother-daughter finan-cial advisory team from our firm, who happened to be standing right next to us. The financial advisors at this conference were from various firms in our industry, so it was unusual to have a mother-daughter partnership from our firm right there at that moment.

The daughter told us that she was thirty years old and that she and her mother worked in a branch on Long Island. Rachel proceeded to ask very thoughtful questions about why and how they had chosen to enter the financial services industry: What were the main factors that attracted them to becoming financial advisors? What was it like working together? And most importantly, what was the social impact they believed they could have as financial advisors? This mother-daughter duo was incredibly kind and warm-hearted toward my daughter and answered all her questions in an extremely thoughtful and meaningful way, which resonated with Rachel.

After fifteen minutes of conversation, I turned to Rachel and said, "Just so you know, I have never met these financial advisors before," and joked that I had not planted them there! It could not have been a more illuminating conversation. Papa, is that you at work? I wondered.

I had previously shared with Rachel that I believed there were many ways she could make a social impact as a financial advisor, but hearing similar information from someone other than her mother was monumental and pivotal. I could see a glimpse of something special unfolding right before my eyes. The mother suggested to Rachel that she could work for a not-for-profit organization and make a social impact, but that may not give her as secure a financial foundation as she could potentially have in the financial services industry, working with me. She said, "You can volunteer your time at nonprofits or charitable organizations you are passionate about while working as a financial advisor." In that moment, understanding the gist of the conversation Rachel was having with this mother-daughter financial advisor team, the executive from our firm turned to Rachel and asked her if she would like to join us for the rest of the conference.

Before the conference, it was made clear to me that Rachel

could attend the firm's dinner, but not the business portion, as that was reserved for top advisors. The executive shared that they had a few cancellations, and it would be perfectly fine for Rachel to be included in the training sessions. Rachel came to the conference with a dual purpose: to celebrate her twenty-fifth birthday and decompress after three years of her intense sales and marketing role. Now she wisely split her time at the conference, attending several of the breakout sessions, including hearing the CEO of the Susan G. Komen Foundation discuss new research around a blood test being developed for the early detection of breast cancer. Rachel saw firsthand many ways that financial advisors can impact their clients and make a social impact on the world at large. I could see Rachel's wheels turning, processing information in a way she had not been able to before about how financial advisors make a social impact in meaningful ways, which was Rachel's greatest career hope.

At the private dinner the next night, we had seating assignments, wedding-style. At a prior conference, I had been seated next to the incoming president of our firm, which was quite an honor and a memorable experience. Seating arrangements at this business summit would prove to be even more significant. Rachel and I were seated at Table 4, and when we sat down, there were two empty seats next to Rachel. A few minutes later, the woman executive Rachel admired sat in one of the seats. I asked the executive if she would like to shift seats to sit next to someone potentially more prominent at our table. The answer was a polite no. Five minutes later, R.J. Shook entered the dining room and sat right next to Rachel. Again, I turned to our firm executive and inquired if she would like to shift seats, and she replied, "No." What ensued was an experience neither Rachel nor I will ever forget.

I witnessed my twenty-five-year-old daughter begin a most

impressive, professional conversation with R.J. Shook as she met him for the first time. I overheard the first part of their conversation, which went something like, "R.J., congratulations on putting on an incredibly impressive conference. Clearly, you have been extraordinarily successful in your professional career. I am curious, at this stage of your career, what fills your cup?" I beamed with delight from ear to ear and let Rachel have this moment to engage in an incredibly meaningful conversation with one of the most senior executives in our industry. Not only did she hold her own, but several minutes into the engrossing conversation, R.J. said, "Rachel, I am truly enjoying our conversation and would really like to continue it, but I am having a difficult time hearing in this acoustically challenged setting. Would you mind stepping into the adjoining open room, which is a bit quieter, so we can continue our conversation?"

I watched this unfold, Rachel and R.J. continuing their conversation in the adjoining room, where roughly forty-five professionals could see and were likely wondering who R.J. was talking with. Dinner was served, and the woman executive at our table called to R.J., "Your dinner has arrived," to which R.J. responded, "Five more minutes!" I smirked to myself, thinking, Oh my goodness, Rachel must be holding her own in an impressive way for her to engage this industry icon in such a lengthy conversation while his filet mignon is getting cold! I waited five more minutes before walking over to R.J. and Rachel to thank him profusely for talking with my daughter at such length. I implored him to come and eat his dinner while it was hot, and he replied, "Five more minutes."

I sensed R.J. had morphed into more of a father figure and role model at that moment; his young-adult daughter was also participating in the conference. I couldn't have been prouder of Rachel or more grateful to R.J. for being such a warm-hearted professional. Finally, they both sat down. I whispered, "Are you hiring her, or am I?" He smiled. We all enjoyed a gourmet dinner and lively conversation with the whole table. The woman executive must have whispered to R.J. that it was Rachel's twenty-fifth birthday because a slice of cake arrived with a candle, and R.J. had the entire room sing "Happy Birthday" to her. R.J. videotaped the whole thing on his cell phone, added a personal birthday message, and then texted it to Rachel on her cell phone. Well, that was an experience not to be forgotten! Rachel must have been incredibly impressive to captivate this business professional's attention.

When Rachel and I got back to the hotel, we looked at each other and burst out laughing, saying, "What just happened!" Rachel shared the gist of her conversation with R.J., which was mostly her inquiring about how he had made a social impact in his career and expressing her interest in doing the same, continuing to display maturity and professionalism well beyond her years.

The next day, back in my Albany office, I had a lengthy conversation with my branch manager, who I had worked alongside for the last thirty-five years, about the conference. We initially worked together as financial advisors; then he became assistant manager while I was the sales manager at our previous firm. He chose a career in branch management, and I chose to stay in a financial advisory role. He shifted to a new firm, and our team followed a year later, based on mutual admiration and trust. What happened next, I will never forget. My manager shared that his own manager had received a call from our firm's woman executive, suggesting that we make Rachel Quinn an employment offer that she could not refuse! I was overwhelmed with emotion.

I took a deep breath and began strategizing with my boss about what it would take to make that happen. Rachel was commanding a high salary as director of sales and marketing. While on sabbatical, she was wondering what kind of professional life she would return to. She wanted to find work-life balance once she resumed her position. I spoke to Rachel about this unexpected development, and we were both very candid about what a suitable role, and compensation package, would have to look like for her to give it serious consideration. I worked with my manager over a series of conversations to explore what could work. Once Rachel glimpsed how she could make a social impact as a financial advisor, she was incredibly strategic in saying, "We are all intelligent professionals. I believe we can come up with something suitable." Rachel originally had more faith in the opportunity than I did, especially with so few women financial advisors being hired in our industry. I had recently introduced my manager to another potential woman team member, but having known my daughter her whole life, he felt Rachel would be a better fit and a solid investment, which I was heartened to hear.

I fought hard to share what I felt would be needed to hire a candidate of Rachel's caliber, knowing I would also have to make a financial investment during a very precarious time in my divorce proceedings. I was absolutely determined to give it my all and dug out the proposal from the national women's task force I had been on prior to the pandemic, which focused on attracting highly qualified women candidates to our industry. It was another informal impact circle I had been part of, which set the stage for this opportunity to unfold. I had sat in on monthly calls with other top women professionals from our firm for over a year, and we came up with a proposal to present to our management team. Little did I know that being involved in that informal impact circle would change the course of my life and my daughter's.

Using the proposal from our task force, the firm came to the table with what I considered a fair offer. I was terrified and exhilarated at the same time. I was convinced, after seeing Rachel in action, that she had the necessary skill set, including three years of opening new markets, multiple promotions, and succeeding at every level despite her youth. I initially thought a suitable candidate would need a minimum of five years of experience in another industry, but I had come to the financial services industry at twenty-four years old with three years of sales experience myself when shifting from computer sales. Was it possible that Rachel was ready at the exact same age? Indeed, she was.

THE CLEANING LADY RETURNS

worked with my best friend and business partner, for twenty-two years before she retired to Florida in 2017, at age fifty-seven. We thoughtfully navigated our personal and professional lives, always prioritizing our friendship above all else. We spoke virtually every Sunday morning, typically while I was out for my morning walk. She was an incredibly amazing friend during all my health-care and personal challenges, and one of my chemotherapy buddies. She had been widowed in her early thirties when her first husband passed away from cancer. She had an exceptional work ethic, putting herself through community college, then earning her BS in Accounting at Siena College and graduating with honors before remarrying. Her story was one of resilience, hard work, and persistence. I was grateful and fortunate to have worked with her for over two decades. With financial security, she embraced the next chapter of her life in a more temperate climate, keeping herself very busy.

Two and a half years into the pandemic, my best friend came for her first visit to see her family in Albany. Her first attempt was thwarted by airline cancellations. A few weeks later, she was able to visit, and we had the opportunity to spend a fabulously fun day together. We drove to Sharon Springs to visit the charming Beekman 1802 Kindness shop, where we petted baby goats, purchased organic skincare products and luscious goat cheese, and ate a few decadent caramels made with dark chocolate, sea salt, and goat's milk. We had lunch at the sweet Black Cat Café and enjoyed an endearing slice of small-town America, visiting the owner of the local, whimsical lavender farm and Sharon Sprigs, a floral gift shop. I had purchased three elegant planters shaped like women's heads on a previous visit and included them in a unique floral arrangement, sending the owner a photo. I had prominently displayed on my back porch the sentimental arrangement, representing three of the women in my family: my mother, my daughter, and myself. When we walked into the lovely little floral gift shop, I was heartened that the owner knew exactly who I was. I was so enamored with my decorative vases and the floral arrangements celebrating three generations of women in my family that I bought two more identical vases to display in my new office, representing my new mother-daughter business partnership—an incredible dream come true!

At one point in our conversation, my best friend mentioned that she was thinking of getting a part-time job working at a local real estate office. I shrieked. "Are you crazy? Why would you want to do that?" As her financial advisor, I knew it wasn't for financial remuneration, so I was truly puzzled. She said she felt she would benefit from more intellectual engagement during her retirement years and wanted to exercise her brain more, just as she was keeping very fit by exercising all the other parts of her body. During her retirement, she enjoyed a variety of hobbies and interests: cooking, baking, sewing, crocheting, knitting, playing card games with friends, and golfing. But now she was exploring employment for increased mental activity. I took a nanosecond to soak in that surprising information, and

I asked, "Do you want to come back to work with me again?"

She immediately responded, "Yes!" I could not believe my ears! Could that be possible?

I inquired further. "What would you want to do?"

She said, "Any administrative work. Anything you want or need me to do."

Oh, my goodness! What just happened? My best friend and former financial advisor–business partner, who had been retired for four years, wanted to come back to work with me part-time. I was speechless and thrilled! I absolutely missed our professional partnership. We both took a deep breath and agreed to revisit the conversation once she was back home.

The next day, my best friend texted me photos of her on a dirt bike with her daughter-in-law and her grandchildren. My best friend on a dirt bike? Who was this new person? I was just trying to process what had transpired and loved everything about it. I tried not to get too excited, as it was uncharacteristic of her to be interested in anything adventurous or professional at this stage of her life. We set up a time to chat. My mind was racing with ideas. I put together a list of serious questions to address and sent them to her in preparation for our scheduled business discussion. She texted me immediately that she had been pondering the exact same questions. We had to postpone our conversation a few days, as I was recovering from laryngitis after talking for over five hours with professionals from my firm at an exquisite outdoor farm-to-table dinner event hosted by the group "Outstanding in the Field" and coincidentally held at the Beekman 1802 farmhouse mansion.

Once I got my voice back, my best friend and I had a series of candid conversations about all the potential downsides to her jumping back onto our business team. We were totally honest with each other about what we were hoping a renewed professional connection would look like. We were extremely clear on our goals, limitations, fears, and concerns but ultimately very excited about re-engaging in a professional way. I had just finished listening to *The Universe Has Your Back* by Gabrielle Bernstein. The author encouraged putting out to the universe what you need, and having an expanded business team was what I had envisioned professionally for many years. My dream was manifesting itself with my daughter on board and potentially also my best friend. We had a follow-up conversation where I gave her full permission to back out before I mentioned anything to my manager or other team members. She didn't back out and was truly excited about the foundation we had laid out for part-time work. She texted me the exact roles we discussed, and I was over-the-moon excited to welcome her back.

When my mom, my daughter, and my best friend were no longer living in the Capital Region, I felt a deep sense of loss, as not only was I an empty nester, the three dominant women in my life were no longer local. The dynamics of our relationships had to evolve into virtual ones, which was not ideal for my extroverted personality, but we made the best of it. This new business development was most definitely a welcome surprise from the universe. My business team of Susan Brown, senior wealth strategy advisor; Edward Piotrowski, senior registered client associate; Rachel Quinn, financial advisor; and my best friend, now in a client associate role, was complete because "the cleaning lady" was back! When I asked permission to refer to her as "the cleaning lady," she said, "Absolutely, I am not embarrassed by that. I am proud that I did what I needed to do at that time in my life." The cleaning lady continues to have my deepest friendship and admiration.

EMBRACING OUR UNIQUENESS

knew it would be tricky to grow from a team of three to a team of five, especially when one team member was my daughter, and the other was my best friend and former business partner. It took finesse and the support of my valued, existing business partners, Ed and Susan, to assimilate our two new team members. Admittedly, there was some trepidation to be expected from all of us, but our team focused on ways to embrace our unique skill sets and on finding the best working partnerships. It was fascinating to watch it unfold, especially as I suggested implementing substantial technological enhancements and marketing efforts within our business practice, which our team simply had not had the bandwidth to tackle before.

I have always attempted to adopt the latest technology both personally and professionally, and I chuckled because I prominently displayed a framed photo and newspaper article of myself with the headline "Power People on the Go." It depicts me as ahead of my time in 1995, using a cutting-edge laptop computer at a local coffee shop. By employing new software systems, our team could focus on business efficiencies and prepare for whenever any team members were on vacation or transitioning to retirement. Working with our expanded team was a delicate balancing act; however, we attempted to keep our informal business impact circle functioning well for the benefit of our clients, our firm, and ourselves. I was fortunate to have them all on my team.

When my business partner, Ed Piotrowski, interviewed with me before my best friend retired, he said, "I am your lump of clay. I will do whatever professional role is needed."

I said, "You are hired," because from my experience, that was the type of attitude required to survive and succeed in the financial services industry. It is an industry of constant change, challenge, regulation, and compliance. Someone who is uncomfortable implementing change is unlikely to be a good fit long-term. Our team's roles and careers have required extremely hard work, dedication, and a willingness to adapt to a variety of roles as needed. I have been extremely grateful to have Ed and Susan on my business team for many years and appreciate their hard work, professional expertise, and excellent client service. We have enjoyed many years of personal lunches, client events, birthday and holiday celebrations, and business strategy sessions, and have done our best to work as a highly functioning team, despite the challenges of significant change we must navigate annually as our industry continues to evolve.

After Rachel passed all five financial advisory exams, she participated in client meetings and discussions, used our firm's software tools for financial planning and analysis, updated our marketing brochures and team website, and created technology solutions to digitize my business practice. The best teams find ways to work cohesively, and we were focused on a collective mission to provide exceptional advice and service to the client families and businesses we served, making for a meaningful financial advisory circle.

CHAPTER TWELVE:
Informal Impact Circles

O ver the course of my thirty-eight-year career in the financial services industry, I created four formal impact circles, each with specific goals and missions: the Professional Women's Network; the Executive Network; Passion, Purpose, and Legacy; and Next Chapter. I have also been actively involved in a variety of informal impact circles: the Business & Professional Women's Club of Schenectady (BPW), the Forum for Executive Women, the Capital Region Chamber's Women's Business Council and Women of Excellence, the YWCA of Northeastern New York, Women of Achievement, Trailblazing Women of the Women's Fund of the Capital Region, the Women's Employment and Resource Center, and the *Albany Business Review's* Women Who Mean Business.

Informally, I have sought unique and creative ways to connect my women friends and business professionals, knowing that magic happens with the right connections. Over the years, my business team has hosted a variety of custom educational forums that have led to deeper friendships and more meaningful business relationships, focused on how we can all contentedly live productive, financially secure, healthy lives. My focus has been on leaving a meaningful legacy. This chapter includes a few of the informal impact circles I encountered or was part of along my life's path.

FORT ORANGE CLUB LITERARY SOCIETY

I have been a member of the Fort Orange Club of Albany since 1995 and one of the first female members since the club began admitting women in 1989. I had been going to the club since 1987, before they admitted women members. Each year, our branch manager would host sales recognition events at the club, and I had to be whisked up the back steps to the private business rooms, because I made the top-advisor list every time. Once I felt I could make a living as a financial advisor, I joined the Fort Orange Club as a Junior Member after having lunch with my professional sponsor and ten businessmen who wanted to ensure I would be a good fit for membership. I actively participated in a variety of committees: membership, finance, library, and general manager search. I also joined an informal monthly women's lunch. But by far my favorite part was being a member of the Fort Orange Club Literary Society. In the monthly newsletter, I saw that Michelle Obama's book *Becoming* was being discussed, which I had just read and loved. Somehow, I hadn't realized it was an actual book club until I showed up that evening.

Given my very busy professional life and dance focus, I didn't know if I would be able to find time to read on a consistent basis, but these women were so welcoming, intellectually savvy, and wonderful that I made a commitment to find the time. I discovered I could multitask by listening to books via the Audible app in my car on my way to and from work, business meetings, and dance lessons, or while walking outside or on the treadmill during the colder months. Not every book was necessarily one I would have chosen to read on my own, but I felt every selection broadened my scope—intellectually, histor- ically, and culturally. At each book club meeting, I deepened my connection with phenomenal women spanning genera- tions who were intelligent, well-read, and caring. They brought a lightheartedness to my otherwise frenzied world, allowing for lovely new friendships that I hadn't anticipated.

Shortly after joining the literary society, my unexpected divorce journey surprisingly paralleled my participation in this book club. Initially, I had assumed I would not actually get divorced, as I fully believed John and I would be able to work through any issues after thirty-three years of marriage. So, I thought there would be no need to share any of my marital challenges with this new group of friends. However, as the months went on, it was clear that was not the case. I knew it would only be a matter of time before I felt safe sharing my divorce journey with this supportive group.

When the Fort Orange Club Literary Society met in November 2021, the selected book was *The Winemaker's Wife* by Kristin Harmel. I was waiting for an appropriate opening in the discussion to share what I was going through personally. The book had a main character who had just gone through an unanticipated divorce, so I thought there would be a natural time. Sadly, there wasn't, so at the end of the formal discussion, I chose to ask the members' permission to share something personal. I had already begun sharing my divorce journey with close confidants once it was clear that my marriage was over, as I knew just how much the stress was affecting my health. I feared that my cancer could come back if I didn't look for some emotional support.

I decided I needed to broaden my level of sharing, as it felt inauthentic not to express the personal anguish I was going through. When I shared my news with my literary society friends, they were genuinely shocked. One woman remarked that I always had such a positive attitude, so it was hard to believe what I had been going through for my entire membership in the book club. I immediately knew this was a strong informal impact circle, as the love and support that emerged from that meeting were palpable. These women were incredibly kind, and I will never forget that several stayed after the discussion to share their fierce support. Others approached me privately to share their own confidences, deepening our relationships. I felt safe in that space. These women were incredibly gracious, showing their true strength. Little did I know this book club would become a meaningful source of support on a journey I could never have anticipated. They were truly a hidden gem of a group, enriching my life in so many ways.

The Fort Orange Club Literary Society was an informal impact circle that welcomed several new members over the years, introducing a mixture of perspectives and backgrounds spanning various ages, willing to engage in diverse opinions and lively discussions on a wide variety of topics, and tackling many genres for discussion with a collaborative effort for intellectual enrichment and fellowship. It was a beautiful part of my Fort Orange Club membership. In contrast to how I navigated my early career, having a book club with mostly women members was a welcome delight.

In 2023, I hosted the Fort Orange Club Literary Society in my home for a book swap and holiday party, welcoming new friends into my home, which was fully decked out for the season. This was a further way to connect on a more personal basis—the whole point of informal impact circles. I grew to admire the women of the Fort Orange Club Literary Society as we discussed important life topics covered in the themes of the selected novels.

CORPORATE WOMEN UNLEASHED

did not have reservations about whether Rachel was well suited for a financial advisory role based on her strong academic background and her sales and marketing skills. However, I was uncertain whether she would find herself making a difference in the world in the way she defined it, which I knew was extremely important to her. I strongly believed I was making a difference in the lives of our client families, so I hoped Rachel's idea of social impact could also align with the deep influence she could have on our client families.

Once Rachel discovered she could continue to volunteer her time in the not-for-profit world and find ways to connect with clients for social impact, my heart soared, as I knew she would have a strong career foundation with me if she desired it. Slowly but surely, as her experience grew, she blossomed in her role and was proactive in using her Babson entrepreneurial, marketing, and technology skill sets, as well as those from her first sales and marketing job. Rachel was like a sponge and learned very quickly, simply by observing my day-to-day role, following my lead, and discovering how to add value in her own way. I could see that she genuinely cared about developing relationships and enhancing connections with the next generation of our client families.

During the early part of our mother-daughter working relationship, Rachel recognized the personal and professional struggles I was experiencing during my intense divorce proceedings. I wanted to ensure I was doing everything I could to give her the best foundation so she could thrive, but I knew I faced a challenge going from a team of three to a team of five in a short time. Both additions were most welcome, but the timing was difficult, as it coincided with my personal challenges.

One day, while walking in my neighborhood, I ran into the husband of a friend who was walking his dog, and we paused to chat. We ended up having a meaningful conversation that would later connect me to another significant informal impact circle. During the conversation, I chose to share that I was personally in transition and finally verbalized that I was navigating a divorce. He was amazingly supportive. The next day, I received an email from him containing a series of YouTube videos. They featured journalist Bill Moyers interviewing Joseph

Campbell for *The Power of Myth*. It's a profound series of interviews, and watching it reminded me deeply of my father and his humanistic approach to life. I watched all the videos back-to-back and felt a wondrous connection to my papa. I reached out to three of my dear friends who had known my father. I asked each of them if they were familiar with the work of Joseph Campbell and these interviews. The first two said yes. My third dear friend not only said yes, she also shared that she had watched all the videos with my father in the late 1980s. I just had a hunch that there was a connection to my father there, another endearing synchronicity. The way my siblings and I were raised was very much aligned with the teachings of Joseph Campbell. I had a strong sense of peace and connection to my wise father.

In the middle of the videos, there was an online advertisement with a professional woman who popped up on the screen to highlight a businesswomen's coaching program on the topic of executive burnout. I was clearly going through the most stressful time of my life, and somehow the woman on my computer pierced my heart, speaking directly to me about how to take control of my life and find true balance. Intrigued, I clicked on the links to learn more. I was incredibly impressed with Kate Byars, CEO of the Goodlife Institute, whose message about work-life balance resonated deeply within my soul. I hadn't engaged in any professional coaching since the very early part of my career. After all, I had been doing financial and life planning throughout my career, and I'd been the coach. I decided I needed to explore this further, and I clicked on the button to set up an appointment.

I shared with my daughter that I had just signed up for an exploratory appointment for executive coaching and asked if she would join the call to be an extra set of ears. She agreed, which is what I felt I needed at that moment. We had a lot riding on our professional working relationship, and I wanted to ensure I was doing everything I could to make it succeed. That included working on myself. I was grateful for Rachel's moral support and unique perspective. I was incredibly impressed with the introductory call, which got immediately to the heart of how my life could improve if I could find a better work-life balance. I was initially reluctant to invest the sum required for this high-level coaching program, but Rachel encouraged me to invest in myself and my emotional well-being, just as I had invested in everyone around me, including her. And so I did.

My experience with the Corporate Women Unleashed program was unparalleled compared to any other coaching program I had seen. It was all online, and there was weekly homework, one-on-one coaching, and group coaching. I was extremely impressed with the caliber of female coaching profession- als who were as tough as nails in providing specific training techniques to confront deep-seated emotions that needed to be addressed. I loved the structure of each week and how we delved deeper into effective strategies and addressed new topics as they arose in my daily life. There was strong atten- tion to personal, foundational issues and how they intertwined with professional roles. The personal and professional parts of our lives were tackled together to break through complicated issues.

At the beginning of the program, I was asked to select one word to focus on as an overarching goal. My word was *serenity*. It was the foundation of my entire training and continues to be my most important focus: having a full, meaningful personal and professional life but doing so with peace of mind. I was so impressed with my personal coaches, Jadine, Melinda, and Ali, and administrative assistant Kitty, who were all extremely skilled professionals. They were kind and relentless in uncov- ering the real root of my personal pain and coming up with strategies to address it, helping me move beyond my pain to peace. I was quite surprised at my willingness to be fiercely vulnerable in a virtual group setting, allowing my tears to flow freely while working through the profound emotional trauma I was feeling. Thankfully, I made meaningful steps forward by the end of the eight-week program and have kept serenity top of mind ever since. I love staying connected with this informal impact circle via an online group. They are part of my passionate group of supporters.

FORUM FOR EXECUTIVE WOMEN

I received a timely call from a representative of the Forum for Executive Women, warmly welcoming me to a group that met periodically for professional and social networking. I was very appreciative of being embraced into a network I didn't have to start or lead. It allowed me to just show up to a variety of wonderful networking events without having to coordinate them myself.

En route to one FEW event in the summer of 2024, it rained profusely on my drive there and back, but it was worth the trip to catch up with business friends and associates. I had just come from back-to-back business meetings—a very full professional day—and was severely exhausted, both mentally and physically. I had considered not attending, which is extremely rare for me, as I always feel an obligation to attend anything I commit to. I know how hard it is to coordinate an event and do all the preparation work, so I chose to show up as I do 99.9 percent of the time. I went on to have meaningful conversations with the other executives present, connecting with several of them for powerful business opportunities, so the event was worth the trip. I knew I needed to keep my focus on serenity top of mind though, and I finally came home to rest and rejuvenate.

Over the course of my participation in this informal impact circle, I felt a growing connection to other business leaders. We discussed a wide variety of topics pertinent to us as professionals in our community, and we engaged in social excursions, which were a welcome respite from our work lives. I especially appreciated meeting an exceptional wellness coach, learning about the potential impact artificial intelligence could have on our careers, and making Thanksgiving pies. Fun, for a change!

BALLROOM DANCE SPHERES

allroom dance connections have undoubtedly been one of my most important informal impact circles. Since day one of my dance journey at age forty, I have developed deep, meaningful relationships, both on and off the dance floor, with a large circle of friends, making for a culturally enriching informal impact circle. I meet people from all walks of life, ages, and ethnicities, forming a dynamic melting pot of wonderful humans, each with a shared interest in using dance as a physical, emotional, and social way of connecting with our community and focusing on fitness, positive interactions, and joy.

In dance circles, I forged deep friendships that extended well beyond the dance floor. Some dance friends developed into clients or were sources of client referrals, merging my love of dance with business. This informal impact circle allowed me to connect with the fellow dancer and physician who introduced me to top national oncology specialists when I desperately needed them. Their second opinions allowed me peace of mind for the rest of my life.

I made several new friends along my dance journey of over twenty years. One of them shared this passage after she saw my lighthearted post "Wonka–Charlie and the Chocolate Factory," about my performance for National Ballroom Dance Week during the third week of September 2024, which touched my soul:

> *Dance disappears almost at the moment of its manifestation. It is an extreme expression of the present, a perfect metaphor for life. Dancers sculpt space in real time, working inside a form that is constantly in a state of vanishing.*
> ~ *Crystal Pite, Canadian dancer and choreographer*

I am grateful for the many new and meaningful relationships I developed in the ballroom dance community. I have done my best to remain consistently supportive of our local dance community, advertising in our local USA Dance *Footnotes* newsletter, sponsoring our annual black-tie community ballroom dance event, and welcoming dancer clients into my financial advisor circle. My ballroom dance community is an extremely meaningful informal impact circle in my life, serving as a support system and proving to be monumental for my health and wellness, both physically and emotionally.

NEIGHBORHOOD CIRCLES

I was fortunate to grow up in the beautiful neighborhood of the historic General Electric Realty Plot in Schenectady from age four until going off to Union College and living on campus for four years, despite being a block from our home, as my parents encouraged that transformative growth experience. In my childhood neighborhood, I forged meaningful relationships with a few close friends, from elementary school through high school, who I am still in contact with, including a pen pal from age four, who I found years later while vacationing in South Carolina. I lived in two apartments before getting married and have now had the privilege of living in the same Albany County suburban neighborhood for over thirty years.

In my current neighborhood, we have had cul-de-sac gatherings, picnics, bonfires, holiday parties, and garage sales, staying connected via an email distribution list and neighborhood Facebook page to share important notifications, resources, and events pertinent to our community. My immediate neighbors were there for me personally and were especially supportive as I navigated my cancer and divorce journeys. My neighbors were also tremendously helpful when, after thirty years, I had two floods in my basement. This was despite many precautions to avoid flooding: new sump pumps, backup sump pumps, a generator, vinyl plank flooring, French drain cleaning, and gutter improvements. My neighbors have been there to provide resources, advice, empathy, and property maintenance suggestions. This makes for wonderful friendships and walking buddies, keeping one another focused on health and wellness. We have happy hours and impromptu S'mores Nights, poolside or on the deck, sharing life's good times and challenges. I am grateful for my incredible neighbors. One of my neighborhood walking buddies even became a member of one of my impact circles and a treasured new friend.

TEA PARTIES

In an attempt to keep serenity and business development top of mind, Rachel and I came up with the idea of hosting a series of tea parties with different themes: a Women's International Tea; a Mother-Daughter Tea; and a Healthy, Wealthy, and Wise Tea—all focused on work-life integration concepts. Rachel created elegant invitations using a customized marketing-software program, which we used to invite business leaders and guests to join us. We chose a potluck-style event, having everyone bring appetizers instead of catering. This was in part to keep costs within our budget, but more importantly, it set a personal tone, allowing for a less formal atmosphere. We held the events in my home, which was now completely mine and imbued with a new sense of freedom.

Rachel, with a home base in Boston, Massachusetts, came to Albany to attend the Capital Region Chamber Annual Dinner, where I formally introduced my newest business partner to leaders in our community. I learned that our marketing efforts, which had introduced my daughter as my business partner, had been effective. When I introduced her in person, most leaders already knew she was my daughter and my newest business partner. They also said they loved seeing the tribute video of my ballroom dance for my mom on LinkedIn, which was heartwarming. Their response reinforced my belief that my more personalized approach to marketing was doing what I hoped it would: highlighting my professional career in a more authentic way. Since I was in the minority as a woman financial advisor in our industry, I knew that I could try the business-development approach of my colleagues or embrace a more unique style. This is what ultimately led to my success. I had forged my own path in the early days of my career and was encouraging my daughter to do the same.

I was extremely proud to be selected as a Trailblazing Woman by the Women's Fund of the Capital Region in 2014. I was presented with a brass compass that I proudly displayed in my office, inscribed with this quote that is often attributed to Ralph Waldo Emerson: "Do not go where the path may lead, go instead where there is no path and leave a trail." It summarized my professional path, and thankfully there was a positive outcome. In 2021, I also received a Women Who Mean Business award through the *Albany Business Review*. I was preparing to go on stage for a panel discussion with other distinguished award recipients when a dear EN friend from my professional circles, who I had known since our children were in daycare together at Bright Horizons at Corporate Woods, came straight over to me and asked, "What's wrong?" Apparently, she could see right through me, as I was going through my heartbreaking divorce in silence, and I was not my usual, bubbly self. I told her I couldn't share anything at that time but would reach out when I could. I was very pleased to receive many compliments on my panel participation, validating that I could maintain my professional persona despite my internal pain.

Rachel and I agreed on most business-development methods but had unique perspectives. We navigated our different approaches to our joint marketing events by planning large and intimate gatherings. Ultimately, we hosted phenomenal events that encouraged creative name tags as icebreakers and used talking-point cards. We lit candles, had a table filled with fabulous appetizers, and served decadent desserts with international teas from my favorite tea shop, Short and Stout Tea Company, in Guilderland. The most valuable parts of our events were the meaningful discussions we had with executives as they shared tips for work-life balance, especially during the aftermath of the pandemic.

When Rachel and I hosted our first Mother-Daughter Summer Tea, we invited select mother-daughter duos and led an intimate discussion with sixteen amazing women. This was a chance to have meaningful conversations and share wisdom about life, finances, career planning, and ideas from one generation to the next. It was a huge hit and allowed Rachel and me a chance to navigate our own mother-daughter relationship while our guests learned from each other.

Our unique events allowed our guests to share their favorite mother-daughter activities with each other by listing them on their name tags, which invited interesting conversations with other guests. We also had each guest write an anonymous question about anything they would like to ask the group. Rachel and I each put in one question. Mine asked, "What does flourishing look like in your family?" Rachel's asked, "Do you talk about money in your family, and if not, how would you like to talk about it?" There were many thought-provoking questions from our guests, making for an enchanting evening. The take-aways were quite profound, as everyone in the room shared with vulnerability and authenticity. Two young women shared how flourishing in their family meant being able to spend more time with their father, who was traveling a lot for business. The whole room felt the sincerity with which this was shared. All guests were genuinely engaged in a meaningful conversation after a few prompts from me, as I led the discussion.

Rachel took on the question "What is your biggest fear for the future?" and handled it honestly and vulnerably from her twenty-six-year-old perspective. She was thoughtful and genuine in her response. It was a perfect way to wrap up our session and allow for follow-up networking with guests who had found someone new to connect with after hearing the answers to the questions. It was quite a philosophical experience, and I was proud of us both. Our first few business-partnership events were a success, despite the hard work and emotional toll it took to prepare for such personal gatherings. My friend and photographer, Joan Heffler, read about our tea party and shared this:

> *Alissa and Rachel, I am in complete awe of your informal yet intimate gatherings. Such a powerful message of bonding, community, and networking with flair! I don't know any financial advisors who would do this and create such meaningful groups of women celebrating themselves, their families, and their peers in such a beautiful way. Brava!*

It was such an incredibly thoughtful and beautiful response to exactly what we were trying to accomplish as mother-daughter financial advisors. We created a sacred space for professionals to deepen their relationships and tap into embracing financial empowerment across generations with wisdom and strength, encouraging all women to participate in comprehensive financial planning.

Next, we hosted a Healthy, Wealthy, and Wise Tea, and this time we invited two outside speakers: Benita Zahn, an NBC-HWC certified health and wellness coach, and Judy Torel, an NBC-HWC certified nutrition and fitness coach. I discussed the "soul of money," referring to a book of the same title by Lynne Twist, which included many financial concepts specific to women, such as money, power, fear, a scarcity mindset, and the importance of proper financial planning. I also introduced the concept of my impact circles and mentioned a second book, *Die With Zero* by Bill Perkins, which underscores spending money on memorable experiences and the concept that there is no linear need to spend money over your lifetime. This was a personal and professional message I felt deeply and wanted to share with participants. We provided booklets for storing comprehensive information as a powerful thank-you to our guests, giving them one place to keep all their important financial content for their loved ones. We had dozens of guests filling my living room.

The tea party events were hugely successful and provided a foundation for Rachel and me to build our signature business events on. They led to new account relationships, financial-planning engagements, and several new 401(k) small business retirement plans. I was delighted that our business partnership was working and that we could continue to build our financial consulting practice with our more personal, collaborative touch, so different from the approach of our colleagues. This allowed us to find our own entrepreneurial spirit and soar. Much of our financial consulting work is with professional couples, but as women financial advisors, we encourage both parties in a relationship to feel heard when discussing financial matters, whether or not they make joint decisions.

S'MORES CIRCLES

*D*uring the summer of 2024, I decided to host a series of impromptu S'mores Nights at my home, poolside, inviting men and women in my circles who were available to be spontaneous and come for whatever portion of a summer evening they could spare. I created serene spaces by playing soft nature music, lighting candles, hanging fairy lights, and using flowing, warm pool water as a backdrop. Guests came from all areas of my life: neighbors, friends, dancers, professional contacts, and clients. I encouraged friends to bring their favorite appetizer, beverage, or dessert to share, saying, "Come as you are." I wanted to create an outdoor haven for people to gather, decompress from their busy lives, and have an opportunity to reconnect with friends or make some new ones.

On my last impromptu S'mores Night of the summer, I chose a serenity theme. I played jazz music for hours, and we enjoyed a delectable array of savory and sweet treats, brainstormed ways to fill our lives with more peace, roasted marshmallows, made s'mores with dark-chocolate, sea-salt caramels, and dangled our legs in the warm pool water. What a wonderful way to connect with special people and let the grace of the evening unfold. These informal S'mores Nights were so simple yet so powerful for helping us decompress from our life challenges. I was heartened to have a lovely, serene evening with wonderful friends, a magnificent remedy for any of life's woes. One business leader guest, after attending a S'mores Night, shared this on social media.

Sometimes you MUST say yes to the impromptu get-together. Not everything can be planned. Remember to live in the moment. Remember to enjoy the fun side of life as much as the work side of life. Thanks, Alissa, for the invitation and encouraging folks to share serenity tips and habits.

That night, we lingered for hours, late into the evening, enjoying a little piece of summer serenity. You never know what the universe has in store when you encourage random friends to gather and deepen their relationships.

The Smore's Nights turned into informal impact circles in ways I could not have imagined: friendships blossomed, and professional connections were enhanced. Long after the warm summer evenings faded, I received a precious thank-you note from another one of my guests, which read:

> *Dearest Alissa,*
>
> *Your spontaneous pool parties and s'mores fests were way more than just the delectable goodies on the table; they were about the friends in the circle. You brought us together around evening lights, and you were a key spark! Thank you for your kindness and for always thinking of me, and for the fellowship you arrange.*

The unique tea parties and Smore's Nights we created became informal impact circles and turned out to be incredibly meaningful based on the feedback we received from our guests and the ensuing business. Ultimately, these formal and informal circles connected people together in fellowship, friendship, and business. Several guests shared that they felt my impact circles provided a framework to minimize loneliness in the world, a heartfelt and beautiful sentiment that summarized my ardent hope.

CHAPTER THIRTEEN:
Healing

ealing came in many forms after my cancer and divorce storms. I found that daily neighborhood walks, yoga stretches, meditation, lighting candles, enjoying cups of tea, ballroom and Argentine tango dancing, flower arranging, home decorating, inspirational reading, and connecting with my family and friends all helped me navigate the challenges I faced along my path. As I faced adversity, I customized my approach to allow myself to heal.

TRAVEL HEALING

he trips I have made over my lifetime were enchanting and nourished my soul with every adventure. I have marveled at phenomenal European artwork in famous museums, exquisite architecture, divine food and delectable pastries, gorgeous flowers, abundantly blooming trees, and color-drenched shrubs in landscapes of beauty beyond my wildest imagination. Traveling has proven to be quite profound, particularly my escape to southern France with Mayela and Rachel, and my vacation to Turkey with Carl's family (his wife Jeanine and their children Kyle, Nico, and Maya) to see my nephew Nico Calabria, co-captain of the U.S. Amputee Soccer Team, compete at the Amputee World Cup in Istanbul in 2023. These were both phenomenal trips of a lifetime. I am in awe of my nephew Nico, who climbed Mt. Kilimanjaro at age thirteen with his father for a coming-of-age trip, raising over $100 thousand for the Free Wheelchair Mission in South Africa, which helps individuals with limb deficiencies. As an adult, Nico raises awareness to help normalize different abilities in K–12 classrooms in the US, as he was born with one leg.

I have had extremely positive experiences that have enriched my soul, in every country I have visited in Europe. Every trip was exquisitely memorable and filled with magnificent adventures. I typically go for seven to ten days, but each experience has filled my heart for a lifetime and provided significant healing therapy. I am open to seeing the rest of the world, but nothing excites me more than the idea of European journeys. I have been fortunate to work with a wonderful travel agent, Jean Gagnon at Plaza Travel, whose daughter Rachel is the namesake of our daughter—the preschool buddy Johnnie named his sister after when he announced, "I want a Rachel of my own!" Jean grew to understand the right balance of experiences for me, including the types of excursions, downtime, best-fit hotels, number of cities, and smooth transportation solutions. I feel extremely blessed with all the fabulous trips I have had over my lifetime and hope to continue traveling for many years to come.

As I have used Facebook to connect with family and friends, my relationships have deepened, not only in my hometown but across the US and throughout my mother's home country of Ecuador, especially when I post photos of my life and travel adventures. I feel as if I am bringing many of my travel friends along with me on my journeys and vice versa. Posting glorious photos of European architecture, exquisite museums, splendid palaces, vibrant flowers, scrumptious food, and enriching explorations has connected me more significantly to those in my informal travel circles, as it fills their souls just as it does mine, capturing the essence of different cultures that somehow resonates with us.

Each time I come back from my traveling, I create digital and physical scrapbooks with approximately a thousand illuminating photos to help me remember the essence of each enchanting journey. I love sharing these with friends and family, who look forward to seeing my trips come to life on the pages upon my return. They salivate at the food photos, swoon at the architecture, admire the flowers, shriek with delight at the desserts, and marvel at the uniqueness of each excursion. This moment of sharing deepens our relationships in ways I could not have imagined, as we gush over my exquisite adventures together. Seeing other parts of the world gives me a global perspective that comes from sharing experiences of different cultures. The most heartwarming stories often come from visiting places our grandparents came from, allowing for meaningful connections to our elders—something that has been deeply personal to me. Travel has been a way to embrace living life to its fullest and experience the magic of informal travel impact circles. This has been a healing therapy for me, showing me abundance.

VENTURING ABROAD SOLO

"Are you alone?" asked the waiter at Hotel Albergo Degli Amici. I thought for a moment and wanted to say "No, I am not alone. All my family and friends are with me, following my travels during my Northern Italy solo pilgrimage." I chose Northern Italy because Cinque Terre was one of the stops my parents had made on their honeymoon in Europe. My mom specifically mentioned the colorful pastel houses being so memorable and hinted I should venture there someday. As I had already been to many other locations in Italy, including Rome, Florence, Venice, Siena, San Gimignano, Lake Como, Sorrento, Positano, Naples, Reggio di Calabria, Taormina in Sicily, and the Amalfi Coast, I felt a calling to see the little pastel buildings my mother had spoken so highly of to continue my connection to her and my father, as well as to further my passion for European travel, hoping for more healing.

This journey was indeed my first solo adventure, but I did not feel alone. I posted photos of my journey on Facebook and felt wrapped in love by friends and family who followed along with me on my excursions. Some intimately understood the significance of traveling on my own and the deep importance of making this journey to heal from the last two and a half years of sorrow, simultaneously navigating divorce and grief. My friends were there cheering me every step of the way, so I felt warmly connected to them.

My excursion started in Santa Margherita Ligure, Northern Italy, as recommended by my travel agent, who shared that she would like to retire there. I could see why. It was a small town on the Ligurian Sea. The landscape was peppered with blooming pink and purple flowering trees, aquamarine waters, architectural wonders, and cobblestone walkways in the old part of town. There were scents of fresh pizza, pasta, and seafood right from the bay with fishermen bringing in a daily haul of treasures from the sea to be consumed by evening's end. My senses were exploding in every positive way. I wandered the narrow streets, which offered magnificent sights and sounds in every direction. I sampled the local fare of lemon-drenched anchovies, warm focaccia bread, and sumptuous pasta made to perfection—just a little firm to the bite. And oh, the gelato of every flavor with a charming gelateria every few streets. Mayela had prescribed two gelatos to be consumed daily. I was a good patient and had no trouble following her instructions, trying stracciatella, sweet cream with chocolate chips, pistachio, and chocolate in any combination imaginable.

I also tried all the regional favorites: trofie pasta with pesto—homemade, long, thin macaroni-like noodles with a famous sauce made with fresh basil, grated Parmigiano-Reggiano and pecorino romano cheeses, pine nuts, and olive oil that tasted as fresh as could be. I have always enjoyed anything with lemon, so my beverage of choice was always fresh-squeezed lemonade, carbonated or not. Both were refreshing for me on warm days. Seeing the lemon and orange trees scattered along my journey just melted my heart, as did the massive flowering trees drenched in deep purple next to houses, shops, and village buildings. Seeing pink flowering trees made my heart sing. Bliss! There was something about the flowers in Europe that encouraged my passion for arranging both fresh and silk flowers. I have been creating artistic arrangements from visions inspired by my travels all over Europe. I loved the soft pastels and muted colors I saw, and I attempted to replicate them in my home, transporting myself to charming European destinations.

The weather in Northern Italy was humid, and I was dripping with perspiration, dripping in ideas, dripping in feelings, and enjoying every second. I came down to breakfast at Hotel Milano Scala, and there was a woman musician playing a large harp right in the quaint dining area. I had not seen anyone playing the harp since my formal dinners at the Fort Orange Club, some thirty years prior at holiday parties. I immediately felt that somehow this Italian harp was a healing harp, as her music was so soothing, and I experienced catharsis. She only played for a short while, but I felt the impact very strongly. I also recalled giving our dog, Harpo, an official name for his birth certificate: "The Happy Irish Harp." This made me smile, thinking of him.

In Europe, I treasured the connection to my parents, who were always willing to express their feelings of love for travel and passion for their family, friends, food, dance music, nature, and life. I felt their passion for life and was determined to find my own for my next life chapter, filled with travel, self-love, family, friends, joyful dance, meaningful work, soulful music, and anything to make my heart sing! It was my choice, my voice, and my passion that would lead my way. And I would bring along my friends and family who wanted to join me on the exquisite experiences that lay ahead. The future would be my time to flourish.

DANCE THERAPY

*M*y soul was meant for passion, fulfilling work, close relationships with family and friends, and making my life meaningful and important. I never gave up on my ballroom dance dreams during my storms, staying connected to something that was physically healthy for my body, mind, and soul. I refused to give up on life, despite health challenges and heartbreak, using ballroom dance as a form of healing therapy.

I found ballroom dance and Argentine tango to be emotionally and physically healing. Dancing was a positive distraction. One evening, a dance couple hosted an Argentine tango milonga dance party at their country home and barn, potluck-style. I was mentally exhausted and wondered if I should just stay home and rest. But I remembered the stories my dad used to share about my mom being very tired on Friday nights after a long week of caring for four children and working part-time. My dad would say, "Come on. Let's go, because as soon as you hear the music, you will perk up." I thought perhaps that might happen to me too, since I had so many things in common with my parents.

I looked in the refrigerator to see if I had anything I could quickly whip up to bring with me to the party. Indeed, I had the ingredients for Italian meatballs, Calabrian-style! I made a batch, changed my outfit, and headed off to the dance. On the long drive to the country farm, I was extremely tired, trying to stay awake at the wheel, which I knew could be very dangerous. I thought, Well, I can just stay for a little bit and head right back home if I need to.

I used the long drive to finish listening to the book *Think Like a Monk* by Jay Shetty, which included incredibly inspirational stories, giving me the opportunity to recharge my energy. I walked up to the residence, heard the music playing in the barn, and immediately smiled. That music was the healing therapy I needed. In an instant, I knew I was meant to be there, just like my mama at folk dancing on Friday nights years ago, dancing with my papa and their beloved dance community.

There was a welcoming crowd, and I immediately saw two of my mom's closest tango friends, John and Lin Melbourne. Lin put me right at ease once she saw my meatballs with the one-liner "And, you had time to make something homemade!" She added, "I only know how to buy from Villa Italia," a favorite local Italian bakery. She was a gem. I saw dancers I had not seen for two years, due to the pandemic, and immediately felt at home. The dancing filled my soul. I was free to dance in a close embrace, otherwise known as a hug in Argentine tango circles, filling my soul with healing. Everyone inquired about how I was doing after my mom's passing, as she was beloved in their tango circle. I shared that until three weeks before she passed at age ninety-four, my mom had still been out dancing Argentine tango two or three nights per week in Minnesota, thriving.

It was healing to reconnect with my mom's Argentine tango dance friends, including her beloved instructors, David Salvatierra and Maia Martinez. My mother was known as the Queen of Tango wherever she went in Argentine tango circles and was awarded Tango Treasure in Minneapolis. I chuckled and shared, "I just want to attempt to be a Princess of Tango." Lin said I qualified, which made my heart soar. She has referred to me as Princess ever since. I know I have a long way to go to earn that title, but I am looking forward to enjoying every step of the journey with my wonderful Argentine tango friends.

I continued my weekly dance lessons at Fred Astaire Dance Studio, where I have danced since 2005, and Dance Fire Studio, where I have danced since 2016, doing showcase performances with my instructors. This was an incredibly enriching escape from my work. Ballroom dance gave me the opportunity to continue my beloved parents' dance legacy as well as focus on stress relief and fitness. The lessons provided forty-five minutes of therapeutic uninterrupted bliss. They could also be hard work, mentally and physically, so I always attempted to balance my experience of improving my craft while enjoying all of the healing and emotional benefits of dance.

SHARED GRIEF

On Sunday, April 21, 2024, just over a year after our divorce had been finalized, I received an unexpected email from my ex-husband, sharing the news that our beloved sixteen-year-old dachshund Harpo had passed away. He shared that he had hoped I would see Harpo before he passed, but his decline was quick. The tone of the email was surprisingly supportive and anticipated the grief I might feel. This was the first communication from my ex-husband in over a year, even though he was living a block from my home with his mother.

I have always acknowledged that John was the primary care-giver for our two treasured dachshunds, having raised several dogs in his youth. John and I navigated profound grief after losing our first four-legged family member, a beloved cocker spaniel called Oliver, when our children were young. It took us ten years to consider getting another dog. I expected Harpo's passing would be challenging for both of us, despite his having lived a long, beautiful life.

Hoping to provide comfort, I immediately sent John all the best photos I had of Harpo, along with videos of our two pups running exuberantly through the backyard. Harpo had mirac-ulously recovered from back surgery a few years prior, after intense physical therapy to get him back to health. Harpo's passing opened a dialogue between my ex-husband and me, a positive step forward.

The next day, I called to check on John and our younger dachshund, Bella, who was thirteen years old. I imagined both were taking Harpo's loss extremely hard, as they were all inseparable. I asked John if I could stop by to see Bella in person, and he agreed. When Bella saw me, I received the very same greeting that I had received from Harpo, despite his hearing difficulties and partial loss of eyesight—squeals of delight and a very long, loving greeting. I knew how hard it had been for me not to see the pups, but I also recognized how hard it was for them, innocent bystanders of divorce. Bella was thrilled to see me, which was so touching; the pups had both missed me tremendously.

I asked John how he was holding up. He openly shared his visible pain. Shocking myself, I asked if I could give him a hug, and he said yes. I gave him a big, genuine, strong hug, surprisingly, as I had still been filled with such heartache, anger, and pain. I did my best to support him. John shared that no one else understood how deeply he felt this loss. He openly communicated details of Harpo's passing and how he hoped he had not let Harpo down. I assured him he had not. I could feel his anguish and grief, just as I was navigating my own sorrow. I was astonished to find I could support my ex-husband with genuine hugs, listening to his mourning. That was certainly a breakthrough moment for me, as we shared grief that could lead to healing. What felt ironic was that I had loved my husband unconditionally since I was fourteen years old, which is why I fought so hard to save our marriage. In the end, it was just extremely sad and heartbreaking on all levels.

The benefit of our connection was that I finally felt a wave of relief calmly coming across my body and soul. Somehow, it became a turning point for me, allowing me to release the incredible pain I had carried far too long. When I got home, I sobbed, as there had been so much heartache inside me for such an exceedingly long time. I needed to finally let it all out.

Soon thereafter, I was heartened to see my two children reconnect with their cousins, aunts, and uncles on my side of the family. Sadly, these relationships had been strained due to the divorce. Coming from a large Italian and Ecuadorian family, my extended family connections have always been extremely important to me. I have always encouraged my children to cultivate special relationships with their extended family, hoping they would form meaningful ties, as I have done my whole life. Our family has been blessed to connect through wonderful family reunions over the years, and I hope those will continue, not only for weddings and funerals.

ROMANIAN GRAND GALA

I found a way to combine my love of dance and European travel for an amazing experience of a lifetime. In the summer of 2024, I traveled with treasured fellow dance students, including impact circle member and friend Amy Aldrich, to meet our exceptional ballroom dance instructors Florin Vlad and Natalia O'Connor at the JW Marriott hotel in Bucharest for a Romanian Grand Gala dance event. I have never pursued competitive ballroom dancing due to the cost and intensity involved, but I chose to step out of my comfort zone and participate in my first international dance competition. I competed in five international standard dances at the open gold level—waltz, tango, foxtrot, Viennese waltz, and quickstep—in addition to doing a lighthearted showcase performance. I created my showcase music from a variety of songs from the musical score of *Wonka*, which is based on one of my favorite childhood movies, *Charlie and the Chocolate Factory*.

I pieced together a medley of songs from this entertaining movie, which connected me to my sweet tooth and fond childhood memories. Florin and I collaborated with professional choreographer Alexandra Perzhu for a fabulously creative showcase. It was an unforgettable experience on an international ballroom dance stage. For the competition portion of the event, I requested we do lead-follow dancing, which was quite unorthodox for a competition of this magnitude. However, to keep my competitive dance experience positive, I felt it was worth trying, as my whole ballroom dance journey was focused on honoring the legacy of my parents, and dancing for joy was my primary goal. Serendipitously, I was giddy with delight upon learning I won first place in all my dances!

After the ballroom dance competition, we toured the highlights of Romania with a private tour guide and bus. Instructors Florin Vlad and Andrei Bires shared the magnificence of their home country with us. We visited exquisite castles, including Cantacuzino Castle, Bran Castle (Dracula's famous castle in Transylvania), the Black Church and Evangelical cathedrals, the Palace of Culture, the Bucharest thermal spa, the captivating Liliac Winery, and Azuga Cellars. We saw the spectacular and serene Barsana Monastery, the fascinating Minerology Museum, and the incredible Turda Salt Mine, a mini underground city of wonder. We rode a massive old-fashioned steam engine through the beautiful Romanian countryside. We admired traditional folk dancers in their costumes and danced to exhilarating Latin music lakeside in Florin's hometown of Baia Mare. It was an enchanting, unforgettable experience! My heart was soaring as all my joys came together beyond my expectations on one magical trip, shared with members of my beautiful dance circle. It was epic.

When I returned home, a client friend encouraged our local newspaper to write a story about my ballroom dance journey.

This turned out to be incredibly heartwarming, as the writer beautifully captured the essence of my loving tribute to my parents' legacy. The article, a meaningful keepsake, was splashed on the front cover of the arts section of Schenectady's *The Daily Gazette* on July 27, 2024. It was also available online, so I could continue to share my dance and travel love affair with members of my community near and far.

NEXT CHAPTER

Focusing on my future life, I decided it was time to start Next Chapter, my fourth formal impact circle. As with my prior formal impact circles, I thought of inviting strong, resilient, intelligent, and compassionate executive women, but this time I approached those in transition—navigating divorce, losing a spouse, losing a parent, losing an executive job, caring for aging parents, or experiencing any significant life transition.

It was completely natural for me to create this impact circle with the goal of connecting like-minded women going through similar experiences: substantial transitions in our personal and professional journeys. This Next Chapter impact circle would include intentional gatherings of women, focused on the common mission of supporting each member's needs with the collective synergy and wisdom that comes from collaborative engagement, a willingness to be vulnerable, and giving and receiving for the greatest good of each individual member and the mission of the group at large. It felt rewarding to connect the right people, who chose to care about fellow members, share their authentic selves and vulnerability, and fiercely support one another. When I created this next formal impact circle, I immediately saw it could be as powerful as my prior three formal impact circles: PWN, EN, and PPL.

I hosted our first Next Chapter lunch meeting, fittingly, on

International Women's Day, May 8, 2024. I started with an introduction about what I hoped our impact circle would be: a haven for executive women with a strong willingness to tackle significant challenges they were navigating personally or professionally, who would feel comfortable giving and receiving input from one another. I said that what makes this impact circle unique is that it is a confidential safety zone for like-minded executive women who are willing to be authentic and vulnerable in their hopes for not only healing but also thriving, despite navigating challenging parts of their lives. As I had hand-selected each member, I knew based on my personal relationship with each of them that it was an extremely trustworthy group of incredible women right from the beginning.

I used my simple, proven formula of going around the table and asking each member to share the challenges they were going through, and then asking the group to share thoughts and ideas on how we could be supportive. The first member I called on immediately began in tears. She shared that she had a client who had been in a car accident in which another person perished. The room stopped cold in its tracks. It launched our first meeting with true vulnerability and a willingness to tackle and embrace real-life issues right away.

A second member shared the deep pain she was experiencing three years after the loss of her husband, which had meant a shift in career focus and solo parenting. The pain she expressed was so profound that all our hearts and minds were open to collaborating and assisting her through such palpable grief in her next life chapter. Members easily shared thoughts and strategies in support of one another, brainstorming ideas we would not have considered by ourselves. We focused on our own foundations of self-care, which in many cases had been neglected because we were predominantly caring for others; this was in our DNA. The powerful concept of focusing on self-care was huge for all of us. Even as executive women, we still had not mastered the concept of self-care, whether we had children or not.

My heart and soul were full, despite the gravity of the conversations, as I witnessed firsthand the power of our first Next Chapter meeting unfold. The openness of the conversation among members was palpable, and everyone shared deep pain, personal or professional, and leaned on the group to discuss helpful strategies. There was enormous strength in the ideas and solutions shared.

In the next few meetings, we discussed many unique challenges: single life after long marriages, the deaths of loved ones, the hurt of lack of communication with adult children, the pain of an elderly parent's resistance to safety measures, the abrupt transition to retirement, the loss of executive jobs, career identity challenges, navigating new personal relationships and breakups and milestone birthdays, and letting go of incredible grief, pain, and heartache. Collectively, there was already a profound sense of community and support for working on issues together in a rare circle of healing and power.

Our Next Chapter impact circle was incredibly open and forthcoming with conversations about extremely private raw transitions, and I was heartened to provide a sanctuary for long-standing friends and trusted executives. This was a solid foundation for exploring the impact we could have on each other and the power we could have on our community at large. One of our members mentioned the potential for having a collective social impact, and I beamed with pride because that was one of my hopes. All members were immediately receptive to that idea, which can be a compelling aspect of any impact circle. Selecting a charitable organization together can be impactful for the community and meaningful for members.

This amazing group of women thought bigger and broader than just their own personal power.

Around the same time, a client asked me to critique a few chapters of a memoir he was in the process of writing. We got together at his favorite café in Stuyvesant Plaza, and I shared my thoughts on his writing. He told me that he was on the board of RISSE, Refugee and Immigrant Support Services of Emmaus, a non-profit organization in Albany, assisting refugees from all over the world who were looking for a haven in our community. He said that RISSE was a family-based center that helped newcomers build sustainable lives. My heart sang, knowing this was an idea to bring to my Next Chapter impact circle members to see what effect we could have on our own community and beyond.

A few months later, treasured Next Chapter member and dear friend Pat Bucklin and I attended World Refugee Day at RISSE, learning about a collaboration with Rensselaer Polytechnic Institute. We listened to music from cultures around the world and learned about the influence RISSE was having on immigrants coming to our Capital Region. Pat and I would share our experience with other members of Next Chapter as one option for consideration when discussing the profound influence we could have on our local community and perhaps the world. Later, we would discuss many more ways we could have an impact.

As our Next Chapter circle evolved, we delved into deeper topics of loss, transition, aging parents, adult children, transitions to retirement, self-identity, life purpose, legacy planning, and more. Each meeting was enhanced by the powerful, wise women present, offering caring ideas and thought-provoking solutions to the delicate needs of its members. Members collaborating for personal impact and greater purpose proved to receive compelling results.

The consistent formula for each of these four formal impact circles was that they allowed for deep, meaningful personal and professional conversations that led to powerful outcomes, impacting each member. Business connections, personal friendships, breakthrough conversations, and letting go of pain and hurt blossomed with each meeting. One-on-one conversations encouraged personal growth that was palpable. Creating these formal impact circles was indeed a source of great personal pride, witnessing the glory of investing in individual relationships, networking in my community, connecting incredible human beings willing to share their authenticity and vulnerability for the greatest form of healing: personal and professional growth.

Here are a few captured comments from members of our Next Chapter impact circle.

"I love that we can be honest, and hearing other women's stories makes me wiser. Plus, their questions make me think through my life."

"Meeting an entirely different group of amazingly supportive women who have so much insight and perspective to offer provided a safe place to express myself and feel listened to!"

"Connection, sharing, and going through similar experiences, helped me remember what is important."

"Zero judgment, holding space, kind, supportive, safe."

"Insights shared by others allowed me to hear what types of transitions others are going through and how similar they are to mine."

These remarks highlighted exactly the type of impact I hoped we could make together.

IMPACT CIRCLE REUNION

On Wednesday, November 6, 2024, I hosted the thirty-fifth reunion of my first formal impact circle, PWN, one day after the presidential election. Twenty local members reunited to reminisce about our early careers and catch up on one another's lives. The evening reminded us of the synergy we had experienced early in our careers and how lasting friendships and business relationships had endured over three decades. My soul was full, revisiting the heartwarming stories of the impact our network had on our members. There was much to celebrate in our strong network of like-minded women.

Here are a few of the comments they shared that evening. What our PWN meant to me:

- *It was a great sounding board for all things professional and personal.*
- *Having women represent many industries was inspiring.*
- *It was a sisterhood of nonjudgmental support, affirmation, and wisdom.*
- *It meant access to the brains and hearts of these women.*
- *Support, guidance, and trust.*
- *Bonding with bright, interesting women who challenged me.*
- *PWN began as a networking group but became a special group of friends.*
- *PWN happened to me at an important time in my life—becoming a new parent and navigating a career transition. The welcome and acceptance were so meaningful. I am thankful for the experience.*
- *We were trailblazers before our time, making a meaningful network of professional connections and long-lasting friendships. It was amazing. So profound. I made meaningful lifelong relationships.*
- *I am not a "joiner," but I've always appreciated the energy.*

Favorite Memories

- *The wonderful tête-à-tête talks among professional women*
- *Friendships that I made through the years*
- *The morning meetings became my favorite. I was taken by the experiences and backgrounds of the members.*
- *When we were on a retreat and broke through from professionals to friends*
- *Participating in the Meyers-Briggs Type Indicator (MBTI) personality test and learning about how I operate*
- *New York City trip in a limousine*
- *The retreat when I was on top of the mountain when I was eight months pregnant*
- *Dancing at the disco in New York City at Polly Esther's with tops pulled up and folded over!*
- *The retreat in 2001 with Mary Browne*
- *Holiday parties—the delight! The party clothes!*
- *The retreats were a highlight to PWN membership—I still have my memory board.*
- *NYC Trip!*
- *Our retreat at Rensselaerville Institute when I felt so connected and heard*
- *Retreat where we did vision boarding. It worked!*
- *Workshops at the Rensselaerville Institute*

My heart was full, witnessing the power of my first impact circle, which I started in 1989, an extraordinary outcome over three decades.

THRIVING

O n the flip side of cancer and divorce is the remarkable truth that I have found joy and meaning in my life, which is filled with the intention to embrace every opportunity with hope and gratitude. Each day is a gift, filled with possibilities. I now look at the challenges I have experienced as opportunities to learn and grow.

I am living my life through a focused lens and making the best of being in the moment. I am dancing with pure bliss in my heart and have set new, bodacious goals for myself, including competing in the most renowned and prestigious ballroom dance competition in the world at Blackpool, England, the mecca of international standard dance. I am brave enough to aspire to lofty experiences, carrying on the dance legacy of my beloved parents, who I know are beaming with pride, watching from Heaven above, knowing their eldest daughter is living out her dreams, picking herself up and dusting herself off after a few life challenges, choosing to live a big, meaningful life, and hoping to inspire others by offering a simple concept to help reduce loneliness in the world.

AFTERWORD

have always been an optimistic person. Born into a loving family, I have worked hard to provide for my own family, be there for my friends, clients, and community, and be grateful, no matter what life has thrown at me. I have always believed that when we are faced with life's challenges, we have a choice as to how we react to issues and how we navigate difficulties. When life presented trials for me, I needed to pause, assess, and strategize options for how best to move through them, ultimately choosing the thriving life I have been blessed to live. I chose to lean on my family, friends, and the four formal impact circles I created, as well as the informal ones I encountered and participated in along my journey. My life has been filled with immeasurable joy. I grew up in a loving household, had amazing parents and siblings, am blessed with two phenomenal children, formed amazing and enduring friendships, and navigated two major life setbacks: cancer and divorce. I benefited immensely from the impact circles I created, and leaned on them during my most challenging years. I found many unseen benefits to deepening relationships with those in all my circles while I ballroom-danced my way through life's storms.

I had the courage to compete in the ninety-ninth Blackpool Dance Festival, held in the Empress Ballroom at Winter Gardens, and placed eighth in the Pro Am B2 Open Gold Standard / International level, dancing with my professional instructor, Florin Vlad, of Dance Fire Studio, to live orchestral music, with my daughter cheering me on—an incredible bucket list item. I felt my parents were watching from heaven above when I saw the flickering lights in two wall sconces in the magnificent ballroom.

My greatest desires were to raise a family and make an impact on my community. My hope is that my children form impact circles of their own as their needs develop over time, and that those circles have as much impact on them as mine had on me.

I have always relished the opportunity to connect with like-minded individuals. I am reminded of Michael Bublé's song "Haven't Met You Yet," which Rachel and Greg foxtrotted to in 2013. It makes me think that perhaps you, dear reader, are a friend I haven't met yet. In that spirit, I invite you to think about how an impact circle could enrich your life. Could you benefit from connecting with other like-minded individuals on a certain topic or issue? Could you create something for the greater good? Are you hoping to leave a meaningful legacy? Do you have a challenge you are hoping to navigate through? If so, consider creating your own impact circle, as it can give you a chance to deepen personal relationships and collaborate for the greater good.

In the appendix is a sample guide to creating an impact circle. There is no right or wrong way to do so. I simply share the process and structure that worked for me and the formal impact circles I created. My hope is that your impact circle will deepen and enrich your life beyond measure. So, I ask you, what impact do you want to make? Imagine the impact we could all have together.

ACKNOWLEDGMENTS

My original concept for writing this book was to have each member of my Passion, Purpose, and Legacy healing impact circle contribute a chapter from their cancer journey to be published as a collection of stories. The book would have included the effect our healing impact circle had on each member and on our group as a whole. However, after losing our matriarch, well-respected community leader, and beloved member Jane Golub, the remaining members were too bereft to undertake our writing project.

A few months after we abandoned our writing project, I wondered if it would be worthwhile to write a book about my personal cancer journey. I had taken one very brief writing class at the Women's Club of Albany with my best friend and business partner, because I was experimenting with journaling as part of my cancer journey and hoping to understand my recovery process once my chemotherapy treatments were behind me.

Next, I decided to take a writing class with author and book coach Coleen Murtagh Paratore, who was leading writing sessions in her Troy home. I first met Coleen when we had elementary school–aged children who were taking piano lessons together at the same music studio in nearby Delmar. I learned that Coleen was the author of *The Wedding Planner's Daughter*, and I read it to my young daughter Rachel, as well as several of Coleen's subsequent children's novels. I loved Coleen's books and was particularly pleased when she published *Dear Writer*, about how to write a book. Using the words "spark, spark, spark," she encouraged first-time writers like me to add flair that jumped off the page! Oh, how I yearned to write like that, but I knew my writing skills had far to go.

It was Coleen who first encouraged me to write my personal story, despite my lack of professional writing skills. Her *Dear Writer* book was the one book I took on my first solo trip to Northern Italy. It was the perfect companion for my journey, inspiring me not only to write but also to focus on deep healing by sharing my story and hoping it would uplift others. Words somehow started coming more easily once I began to let go of the strong need to keep myself free from pain. Coleen suggested that if I finally started to let go of my hurtful past, I would give myself space and freedom, and the words would flow. Indeed, new feelings were emerging from my soul.

With Coleen's encouragement, I began writing about my cancer journey, but then, surprisingly, I started including stories from my childhood and just kept on writing. I considered writing about how I had danced through my cancer storm and calling my book *Dancing Through the Storm*. When I experienced my unanticipated second storm, divorce, I thought the new title could be *Dancing Through the Storms*. However, when I began my research, I found other books written with similar themes and titles, and I wanted my message to be unique.

Once I began seriously considering writing a memoir, I reached out to Susan Novotny, the owner of the Book House of Stuyvesant Plaza, an independently owned local bookstore, for guidance. Susan had hosted a book signing for my father Frank when he published his memoir *Let It Be a Dance*. Susan pointed me in the direction of a list of potential editors to assist with my next stage of writing. I discovered what I needed was a developmental editor.

I was extremely fortunate to find Ayshea Wild of Write Wild, who immediately embraced the concept of my memoir. Building on Coleen's initial encouragement, I began to organize the hundreds of raw pages about my life's journey, including both exceedingly difficult storms of cancer and divorce in addition to the joyful, wonderful parts of my blessed life. Once I understood what a developmental editor could assist with, Ayshea and I worked together on revisions and edits back and forth until we found a structure that would lay the foundation for my fresh writing. I finally embraced writing from my heart, sharing my joy, pain, and vulnerability as part of my healing journey. Ayshea introduced me to the concept of incorporating the formal impact circles I have created over my lifetime into a central theme, and this resonated deeply with me. The goal of inspiring readers in a meaningful way by sharing my own journey was paramount to me.

Over the course of my writing, I discovered how much the four formal impact circles I created influenced my life and the lives of the women in my circles. I hoped this concept would bring my story from a personal memoir to a more meaningful concept and inspire readers to form their own impact circles, helping them navigate the challenges in their own lives. Ayshea gently encouraged me, saying, "The world needs your book," so I kept diligently writing and revising as much as I could in between full-time work and my ballroom dance passion. I grew to love and respect Ayshea, who encouraged me when needed and was fiercely supportive when I was ready to abandon my writing, especially when I didn't feel confident there was something meaningful in it for my readers. I was extremely grateful for her exceptional editing expertise, but more importantly, for her humanity and compassion, as I released so much pain in my writing journey. She was exceptional at her professional craft and quick to support my every effort, week by week, with encouragement and sage advice. Ayshea provided unwavering commitment and exceptional expertise to my entire writing project, fully dedicated through the tedious final editing stage. I owe her my deepest and profound gratitude.

With heartfelt gratitude, I also acknowledge Nadia Geagea Pupa, Editorial and Graphic Design Consultant at Pique Publishing, whose expert guidance, creative vision, and steady stewardship were instrumental throughout the entire editorial and production process. From the first conversation to the final layout, Nadia's dedication, insight, and artistry helped bring this book to life with exceptional design, elegance, and purpose. I hugged my first hardcover copy as my phenomenal editor, Ayshea Wild, suggested. Ayshea, thank you for introducing me to Nadia!

A special thank you to Robert A. Lane, whose professional audiobook coaching and unwavering encouragement gave me the confidence to narrate *The Power of Impact Circles* in my own voice. His belief in the strength of authenticity reminded me that sometimes the most impactful way to share a message is simply to speak it from the heart.

You were all the dream team.

I would also like to acknowledge dear friends Pat Bucklin and Diane Cameron Pascone, treasured members of my Next Chapter impact circle, for reviewing content and offering support and encouragement throughout my entire writing process. Lastly, I would like to thank my sister, Mayela Harris, who stayed up late into the evening to read my full manuscript in one sitting and shared four hours of fine-tuning insights with me the next day. I was elated to receive very high praise, which I hadn't anticipated from her, the better writer in our family.

My life's purpose has always been to make an impact on the world while I am a part of it, and my fervent wish is to make a difference for my children and others along my path. If I can assist in helping you, my reader, to create an impact circle of your own, please look for more information at https://www.ThePowerOfImpactCircles.com.

APPENDIX
Life Lessons, Tips, and Takeaways

HEALTH AND WELLNESS

- *Choose self-care, making yourself—body, mind, and soul—a top priority.*

- *Live a healthy lifestyle; you are in control of your choices.*

- *Be your own health-care advocate, because it could significantly impact your life.*

- *Prioritize a good night's rest, because with quality sleep, you can make better decisions.*

- *Invest in your mental, emotional, and physical wellness, whether with professional guidance or self-help.*

- *Make some form of exercise you are likely to do consistently a top priority.*

- *Find an accountability buddy to help keep your fitness routine fun and consistent.*

- *Eat nutritious whole foods, supplementing with vitamins and herbs if helpful.*

- *Spend time in nature every day, or as much as possible, to fuel your soul.*

- *Do daily stretches for your body, including any type of yoga, tai chi, or Pilates.*

- *Practice meditation for your mind at any time of day, for any length of time.*

- *Use integrative, complementary, or holistic healing modalities, including chiropractic, acupuncture, active release, massage, craniosacral, reiki, or other bodywork therapies when helpful.*

- *Build in micro-habits to effect change.*

SOCIAL WELL-BEING

- *Spend time with people worthy of your time, friendship, and love.*

- *Surround yourself with things and people that bring you joy or add meaning to your life.*

- *Make time for meaningful relationships and invest in a few exceptional ones, as they can enrich your life beyond measure.*

- *Friends may not be family by blood, but they can be family by love.*

- *Be willing to strike up a conversation with someone new; perhaps they are a friend you haven't met yet.*

- *Just because you are on your own, it does not mean you are alone.*

- *When someone offers help, accept it graciously; it will give you an opportunity to connect with them on a deeper level and form a more meaningful relationship.*

- *Minimizing negative influences—people or information—allows for more enriching experiences.*

MENTAL WELL-BEING

- *The most important relationship you have is with yourself.*

- *Be open to building a life on your own—you are enough!*

- *Be open to new relationships if the right ones come along, or be willing to seek them out.*

- *Be willing to be your authentic, vulnerable self, because this allows you to be true to yourself and to deepen relationships with others.*

- *Listen attentively and share authentically.*

- *Know when to apologize and do so genuinely.*

- *Figure out when, or if, it is time to move on with the next chapter of your life.*

- *Tackle hard things head-on; come up with a strategy or approach that works for you.*

- *Find excellent professional life coaches, psychologists, therapists, medical professionals, or integrative care specialists to help with all aspects of your life.*

- *Ask for help when suitable; it is not a sign of weakness, but an opportunity to strengthen relationships.*

- *Declutter your life of things and people that are unnecessary or hurtful, as it will help clear a path to your greatest potential.*

- *Consider keeping a written or voice journal, a safe place to express your feelings.*

- *Marvel at how you can do hard things.*

SPIRITUAL / UNIVERSAL CONNECTIONS

- *Consider your relationship with a higher power, religious organization, church, synagogue, nature, the universe, or other forms of spiritual connection.*

- *Practice spiritual mindfulness as often as possible, if only for a few minutes daily.*

- *Allow grief to happen, and grieve as fully as possible in the early stages, as it will allow you to move to the other side of grief more meaningfully.*

- *Choose joy along your life path, despite life's challenges.*

- *Embrace feeling a variety of emotions simultaneously; sorrow, grief, and anger can be experienced together with joy, hope, and love.*

- *Laughter is powerful medicine, so find more ways to add laughter to your life.*

- *Look for silver linings and positive outcomes to difficult situations.*

- *You are stronger than you think: physically, intellectually, emotionally, and spiritually.*

LIFE PURPOSE

- *Find a profession or life journey that is meaningful to you and will give you purpose and peace of mind.*

- *Make time for your top life priorities, whatever they may be.*

- *Be present in everyday moments.*

- *Find a hobby, pastime, or creative outlet that brings you excitement or joy.*

- *Use technology to enhance your life, not detract from it.*

- *Keep your physical spaces at home and at work organized, allowing for new energy and positive possibilities.*

- *Natural rhythms and routines can help keep you calm and focused.*

- *Practice gratitude every day for anything positive, little or big, and build a lifetime of appreciation.*

CULTURAL ENRICHMENT

- *Traveling can be a window to the world and a magical place of other cultures, traditions, architecture, flowers, tastes, smells, music, dance, and people.*

- *Smiling is the best international language, but learning a few phrases from the country you are visiting is a sign of respect.*

- *Consider traveling solo, as it can be a spectacular adventure.*

- *Embrace the cultures of other parts of the world through art, music, or dance.*

- *Try new foods, new experiences, and new adventures because you never know when you might discover something brilliant.*

- *Do creative things that provide an outlet for freedom of expression, including gardening, knitting, baking, cooking, decorating, beading, card-making, painting, sculpting, dancing, playing music, songwriting, poetry, flower arranging, pottery, jewelry-making, and woodworking.*

- *Challenge yourself to learn new things on a regular basis by reading, listening to audiobooks, doing library research, or exploring the internet.*

SOCIAL IMPACT

- *Find charitable causes you care about and volunteer in your community by giving your time, talent, or treasure.*

- *Be mindful of your personal carbon footprint and find ways to be more environmentally friendly, as we all live on one planet and are stewards for the generations to come.*

- *Find a way to impact your community at large and enrich your own soul.*

GUIDELINES FOR CREATING
an Impact Circle

1. Think of a topic you would like to focus on, such as business development; healing from trauma; personal development; life transitions; philanthropy; parenting; caring for aging parents; caring for children with special needs; neighborhood harmony; diversity, equity, and inclusion; career or professional advancement; remote work; work-life integration; financial literacy; physical or nutritional wellness; emotional or spiritual connections.

2. Consider like-minded people who might have an interest in the selected topic and could personally benefit from connecting and collaborating with each other.

3. Create a short list of people who you already know would be interested in exploring the topic and people you think might be interested.

4. Consider whether you would like to start with a small group of three to five people or whether you would feel more comfortable with a larger group of six to ten people.

5. Gather contact information, including email addresses and cell phone numbers, and create a list of potential members.

6. Connect with potential members, either by phone or email, and share your initial thoughts and ideas about creating an impact circle for your selected topic.

7. Decide on a date and time, and book the first meeting at a central location, such as a coffee shop, restaurant, private meeting room, library, office, or home setting.

8. Use your first meeting to brainstorm the concept for your

impact circle, including hopes and goals for members and the whole group.

9. Develop an initial mission statement for your impact circle.

10. Decide on a structure for meetings, including the ideal number of members, how often to meet, where to meet, potential financial costs, and what is expected of members.

11. Host regular meetings at determined intervals to focus on individual member needs first and then collective group goals.

12. Revisit the mission statement and goals to ensure expectations are being met for all members.

13. Solicit input from all members about how your impact circle is enhancing their lives.

14. Share success stories and celebrate when personal and group goals are achieved.

15. Consider donating time, treasure, or talent to an organization that resonates with members to make a positive impact.

16. Pay it forward by caring deeply about each member and helping members make a difference to each other and the world.

A SAMPLE OVERVIEW FOR
an Impact Circle

MISSION / PURPOSE OF THE ORGANIZATION

The goals of the _____ Impact Circle are to . . .

- Be a "sounding board of directors" for each member on a personal or professional level.
- Use individual networking and the collective insights of the group to fulfill each member's needs.
- Enhance each member's professional or personal development.
- Elevate the well-being and development of each member.
- Focus on creating synergy the group can use to impact the wider community or a selected not-for-profit organization.

MEMBERSHIP ELIGIBILITY

To achieve the goals of the impact circle, seek members who are open to a forum where new ideas, practical recommendations, and information can be exchanged. Candidates for membership should be able to both contribute to and benefit from a broad network that seeks to attract members interested in _____.

STRUCTURE AND RESPONSIBILITIES

- Choose a meeting facilitator or leader to preserve the group's mission.
- Coordinate meetings, networking events, or social gatherings.
- Fine-tune meetings as needed.
- Actively seek potential members if desired.
- Meet with prospective members in advance to ascertain if they are a suitable fit for the group.
- Set a calendar and book meeting locations for the year.
- Email reminder notices for upcoming meetings.
- Maintain and update the membership list and distribute it to members periodically.

MEMBERSHIP

To reap the benefits of the impact circle, members should make efforts to attend the majority of meetings with the goal of giving back to other members. All discussions are . . .

- Strictly confidential
- Member-focused
- Meant to provide a safe haven for meaningful conversation
- Concentrated on personal and professional updates
- Focused on answering these questions:
  - What's New?
  - What Do You Need?
  - What Do You Have to Give?
- Focused on the collective social impact of the group

READING GROUP GUIDE

1. What power do you believe impact circles can have?

2. How is engaging with collective wisdom through a common interest an effective way to reach individual goals as well as collective goals?

3. Are you currently part of a formal or informal impact circle? If so, what impact has it had on your life?

4. What impact has cultural enrichment such as exposure to the art, food, dance, and music of people from other cultures had on your life?

5. How could you use impact circles to help navigate your life's storms?

6. How might an impact circle make a difference for any wellness or health concerns you might have now or in the future?

7. How can you advocate for your personal health-care needs better so you have more control over your life?

8. Have you experienced any signs from the universe after a loved one's passing? If so, what impact has this had on your life?

9. How does knowing that you could potentially be connected to loved ones after they pass affect your relationships with them today?

10. What benefits can you imagine from creating your own impact circle to live your best life going forward?

11. How do you think creating an impact circle could help you leave a meaningful legacy?

12. What value do you believe impact circles could have on generations to come?

13. What societal influence do you believe you could have if you created your own impact circle?

ABOUT THE AUTHOR

Alissa Quinn successfully blazed a trail as the only woman advisor in her Albany, New York, wealth-management office in 1987. During her NYC World Trade Center training, she was the only woman out of eleven on the whole East Coast to complete the program in her class of fifty-one. She lives by the motto "People don't care how much you know until they know how much you care," which has served her well for over three decades as Senior Vice President / Financial Advisor leading The Quinn Wealth Management Group. Alissa is a graduate of Union College with a Bachelor of Science degree in Industrial Economics, a program combining mechanical engineering and economics.

Alissa's greatest joy has come from raising two children, a son and daughter, who are both Babson College business school graduates. She beams with pride as she works alongside her financial advisor daughter, who joined her business team in 2022. Alissa strives to make a difference for others, creating and leading unique impact circles for executive women in business, professional women prioritizing parenting, women leaders touched by cancer, and women navigating life transitions.

Alissa is an international-award-winning ballroom dance enthusiast, inspired by her mother, a South American immigrant, and her father of Italian heritage, who met on the dance floor. Dancing her way through life's storms, Alissa is an optimist who has learned that, in the words of Robert Brault, "Taking a step backward after taking a step forward is not a disaster, it's a cha-cha!" With her indomitable spirit, insatiable sweet tooth, and nickname of Auntie Bling, Alissa adds passion and a little sparkle to everything she adores: her family, friends, work, ballroom dance, flower arranging, entertaining, and creating impact circles to help others thrive and live life to the fullest!

AWARDS / ACCOLADES

- Trailblazing Shero Panelist, Women's Fund of the Capital Region, 2022
- Women Who Mean Business Award, Albany Business Review, 2021
- President's Circle Award, YWCA of Northeastern NY, 2020
- Pearls of Wisdom Award, Women's Employment & Resource Center, 2019
- Visions of Strength Award, Northeast Health / Karen Mosseau Foundation, 2017
- Trailblazers Award, The Women's Fund of the Capital Region, 2014
- Community Leadership Award, New England Region, 2013
- Advancement of Women in the Workplace Award, Women's Employment & Resource Center, 2011
- Women of Excellence Award, Capital Region Chamber of Commerce, 1993
- Women of Achievement Award, YWCA of Schenectady, 1990
- Enterprising Women's Leadership Institute Award, 1989

COMMUNITY ENGAGEMENT AND PROFESSIONAL SOCIETIES

- Founder, Next Chapter Impact Circle, 2024–present
- Founder, Passion, Purpose, & Legacy Impact Circle, 2014–present
- Honorary Co-chair, Women of Achievement Awards, YWCA of Northeastern NY, 2019–2020
- Babson College Business Coaching, Leadership & Training Program, 2011–2016
- Honorary Co-chair, Women of Excellence Awards, Regional Chamber of Commerce, 2016–2017
- Ambassador, American Heart Association Circle of Red, 2011–2016
- Nomination Committee Chair, USA Dance, 2010–2014
- Founder, Zoller Ballroom Kids: Inner-City Children's Ballroom Dance Program, 2005–2012
- Corporate Committee Chair, Albany Institute of History & Art, 1997
- Founder, Executive Network Impact Circle, 1996–2018
- Volunteer, Girl's Inc., 1995–2010
- Member, Fort Orange Club, 1994–present, Library Committee 2000–2003, Membership Committee 2003–2010, Finance Committee 2013–2015, General Manager Search Committee 2016, Literary Society 2019–present
- Board Member, Junior Achievement, 1994–1997
- Founder, Professional Women's Network Impact Circle, 1989–2017
- Member, Capital Region Chamber of Commerce, 1987–present
- Omicron Delta Epsilon Honorary Society of Economics–Union College, 1984
- Society of Women Engineers–Union College, 1981

www.ingramcontent.com/pod-product-compliance
Lightning Source LLC
Chambersburg PA
CBHW011220120626
46545CB00010B/3079